OXFORD READING

Series Editor C

THE PHILOSOPHY OF SCIENCE

Also published in this series

Theories of Ethics edited by Philippa Foot
Knowledge and Belief edited by A. Phillips Griffiths
The Theory of Meaning edited by G. H. R. Parkinson
Political Philosophy edited by Anthony Quinton
Philosophical Logic edited by P. F. Strawson
The Philosophy of Perception edited by G. J. Warnock
The Philosophy of Action edited by Alan R. White

Other volumes are in preparation

THE PHILOSOPHY OF SCIENCE

Edited by
P. H. NIDDITCH

OXFORD UNIVERSITY PRESS
1968

Oxford University Press, Ely House, London W. 1
GLASGOW NEW YORK TORONTO MELBOURNE WELLINGTON
CAPE TOWN SALISBURY IBADAN NAIROBI LUSAKA ADDIS ABABA
BOMBAY CALCUTTA MADRAS KARACHI LAHORE DACCA
KUALA LUMPUR HONG KONG TOKYO

FILMSET BY ST. PAUL'S PRESS, MALTA
PRINTED IN GREAT BRITAIN
AT THE UNIVERSITY PRESS, OXFORD
BY VIVIAN RIDLER
PRINTER TO THE UNIVERSITY

CONTENTS

INTRODUCTION

THE papers reprinted in this volume illustrate topics and methods of analysis and discussion which have been dominant in the philosophy of science during the past twenty years or so; all the original publication dates belong, as it happens, to the period since 1958. As a rule, I have aimed to avoid including papers already reprinted in other collections, and also those which are about philosophical issues limited to one particular branch of science; further, I have excluded those which require a knowledge of parts of advanced mathematics (including mathematical logic) to be properly understood and evaluated. The contributions to be found here are concerned with questions of widespread and central interest in the current philosophy of the natural and human sciences,[1] and the answers they suggest are so presented as to be comprehensible to the ordinary philosophical reader. The papers reproduced treat some of the fundamental questions of theory construction and evaluation; the notion and criteria of meaning with respect to science; the structure of explanation; teleological explanation; the possibility of human action as subject to causal, scientific explanation; simplicity and the choice of scientific hypotheses; the problem of induction; Nelson Goodman's new problem of induction; and the paradoxes of confirmation. It is intended that there will be a separate volume on the philosophy of mathematics in this series.

There are two related topics which have been purposely omitted, and to which I should make some reference: the nature of probability and the logical foundations of statistical inference. A consideration of them, beyond the superficialities, presupposes an acquaintance with a fair number of interlocked and sophisticated technicalities. Unless such technicalities have been firmly grasped, one is not equipped critically to compare existing alternative theories of a philosophical kind, any better than a layman would be equipped to deal with philosophical issues of modern physics. Where the reader lacks that knowledge in these matters, he is not able to cope

[1]The term 'human sciences' is used here to cover the recognised social sciences (anthropology, economics, political science, sociology, &c.) together with such other studies of man as history, linguistics, and human psychology. (I have elsewhere introduced the name 'anthroponomy' for this area of science.)

philosophically at all: philosophical criticism and construction here rest on having sufficient technical mastery to be able to understand and evaluate competing proposals. As a result of the principles of selection I have adopted, no material on the philosophy of probability and statistics has been provided in the text, and the space thus saved has been devoted to other questions. I have listed in the Bibliography a number of writings on these topics which anyone who may be interested in them should consult; see, in particular, Braithwaite [10] (Chapters 5–7), Carnap [17], Hacking [41], Kyburg [53], Kyburg and Smokler [56], and von Wright [85], all of which contain further references to the literature.

The coverage of the philosophy of science is extensive and diverse, much more so, I think, than is true of most other parts of philosophy. Science is not simple nor uniform; it is constituted by a wide range of activities, discoveries, and modes of thought which are themselves extraordinarily varied and whose tendency is progressive proliferation. Hence, no brief classification of what is covered by the philosophy of science is likely to be exactly informative. What perhaps would be needed is to put together a series of complementary orderings of its contents. One possibility is to make a number of distinct specifications in terms of divisional contrasts: (1) the logic of science *vis-à-vis* the epistemology of science; (2) the philosophy of the natural sciences *vis-à-vis* the philosophy of the human sciences; and (3) the philosophy of science *vis-à-vis* the study of philosophical issues of a particular science. To these three it is likely to be helpful to add a rather different sort of pairing: (4) the philosophy of science *vis-à-vis* the history of science. Of course, there is no claim here to be supplying an exhaustive pattern, or the only kind, of treatment of how the subject may be described; those four groups of categories separately do not embrace, for example, an all-round study of the relations between science and religion which also, I suppose, comes within the scope of the philosophy of science.[1] The remarks that follow discuss primarily the first of the above divisions, one or two of the remainder just being touched on.

Broadly speaking, philosophers of science have, since the end of the Second World War, been chiefly occupied with the logic of science. They interpret science as a body of deductive, or quasi-deductive, systems of assertions; these systems and their components are analysed and judged by using concepts and rules (e.g. *modus tollens*)

[1] A useful introductory survey of the relations between science and religion is given by Barbour [5].

belonging to the study of formal inference and implication, or to some extension of this, e.g. the probability calculus, or are analysed into something modelled on it, e.g. a formal theory of simplicity. This situation is typified by the fact that explanation is widely regarded as the primary explicandum for the philosophy of science, while the best known explications offered mould scientific explanations along deductive lines. Another variety of logic, commonly practised by philosophers of science, is the drawing, and pursuit, of distinctions of meaning.

What is an explanation? 'To explain', said Duhem (1906), 'is to strip reality of the appearances covering it like a veil, in order to see the bare reality itself.'[1] From giving accounts of explanation in metaphorical, metaphysical, or psychological terms, philosophers have tended to move towards an analysis in logical terms. By the 1950's, a determinate, logical diagnosis had become established, owed chiefly to a succession of papers by Hempel. In the first of these papers, he maintains that 'the scientific explanation of the occurrence of an event of some specific kind E ... consists of (1) a set of statements asserting the occurrence of certain events $C_1, \ldots C_n$ at certain times and places, (2) a set of universal hypotheses, such that (a) the statements of both groups are reasonably well confirmed by empirical evidence, (b) from the two groups of statements the sentence asserting the occurrence of event E can be logically deduced'; group (1) describes the initial and boundary conditions for the occurrence of E, while group (2) contains the general laws on which the explanation is based.[2]

All except the first of the papers reprinted in the present volume clearly represent this concern with the logic of science. Unfortunately, there is an awkward absence from our philosophical vocabulary of a brief and suitable expression, with appropriate derivatives, which could be used to refer to the logical study of concepts and conceptions; 'conceptual analysis' is unsatisfactory in the two relevant respects that have just been indicated; so, to fill the gap, I introduce the term 'noematology'. Now, in earlier generations a main, if not

[1] Pierre Duhem, *The Aim and Structure of Physical Theory*, translated by Philip P. Wiener (Princeton University Press, Princeton, 1954); the original edition of this book first appeared in 1906, bringing together papers by Duhem published in 1904–5. But cf. below, page 11.

[2] Carl G. Hempel: 'The function of general laws in history', *The Journal of Philosophy*, 39 (1942), 35–48; Hempel's formulation of the nature of explanation in this paper has been modified in the course of his subsequent papers on this topic; cf. pages 54ff. below, Hempel [46], and see also Popper [65], 59–60.

the main, task of the philosophical treatment of the sciences was taken to be the provision of a full natural-history-cum-logical-account of scientific method; for Herschel, Whewell, Mill, Jevons, and their successors, this meant (1) delineating a general pattern of scientific discovery and (2) establishing comprehensive and universally applicable canons of validation for scientific hypotheses. (1) and (2) overlap to some extent because conducting appropriate tests of validity is required at some stage in the total process of scientific discovery. The tradition founded by the writers just mentioned has ceased to flourish among philosophers so far as it involves (1). But it is still alive in some quarters. Picking rather at random, I quote the following from the introductory chapter of a modern, American text on biology.

Everything that is science ultimately has its basis in the scientific method. Both the powers and the limitations of science are defined by this method. And wherever the scientific method cannot be applied, there cannot be science . . .

All science begins with *observation*, the first step of the scientific method. At once this delimits the scientific domain; something that cannot be observed cannot be investigated by science. . . It is necessary, furthermore, that an observation be *repeatable*, actually or potentially . . . Correct observation is a most difficult art, acquired after only long experience and many errors. . .

After an observation has been made, the second step of the scientific method is to define a *problem*. In other words, one asks a question about the observation. How does so and so come about? . . . More significantly, not everyone sees that there may actually be a problem connected with an observation. . . Anyone can ask questions. However, good questioning, like good observing, is a high art. To be valuable scientifically, a question must be *relevant* and it must be testable . . . Einstein's fame rests, in part, on showing that it is impossible to test whether or not the earth moves through an 'ether', an assumption held for many decades. All questions about an ether therefore become nonscientific, and we must reformulate associated problems until they become testable . . .

Having asked a proper question, the scientist proceeds to the third stop of the scientific method. This involves the seemingly quite unscientific procedure of guessing. One guesses what the answer to the question might conceivably be. Scientists call this postulating a *hypothesis*. . . . The scientist will not know whether his guess was or was not correct until he has completed the fourth step of the scientific method, *experimentation*. It is the function of every experiment to test the validity of a scientific guess . . . On the other hand, experiments do not guarantee a scientific conclusion. For there is ample room within experimentation and in succeeding steps to become unscientific again. Experimentation is by far the hardest part of scientific procedure. There are no rules to follow; each experiment is a case unto itself. Knowledge and experience usually help technically, but to design the experiment . . ., that separates the genius from the dilettante . . . The result of any experiment represents *evidence*; that is, the original guess in answer to a problem is confirmed as correct or is invalidated. If invalidated, a new hypothesis, with new experiments, must be thought up. . .

Experimental evidence is the basis for the fifth and final step in the scientific method, the formulation of a *theory* . . . Every good theory has *predictive* value. It prophesies certain results. In contrast to nonscientific prophecies, scientific ones always have a substantial body of evidence to back them up. Moreover, the scientific prophecy does not say that something will certainly happen, but only that something is *likely* to happen, with a stated degree of probability.[1]

Such an account of the scientific method is not easily to be found in the writings of contemporary philosophers of science; usually, they are careful to refrain from committing themselves to an empirically testable description of the total, temporally successive stages of a scientific inquiry, concentrating instead on a noematological analysis of the *structure* of scientific explanations and arguments, regardless of the detailed psychological and historical conditions, and development, of scientific thinking.[2] One reason for refraining from so committing themselves lies in the dominant conception of the nature of philosophy among philosophers in the English-speaking world;[3] according to this, philosophical problems are not empirical, and philosophical utterances offered by way of solutions and supports to these solutions are not empirical; their non-empirical character is bound up with their being in some special senses 'explanatory'. This conception arose by virtue of the desire not to fall into metaphysics on the one hand nor into armchair science on the other. However, it is not maintained in that simple form, if only because the analytical philosopher has to seek actual material on which to reflect, for he has no other; and, being thus prompted by actual material, the

[1] Paul B. Weisz, *Elements of Biology* (McGraw-Hill, New York, 1961), pp. 4–8. Quoted by permission of McGraw-Hill Book Company.

[2] But there have been occasions when the structure of scientific thought has been examined in combination with a detailed study of historical circumstances; see, e.g., Ellis' paper in Colodny [22], Grünbaum's paper in Volume 2 of Baumrin [8], Hanson [42], and Mary Hesse's *Forces and Fields*, (Nelson, London, 1961); cf. also A. C. Crombie's *Robert Grosseteste and the Origins of Experimental Science 1100–1700* (Clarendon Press, Oxford, 1953).

[3] In all that follows, it is only such philosophers that I shall have in mind; quite different remarks would need to be directed to, say, French philosophers, or to Russian ones.

adequacy and accuracy of his noematological analyses will (unlike the pure mathematician's) depend on his perceptiveness and discriminatory powers, and on the scope of his investigations, in relation to certain *phenomena*. Let me give an example from the philosophy of science of (implicit) reliance on psychological or sociological phenomena. Braithwaite writes: 'If the hypothesis that all men are mortal is regarded as supported solely by the direct evidence that men have died, then *it will not be regarded* as a law of nature; but if it is regarded as also being supported by being deduced from the higher-level hypothesis that all animals are mortal, the evidence for this being also that horses have died, dogs have died, &c., then *it will be accorded* the honorific title of "law of nature" which will then indicate that there are other reasons for believing it than evidence of its instances alone . . . A hypothesis to be regarded as a natural law must be a general proposition which can be thought to explain its instances; if the reason for believing the general proposition is solely direct knowledge of the truth of its instances, *it will be felt* to be a poor sort of explanation of these instances.'[1] Only a momentary relief is gained if '*will*' is implausibly translated throughout as 'should', for can the resulting hypothetical commands be justified otherwise than by an alleged consensus? That there are also explicit appeals to scientific practice is illustrated by passages in Ackermann's paper below; see pages 124ff.

The philosopher's accounts are, therefore, subject to criticism on empirical grounds, when, for instance, he does not notice relevant facts. Once it is granted that the philosopher's data are empirically accessible, it looks as if the status of the philosophical theories about them must be not quite non-empirical; for example, the theories may fail to be sufficiently widely applicable or to be in accord with undeniable facts. It is then difficult to escape the conclusion that much that is involved in the philosopher's investigations does not differ altogether in principle from what is appropriate to the pursuit of empirical knowledge in the natural and human sciences.

Philosophers of science have certainly tried to take cognizance of what are judged to be key points in a whole structure of scientific thought as a real (and not imagined) datum. Thus, when it appeared that probabilistic laws were employed in modern science, an attempt was made to formulate a suitable scheme of scientific explanation, alternative to that where all the cited laws are of strictly universal

[1] Braithwaite [10], 302; italics as printed are mine; in the original, 'explain' is italicised, and, at the end, there is a footnote reference to p. 322.

form, so as to accommodate those cases in which probabilistic laws are incorporated. Nevertheless, it must, I think, be admitted that many philosophers of science have delayed too long, or failed more or less completely, to give due recognition to this and other innovations in the conduct and elaboration of science. Too few case studies and other factual inquiries are undertaken, to serve as a check of correctness and as a stimulus to more profound and refined accounts concerning concept-formation in science; the character and role of observation; classification; laws and theories; prediction; the testing of hypotheses; the conditions of theory retention; and other topics discussed in the philosophy of science. The occasional citation of selected passages from scientific literature does not in itself constitute a fair basis of relevant evidence. I do not deny that some problems in the philosophy of science—the problem of induction is one of them—are hardly bound up with the actualities of science, and to that extent their discussion does not call for evidence; however, opinions may differ about whether the weight of interest such problems carry is as great as that of the remainder, which do have an empirical basis. What I am maintaining is that in so far as problems or solutions rest on the changes and practices of the sciences, rationality demands that these changes and practices be properly investigated and not merely disregarded or effortlessly prejudged.

Although philosophers of science nowadays tend to avoid offering what is meant to be a general chronicle of any scientific discovery, their neglect of this chronicle as distinct from a logical reconstruction of scientific thought—their interest being in procedure rather than in process—is a legitimate curtailment of the study of scientific inquiry. Hyperbole such as that in the version of scientific method quoted above is hard to escape; the hyperbole is illustrated by the simple distinction drawn, in the penultimate paragraph quoted, between the dilettante and the genius—as if only a genius can successfully devise, or devise successful, experiments. That version should provoke scepticism and criticism by its suggestions that all the sciences at any period are essentially homogeneous, and that there is a fixed order, beginning with observation, in which uncombined elements of the scientific method function. Are there no constraints on the making of good theories other than a theory's possessing evidential backing and predictive value? Is it the case, or could it even be the case, that the formulation of every theory is accompanied by a stated degree of its probability?

In general, philosophers of science have assumed that there are certain indispensable components of a unique scientific method: *inter alia*, devising hypotheses, deducing predictions from them, and empirically testing the hypotheses via the predictions; and they have propounded what they think these various components are; in this way, noematology within the philosophy of science includes important phases of methodology. It might, however, be argued, as Bridgman has done, that the very existence of scientific method is doubtful and is something not to be acknowledged as a datum. 'The scientific method, as far as it is a method, is nothing more than doing one's damnedest with one's mind, no holds barred. What primarily distinguishes science from other intellectual enterprises in which the right answer has to be obtained is not method but the matter.'[1] I find this an attractive opinion, to which I would add two glosses. Firstly, its acceptance does not preclude recognising the importance of those features of the empirical sciences—observation, explanation, prediction, and the rest—which are discussed in the current logic of science; it does imply that these do not form the whole or the only matrix for describing, interpreting, and correlating facts about science. Secondly, it does not follow that there are not factors systematically differentiating some ranges of subject-matter from others; among other things, it leaves open the possibility that certain sciences—the human ones—are in significant respects dissimilar from and irreducible to the natural sciences.

The occupation of the centre of attention by the logic of science within the past generation has led to the displacement of the epistemology of science from that position. These two aspects of the philosophy of science are not, admittedly, mutually exclusive, either constitutionally or practically. Logical methods may be deployed in an epistemological context; and, conversely—epistemology being concerned with the nature and scope of human knowledge—it is plausible to maintain that logical analysis of concepts related to the sciences proceeds on epistemological assumptions. All the same, noematology and epistemology are largely different, owing to largely distinct emphases in the sorts of questions each raises. Even so, there are overlaps, e.g. the problem of induction. It may be added further that some issues of the epistemology of science and some of methodology coincide, as in Feyerabend's paper below (pages 12ff.) and in Popper [65].

Much of Broad's *Scientific Thought* (1923) is about 'the sensational and perceptual bases of our scientific concepts'. By the 1950's, the

[1] *Reflections of a Physicist* (New York Philosophical Library, New York, 1950), p. 370.

most common attitude among English-speaking philosophers of science was that the philosophy of perception is irrelevant to their domain.[1] Dealing logically with the nature of scientific laws and how these are related to observed facts, it has been supposed that the notion of an 'observed fact' is uncontroversial and that all observed facts can be described independently of any scientific-theoretical interpretations; the relation of observed facts to scientific laws is treated simply in terms of such logical concepts as those of generalisation and deductive inference. There is, however, a notable group of exceptions: a number of philosophers—P. K. Feyerabend, A. Grünbaum, and the late N. R. Hanson among others—who have a special interest in the philosophy of physics. Also pertinent are writings in recent years by philosophically-minded physicists, among whom Bohm, Bohr, Fock, Heisenberg, and Pauli may be mentioned.[2] The discussions of this type have mostly been about fundamentals of classical physics (especially Newton's laws of motion); the nature of space and time; the status, legitimacy, and possible replacements of Einstein's principle of equivalence in the general theory of relativity; the bases and implications of Heisenberg's indeterminacy principle and of Bohr's complementarity principle in quantum mechanics, with particular reference to the epistemological relationship between observer and observations. In relation to fields of the natural and human sciences other than physics, philosophical work of comparable magnitude and quality has not been forthcoming, and only concerning physics have both professional practitioners and philosophers been active and in mutual dialogue. One might guess that philosophical problems of biology will soon attract similar attention.[3]

A wider consideration, running over all the main epistemological issues raised by science as a whole and by individual sciences, has come to seem to most philosophers of science to be much less important

[1] But Sellars [75] is an exception. See also, for a sketch of a distinctive approach to many epistemological issues, Carnap's 'Empiricism, semantics, and ontology' reprinted in his *Meaning and Necessity*, 2nd. edition (Chicago University Press, Chicago, 1956) and in Wiener [83].

[2] For recent literature on the philosophy of physics, see e.g. papers, and references cited, in Colodny [21] and [22], Danto & Morgenbesser [24] Part Three, Feigl & Maxwell [31], Körner [50], and A. Grünbaum: *Philosophical Problems of Space and Time* (Knopf, New York, 1963). For the work of Fock and of other Soviet physicists and philosophers, cf. S. Müller-Markus: *Einstein und die Sowjetphilosophie*, 2 volumes (Reidler, Dordrecht, 1960–66), and G. A. Wetter: *Dialectical Materialism: A Historical and Systematic Survey of Philosophy in the Soviet Union*, tr. Peter Heath (Routledge and Kegan Paul, London, 1958); pp. 405–32.

[3] For certain philosophical issues of psychology and of cybernetics, see Taylor [77], and S. Hook (editor): *Dimensions of Mind* (Collier Books, New York, 1960).

than it used to. It is no accident that only one new, elaborate treatise of this sort has appeared since before the Second World War, its author—Michael Polanyi—not being a recognized philosopher.[1] His book goes a little way in some respects towards providing an adequate account of certain matters it raises; its chief value lies in its criticism of 'objectivism' (i.e. the doctrine that all scientific beliefs are determined solely by observed facts) and in focusing on certain aspects of heuristics which have been overlooked or neglected. One of Polanyi's theses is that an understanding of the character of scientific knowledge (with all that this embraces) can be gained only by viewing this comprehensively in relation to the process of discovery. Discoveries are made in the context of already established discoveries. At any rate one major problem posed by science is its progressiveness; yet the way science advances is not satisfactorily accounted for by the usual, logical analyses of scientific structure, most of which, in any case, scarcely touch, still less come to grips with, the problem; for they start from what are regarded as completed scientific theories as data.

The analysis of a scientific theory as a hypothetico-deductive system involves a *static* conception of the theory; for this standpoint there are serious difficulties in dealing with a changing scientific theory—and all theories of living interest are continually being modified by amendment and extension. And there is a continued increase in observational knowledge too. Certainly, beyond a statics, a dynamics of science is also required; there have been some efforts to supply one, of which probably the best known is Popper's.[2] Popper's dynamics is, however, ineffective: it does not satisfactorily elucidate the usually *coherent* growth of scientific knowledge; it suggests that science may advance by the adoption and falsification of a succession of mutually isolated sets of hypotheses. Popper has proposed the use of simplicity to guide the choice of hypotheses: the simpler hypothesis is the more preferable. This part of his epistemology-cum-methodology is exposed to at least two different attacks. He equates methodological simplicity with degree of falsifiability; and one attack, aiming to

[1] Polanyi [63]. See also Grene [39], which is a study of some significant episodes in the history of epistemology making use of Polanyi's ideas; it also contains a provocative discussion of some problems in the philosophy of Biology. Palter [61] is a critical exposition of an older attempt to construct a large-scale epistemology of science. (I have not overlooked Russell's *Human Knowledge: Its Scope and Limits* (1948). Popper [65] would have counted if it were not a translation, with addenda, of his *Logik der Forschung: Zur Erkenntnistheorie der modernen Naturwissenschaft* (imprint '1935', actually published in 1934).

[2] Popper [65], especially Chapters 6 and 7.

undermine the whole edifice of his system, is on weaknesses in his notion of falsifiability. The other attack throws doubts and difficulties directly on Popper's path connecting simplicity with falsifiability.[1] A quite different approach to the dynamics of science is the view of scientific theories as essentially models of segments of reality; a model is a system of concepts and n-place predicates which are thought to be analogous to the basic entities, their properties, and relations occurring in the modelled segment of reality. This view rightly rejects the thesis that all scientific theories, even in physics, are merely interpreted axiomatic systems.[2] According to Duhem, 'A physical theory is not an explanation. It is a system of mathematical propositions, deduced from a small number of principles, which aim to represent as simply, as completely, and as exactly as possible a set of experimental laws.'[3] However, the axiomatic account of scientific theories fails to clarify the nature and role of discovery in science and hence also is unable to contribute much to the understanding of the dynamics of science. This account has been attractive to philosophers and philosophical physicists who are unduly disturbed by the threat of metaphysical incursions into physics, not realizing that physics is well able to curb the more fanciful flights of the metaphysical imagination and to convert any thoroughgoing concern with the details of physical reality to its own ends. (But possibly the stringencies of the axiomatic method, combined with a rigorous empiricism, will continue for some time to be salutary for certain branches of the human sciences.)

[1] For criticisms of Popper's account of simplicity, see the papers by Nelson Goodman and Robert Ackermann reprinted below (pages 121 ff., 124 ff.; cf. also, Harsanyi [45]. For criticisms of other doctrines in Popper [65], see e.g. the review by Haskell Fain, *Philosophy of Science*, 28 (1961), 319–24.

[2] Cf. Hesse [48].

[3] Duhem, op. cit., p. 19.

I

HOW TO BE A GOOD EMPIRICIST—A PLEA FOR TOLERANCE IN MATTERS EPISTEMOLOGICAL

P. K. FEYERABEND

'Facts?' he repeated. 'Take a drop more grog, Mr. Franklin, and you'll get over the weakness of believing in facts! Foul play, Sir!'

Wilkie Collins, *Moonstone*

1. Contemporary Empiricism Liable to Lead to Establishment of a Dogmatic Metaphysics

Today empiricism is the professed philosophy of a good many intellectual enterprises. It is the core of the sciences, or so at least we are taught, for it is responsible both for the existence and for the growth of scientific knowledge. It has been adopted by influential schools in aesthetics, ethics, and theology. And within philosophy proper the empirical point of view has been elaborated in great detail and with even greater precision. This predilection for empiricism is due to the assumption that only a thoroughly observational procedure can exclude fanciful speculation and empty metaphysics as well as to the hope than an empiristic attitude is most liable to prevent stagnation and to further the progress of knowledge. It is the purpose of the present paper to show that empiricism in the form in which it is practised today cannot fulfil this hope.

Putting it very briefly, it seems to me that the contemporary doctrine of empiricism has encountered difficulties, and has created contradictions which are very similar to the difficulties and contradictions inherent in some versions of the doctrine of democracy. The latter are a well-known phenomenon. That is, it is well known that essentially totalitarian measures are often advertised as being a necessary consequence of democratic principles. Even worse—it not so rarely happens that the totalitarian character of the defended measures is

From *Philosophy of Science, The Delaware Seminar*, Vol. 2, ed. B. Baumrin (Interscience Publishers, 1963), pp. 3–39. This is a revised version of a paper originally published in *Inquiry*. Reprinted by permission of the University of Delaware.

not explicitly stated but covered up by calling them 'democratic', the word 'democratic' now being used in a new, and somewhat misleading, manner. This method of (conscious or unconscious) verbal camouflage works so well that is has deceived some of the staunchest supporters of true democracy. What is not so well known is that modern empiricism is in precisely the same predicament. That is, some of the methods of modern empiricism which are introduced in the spirit of anti-dogmatism and progress are bound to lead to the establishment of a dogmatic metaphysics and to the construction of defence mechanisms which make this metaphysics safe from refutation by experimental inquiry. It is true that in the process of establishing such a metaphysics the words 'empirical' or 'experience' will frequently occur; but their sense will be as distorted as was the sense of 'democratic' when used by some concealed defenders of a new tyranny.[1] This, then, is my charge: Far from eliminating dogma and metaphysics and thereby encouraging progress, modern empiricism has found a new way of making dogma and metaphysics respectable, viz., the way of calling them 'well-confirmed theories', and of developing a method of confirmation in which experimental inquiry plays a large though well controlled role. In this respect, modern empiricism is very different indeed from the empiricism of Galileo, Faraday, and Einstein, though it will of course try to represent these scientists as following its own paradigm of research, thereby further confusing the issue.[2]

From what has been said above it follows that the fight for tolerance in scientific matters and the fight for scientific progress must still be carried on. What has changed is the denomination of the enemies. They were priests, or 'school-philosophers', a few decades ago. Today

[1] K. R. Popper, *The Open Society and Its Enemies*, Princeton University Press, Princeton, New Jersey, 1953.

[2] It is very interesting to see how many so-called empiricists, when turning to the past completely fail to pay attention to some very obvious facts which are incompatible with their empiristic epistemology. Thus Galileo has been represented as a thinker who turned away from the empty speculations of the Aristotelians and who based his own laws upon facts which he had carefully collected beforehand. Nothing could be further from the truth. *The Aristotelians could quote numerous observational results in their favour*. The Copernican idea of the motion of the earth, on the other hand, did not possess independent observational support, at least not in the first 150 years of its existence. Moreover, it was inconsistent with facts and highly confirmed physical theories. And *this* is how modern physics started: not as an observational enterprise *but as an unsupported speculation that was inconsistent with highly confirmed laws*. For details and further references see my 'Realism and Instrumentalism', in *The Critical Approach: Essays in Honor of Karl Popper*, ed. M. Bunge, The Free Press, Glencoe, Illinois, 1964.

they call themselves 'philosophers of science', or 'logical empiricists'.[1] There are also a good many scientists who work in the same direction. I maintain that all these groups work against scientific progress. But whereas the former did so openly and could be easily discerned, the latter proceed under the flag of progressivism and empiricism and thereby deceive a good many of their followers. Hence, although their presence is noticeable enough they may almost be compared to a fifth column, the aim of which must be exposed in order that its detrimental effect be fully appreciated. It is the purpose of this paper to contribute to such an exposure.

I shall also try to give a positive methodology for the empirical sciences which no longer encourages dogmatic petrification in the name of experience. Put in a nutshell, the answer which this method gives to the question in the title is: You can be a good empiricist only if you are prepared to work with many alternative theories rather than with a single point of view and 'experience'. This plurality of theories must not be regarded as a preliminary stage of knowledge which will at some time in the future be replaced by the One True Theory. Theoretical pluralism is assumed to be an *essential feature* of all knowledge that claims to be objective. Nor can one rest content with a plurality which is merely abstract and which is created by denying now this and now that component of the dominant point of view. Alternatives must rather be developed in such detail that problems already 'solved' by the accepted theory can again be treated in a new and perhaps also more detailed manner. Such development will of course take time, and it will not be possible, for example, at once to construct alternatives to the present quantum theory which are comparable to its richness and sophistication. Still, it would be very unwise to bring the process to a standstill in the very beginning by the remark that some suggested new ideas are undeveloped, general, metaphysical. *It takes time to build a good theory* (a triviality that seems to have been forgotten by some defenders of the Copenhagen point of view of the quantum theory); and it also takes time to develop an alternative to a good theory. The *function* of such concrete alternatives is, however, this: They provide means of criticizing the accepted theory in a manner which goes *beyond* the criticism provided by a

[1] One might be inclined to add those who base their pronouncements upon an analysis of what they call 'ordinary language'. I do not think they deserve to be honoured by a criticism. Paraphrasing Galileo, one might say that they 'deserve not even that name, for they do not talk plainly and simply but are content to adore the shadows, philosophizing not with due circumspection but merely from having memorized a few ill-understood principles'.

comparison of that theory 'with the facts'; however closely a theory seems to reflect the facts, however universal its use, and however necessary its existence seems to be to those speaking the corresponding idiom, its factual adequacy can be asserted only *after* it has been confronted with alternatives *whose invention and detailed development must therefore precede any final assertion of practical success and factual adequacy*. This, then, is the methodological justification of a plurality of *theories:* Such a plurality allows for a much sharper criticism of accepted ideas than does the comparison with a domain of 'facts' which are supposed to sit there independently of theoretical considerations. The function of unusual *metaphysical* ideas which are built up in a nondogmatic fashion and which are then developed in sufficient detail to give an (alternative) account even of the most common experimental and observational situations is defined accordingly: They play a decisive role in the criticism and in the development of what is generally believed and 'highly confirmed'; and they have therefore to be present at *any* stage of the development of our knowledge.[1] A science that is free from *metaphysics* is on the best way to become a *dogmatic* metaphysical system. So far the summary of the method I shall explain, and defend, in the present paper.

It is clear that this method still retains an essential element of *empiricism:* The decision between alternative theories is based upon *crucial experiments*. At the same time it must *restrict* the range of such experiments. Crucial experiments work well with theories of a low degree of generality whose principles do not touch the principles on which the ontology of the chosen observation language is based. They work well if such theories are compared with respect to a much more general background theory which provides a stable meaning for the observation sentences. However, this background theory, like any other theory, is itself in need of criticism. Criticism must use alternatives. Alternatives will be the more efficient the more radically they differ from the point of view to be investigated. It is bound to happen, then, that the alternatives do not share a single statement with the theories they criticize. Clearly, a crucial experiment is now impossible.

[1] It is nowadays frequently assumed that 'if one considers the history of a special branch of science, one gets the impression that non-scientific elements . . . relatively frequently occur in the earlier stages of development, but that they gradually retrogress in later stages and even tend to disappear in such advanced stages which become ripe for more or less thorough formalization'. (H. J. Groenewold, *Synthèse*, 1957, p. 305). Our considerations in the text would seem to show that such a development is very undesirable and can only result in a well-formalized, precisely expressed, and completely petrified metaphysics.

It is impossible, not because the experimental device is too complex, or because the calculations leading to the experimental prediction are too difficult; it is impossible because there is no statement capable of expressing what emerges from the observation. This consequence, which severely restricts the domain of empirical discussion, cannot be circumvented by any of the methods which are currently in use and which all try to work with relatively stable observation languages. It indicates that the attempt to make empiricism a universal basis of all our factual knowledge cannot be carried out. The discussion of this situation is beyond the scope of the present paper.

On the whole, the paper is a concise summary of results which I have explained in a more detailed fashion in the following essays: 'Explanation, Reduction, and Empiricism'; 'Problems of Microphysics'; 'Problems of Empiricism'; 'Linguistic Philosophy and the Mind-Body Problem.'[1] All the relevant acknowledgements can be found there. Let me only repeat here that my general outlook derives from the work of K. R. Popper (London) and David Bohm (London) and from my discussions with both. It was severely tested in discussion with my colleague, T. S. Kuhn (Berkeley). It was the latter's skilful defence of a scientific conservatism which triggered two papers, including the present one. Criticism by A. Naess (Oslo), D. Rynin (Berkeley), Roy Edgley (Bristol), and J. W. N. Watkins (London) have been responsible for certain changes I made in the final version.

2. Two Conditions of Contemporary Empiricism

In this section I intend to give an outline of some assumptions of contemporary empiricism which have been widely accepted. It will be shown in the sections to follow that these apparently harmless assumptions which have been explicitly formulated by some logical empiricists, but which also seem to guide the work of a good many physicists, are bound to lead to exactly the results I have outlined above: dogmatic petrification and the establishment, on so-called 'empirical grounds', of a rigid metaphysics.

One of the cornerstones of contemporary empiricism is its *theory of explanation*. This theory is an elaboration of some simple and very plausible ideas first proposed by Popper[2] and it may be introduced

[1] These essays were published in Volume III of the *Minnesota Studies in the Philosophy of Science*; in Volumes I and II of the *Pittsburgh Studies in the Philosophy of Science*; and in *Problems of Philosophy, Essays in Honor of Herbert Feigl*, respectively.

[2] See K. R. Popper, *Logic of Scientific Discovery*, New York, 1959, Section 12 (this is a translation of his *Logik der Forschung* published in 1935). The decisive feature of Popper's theory, a feature which was not at all made clear by earlier writers on the

as follows: Let T and T' be two different scientific theories, T' the theory to be explained, or the explanandum, T the explaining theory, or the explanans. Explanation (of T') consists in the *derivation* of T' from T and initial conditions which specify the domain D' in which T' is applicable. Prima facie, this demand of derivability seems to be a very natural one to make for 'otherwise the explanans would not constitute adequate grounds for the explanation'.[1] It implies two things: first, that the consequences of a satisfactory explanans, T, inside D' must be compatible with the explanandum, T', and secondly, that the main descriptive terms of these consequences must either coincide, with respect to their meanings, with the main descriptive terms of T', or at least they must be related to them via an empirical hypothesis. The latter result can also be formulated by saying that the meaning of T' must be unaffected by the explanation. 'It is of the utmost importance to observe', writes Professor Nagel,[2] emphasizing this point, 'that the expressions peculiar to a science will possess meanings that are fixed by its *own* procedures, and that are therefore intelligible in terms of its own rules of usage, whether or not the science has been or will be [explained in terms of] the other discipline.'

Now if we take it for granted that more general theories are always introduced with the purpose of explaining the existent successful theories, then every new theory will have to satisfy the two conditions just mentioned. Or, to state it in a more explicit manner,

(1) only such theories are then admissible in a given domain which either *contain* the theories already used in this domain, or which are at least *consistent* with them inside the domain[3]; and

---

subject of explanation, is the emphasis he puts on the initial conditions and the implied possibility of two kinds of laws, viz., (1) laws concerning the temporal sequence of events; and (2) laws concerning the space of initial conditions. In the case of the quantum theory, the laws of the second kind provide very important information about the nature of the elementary particles and it is to *them* and *not* to the laws of motion that reference is made in the discussions concerning the interpretation of the uncertainty relations. In general relativity, the laws formulating the initial conditions concern the structure of the universe at large and only by overlooking them could it be believed that a purely relational account of space would be possible. For the last point, cf. E. L. Hill, 'Quantum Physics and Relativity Theory', in H. Feigl and G. Maxwell, eds., *Current Issues in the Philosophy of Science*, Holt, Rinehart and Winston, New York, 1961.

[1] C. G. Hempel, 'Studies in the Logic of Explanation', reprinted in H. Feigl and M. Brodbeck, eds., *Readings in the Philosophy of Science*, New York, 1953, p. 321.

[2] E. Nagel, 'The Meaning of Reduction in the Natural Sciences', reprinted in A. C. Danto and S. Morgenbesser, eds., *Philosophy of Science*, New York, 1960, p. 301.

[3] It has been objected to this formulation that theories which are consistent with a given explanandum may still contradict each other. This is quite correct, but it does

(2) meanings will have to be invariant with respect to scientific progress; that is, all future theories will have to be phrased in such a manner that their use in explanations does not affect what is said by the theories, or factual reports to be explained.

These two conditions I shall call the *consistency condition* and the *condition of meaning invariance*, respectively.

Both conditions are *restrictive* conditions and therefore bound profoundly to influence the growth of knowledge. I shall soon show that the development of actual science very often violates them and that it violates them in exactly those places where one would be inclined to perceive a tremendous progress of knowledge. I shall also show that neither condition can be justified from the point of view of a tolerant empiricism. However, before doing so I would like to mention that both conditions have occasionally entered the domain of the sciences and have been used here in attacks against new developments and even in the process of theory construction itself. Especially today, they play a very important role in the construction as well as in the defence of certain points of view in microphysics.

Taking first an earlier example, we find that in his *Wärmelehre*, Ernst Mach[1] makes the following remark:

> Considering that there is, in a purely mechanical system of absolutely elastic atoms no real analogue for the *increase of entropy*, one can hardly suppress the idea that a violation of the second law . . . should be possible if such a mechanical system were the *real* basis of thermodynamic processes.

And referring to the fact that the second law is a highly confirmed physical law, he insinuates (in his *Zwei Aufsaetze*[2]) that for this reason the mechanical hypothesis must not be taken too seriously. There were many similar objections against the kinetic theory of heat.[3] More recently, Max Born has based his arguments against the possibility of a return to determinism upon the consistency condition and the assumption which we shall here take for granted, that wave mechanics is incompatible with determinism.

If future theory should be deterministic, it cannot be a modification of the present one but must be essentially different. How this should be possible

---

not invalidate my argument. For as soon as a single theory is regarded as sufficient for explaining all that is known (and represented by the other theories in question), it will have to be consistent with all these other theories.

[1]E. Mach, *Wärmelehre*, Leipzig, 1897, p. 364.

[2]E. Mach, *Zwei Aufsaetze*, Leipzig, 1912.

[3]For a discussion of these objections, cf. ter Haar's review article in *Reviews of Modern Physics*, 1957.

without sacrificing a whole treasure of well-established results [i.e., without contradicting highly confirmed physical laws and thereby violating the consistency condition] I leave to the determinists to worry about.[1]

Most members of the so-called Copenhagen school of quantum theory would argue in a similar manner. For them the idea of complementarity and the formalism of quantization expressing this idea do not contain any hypothetical element as they are 'uniquely determined by the facts.'[2] Any theory which contradicts this idea is factually inadequate and must be removed. Conversely, an explanation of the idea of complementarity is acceptable only if it either contains this idea, or is at least consistent with it. This is how the consistency condition is used in arguments against theories such as those of Bohm, de Broglie, and Vigier.[3]

The use of the consistency condition is not restricted to such general remarks, however. A decisive part of the existing quantum theory *itself*, viz., the projection postulate,[4] is the result of the attempt to give an account of the definiteness of macro objects and macro events that is in accordance with the consistency condition. The influence of the condition of meaning invariance goes even further.

> The Copenhagen interpretation of the quantum theory [writes Heisenberg[5]] starts from a paradox. Any experiment in physics, whether it refers to the phenomena of daily life or to atomic events, is to be described in the terms of classical physics ... *We cannot and should not replace these concepts by any others* [my italics]. Still the application of these concepts is limited by the relations of uncertainty. We must keep in mind this limited range of applicability of the classical concepts while using them, but we cannot and should not try to improve them.

This means that the meaning of the classical terms must remain invariant with respect to any future explanation of microphenomena. Microtheories have to be formulated in such a manner that this invariance is guaranteed. The principle of correspondence and the formalism of quantization connected with it were explicitly devised for satisfying this demand. Altogether, the quantum theory seems to be the first theory after the downfall of the Aristotelian physics that

[1] M. Born, *Natural Philosophy of Cause and Chance*, O. U. P., New York, 1948, p. 109.

[2] L. Rosenfeld, 'Misunderstandings about the Foundations of the Quantum Theory' in *Observation and Interpretation*, London, 1957, p. 42.

[3] Cf. the discussions in *Observation and Interpretation* (see previous note).

[4] For details and further literature, cf. Section 11 of my paper 'Problems of Microphysics'.

[5] W. Heisenberg, *Physics and Philosophy*, New York, 1958, p. 46.

has been quite explicitly constructed with an eye both on the consistency condition and the condition of (empirical) meaning invariance. In this respect it is very different indeed from, say, relativity which violates both consistency and meaning invariance with respect to earlier theories. Most of the arguments used for the defence of its customary interpretation also depend on the validity of these two conditions and they will collapse with their removal. An examination of these conditions is therefore very topical and bound deeply to affect present controversies in microphysics. I shall start this investigation by showing that some of the most interesting developments of physical theory in the past have violated both conditions.

3. These Conditions Not Invariably Accepted by Actual Science

The case of the consistency condition can be dealt with in a few words: it is well known (and has also been shown in great detail by Duhem[1]) that Newton's theory is inconsistent with Galileo's law of the free fall and with Kepler's laws; that statistical thermodynamics is inconsistent with the second law of the phenomenological theory; that wave optics is inconsistent with geometrical optics; and so on. Note that what is being asserted here is *logical* inconsistency; it may well be that the differences of prediction are too small to be detectable by experiment. Note also that what is being asserted is not the inconsistency of, say, Newton's theory and Galileo's law, but rather the inconsistency of *some consequences* of Newton's theory in the domain of validity of Galileo's law, and Galileo's law. In this last case the situation is especially clear. Galileo's law asserts that the acceleration of the free fall is a constant, whereas application of Newton's theory to the surface of the earth gives an acceleration that is not a constant but *decreases* (although imperceptibly) with the distance from the centre of the earth. Conclusion: If actual scientific procedure is to be the measure of method, then the consistency condition is inadequate.

The case of meaning invariance requires a little more argument, not because it is intrinsically more difficult but because it seems to be much more closely connected with deep-rooted prejudices. Assume that an explanation is required, in terms of the special theory of relativity, of the classical conservation of mass in all reactions in a closed system S. If m', m'', m''', . . . , m^i, . . . are the masses of the

[1] P. Duhem, *La Théorie Physique: Son Objet, Sa Structure*, Paris, 1914, Chs. IX and X. See also K. R. Popper, 'The Aim of Science', *Ratio*, Vol. I (1957).

parts P', P'', P''', . . . P^i, . . . of S, then what we want is an explanation of

$$\Sigma m^i = \text{const.} \tag{1}$$

for all reactions inside S. We see at once that the consistency condition cannot be fulfilled: According to special relativity Σm^i will vary with the velocities of the parts relative to the co-ordinate system in which the observations are carried out, and the total mass of S will also depend on the relative potential energies of the parts. However, if the velocities and the mutual forces are not too large, then the variation of Σm^i predicted by relativity will be so small as to be undetectable by experiment. Now let us turn to the *meanings* of the terms in the relativistic law and in the corresponding classical law. The first indication of a possible change of meaning may be seen in the fact that in the classical case the mass of an aggregate of parts equals the sum of the masses of the parts:

$$M(\Sigma P^i) = \Sigma M(P^i).$$

This is not valid in the case of relativity where the relative velocities and the relative potential energies contribute to the mass balance. That the relativistic concept and the classical concept of mass are very different indeed becomes clear if we also consider that the former is a *relation*, involving relative velocities, between an object and a co-ordinate system, whereas the latter is a *property* of the object itself and independent of its behaviour in co-ordinate systems. True, there have been attempts to give a relational analysis even of the classical concept (Mach). None of these attempts, however, leads to the relativistic idea with its velocity dependence on the co-ordinate system, which idea must therefore be added even to a *relational* account of classical mass. The attempt to identify the classical mass with the relativistic rest mass if of no avail either. For although both may have the same numerical value, the one is still dependent on the co-ordinate system chosen (in which it is at rest and has that specific value), whereas the other is not so dependent. We have to conclude, then, that $(m)_c$ and $(m)_r$ mean very different things and that $(\Sigma m^i)_c = \text{const.}$ and $(\Sigma m^i)_r = \text{const.}$ are very different assertions. This being the case, the derivation from relativity of either equation (1) or of a law that makes slightly different quantitative predictions with Σm^i used in the classical manner, will be possible only if a further premiss is added which establishes a relation between the $(m)_c$ and the $(m)_r$. Such a 'bridge law'—and this is a major point in Nagel's theory of reduction—is a hypothesis according to which the occurrence of the properties designated by some expression in the premises of the [explanans] is a sufficient, or a necessary and sufficient, condition for the occurrence of the properties designated by the expression of the [explanandum].[1]

Applied to the present case this would mean the following: Under certain conditions the occurrence of relativistic mass of a given magnitude is accompanied by the occurrence of classical mass of a corresponding magnitude; this assertion is inconsistent with another part of the explanans, viz., the theory of relativity. After all, this theory asserts that there are no invariants which are directly connected with mass measurements and it thereby asserts that '$(m)_c$' does not express real features of physical systems. Thus we inevitably arrive at the conclusion that mass conservation cannot be explained in terms of relativity (or 'reduced' to relativity) without a violation of meaning invariance. And if one retorts, as has been done by some critics of the ideas expressed in the present paper,[2] that meaning invariance is an essential part of both reduction and explanation, then the answer will simply be that equation (1) can neither be explained by, nor reduced to relativity. Whatever the *words* used for describing the situation, the *fact* remains that actual science does not observe the requirement of meaning invariance.

This argument is quite general and is independent of whether the terms whose meaning is under investigation are observable or not. It is therefore stronger than may seem at first sight. There are some empiricists who would admit that the meaning of theoretical terms may be changed in the course of scientific progress. However, not many people are prepared to extend meaning *variance* to observational terms also. The idea motivating this attitude is, roughly, that the meaning of observational terms is uniquely determined by the procedures of observation such as looking, listening, and the like. These procedures remain unaffected by theoretical advance.[3] Hence, observational meanings, too, remain unaffected by theoretical advance. What is overlooked, here, is that the 'logic' of the observ-

[1]E. Nagel, 'The Meaning of Reduction in the Natural Sciences', loc. cit., p. 302.

[2]Cf. Section 4.7 of M. Scriven's paper 'Explanations, Predictions, and Laws', in Vol. III of the *Minnesota Studies in the Philosophy of Science*. Similar objections have been raised by Kraft (Vienna) and Rynin (Berkeley).

[3]For an exposition and criticism of this idea cf. my 'Attempt at a Realistic Interpretation of Experience', *Proceedings of the Aristotelian Society*, New Series, LVIII, 143–70 (1958).

ational terms is not exhausted by the procedures which are connected with their application 'on the basis of observation'. As will turn out later, it also depends on the more general ideas that determine the 'ontology' (in Quine's sense) of our discourse. These general ideas may change without any change of observational procedures being implied. For example, we may change our ideas about the nature, or the ontological status (property, relation, object, process, &c.) of the colour of a self-luminescent object without changing the methods of ascertaining that colour (looking, for example). Clearly, such a change is bound profoundly to influence the meanings of our observational terms.

All this has a decisive bearing upon some contemporary ideas concerning the interpretation of scientific theories. According to these ideas, theoretical terms receive their meanings via correspondence rules which connect them with an observational language *that has been fixed in advance* and independently of the structure of the theory to be interpreted. Now, our above analysis would seem to show that *if we interpret scientific theories in the manner accepted by the scientific community*, then most of these correspondence rules will be either false, or nonsensical. They will be *false* if they *assert* the existence of entities denied by the theory; they will be *nonsensical* if they *presuppose* this existence. Turning the argument around, we can also say that the attempt to interpret the calculus of some theory that has been voided of the meaning assigned to it by the scientific community with the help of the double language system, will lead to a very different theory. Let us again take the theory of relativity as an example: It can be safely assumed that the physical thing language of Carnap, and any similar language that has been suggested as an observation language, is not Lorentz-invariant. The attempt to interpret the *calculus* of relativity on *its* basis therefore cannot lead to the *theory* of relativity as it was understood by Einstein. What we shall obtain will be at the very most *Lorentz's interpretation* with its inherent asymmetries. This undesirable result cannot be evaded by the *demand* to use a different and more adequate observation language. The double language system assumes that theories which are not connected with some observation language do not possess an interpretation. The demand assumes that they do, and asks to choose the observation language most suited to it. It reverses the relation between theory and experience that is characteristic for the double language method of interpretation, which means, it gives up this method.

Contemporary empiricism, therefore, has not led to any satisfactory account of the meanings of scientific theories.[1]

What we have shown so far is that the two conditions of Section 2 are frequently violated in the course of scientific practice and especially at periods of scientific revolution. This is not yet a very strong argument. True: There are empirically inclined philosophers who have derived some satisfaction from the assumption that they only make explicit what is implicitly contained in scientific practice. It is therefore quite important to show that scientific practice is not what it is supposed to be by them. Also, strict adherence to meaning invariance and consistency would have made impossible some very decisive advances in physical theory such as the advance from the physics of Aristotle to the physics of Galileo and Newton. However, how do we know (independently of the fact that they do exist, have a certain structure, and are very influential—a circumstance that will have great weight with opportunists only[2]) that the sciences are a desirable phenomenon, that they contribute to the advancement of knowledge, and that their analysis will therefore lead to reasonable methodological demands? And did it not emerge in the last section that meaning invariance and the consistency condition *are* adopted by some scientists? Actual scientific practice, therefore, cannot be our last authority. We have to find out whether consistency and meaning

[1] It must be admitted, however, that Einstein's original interpretation of the special theory of relativity is hardly ever used by contemporary physicists. For them the theory of relativity consists of two elements: (1) the Lorentz transformations; and (2) mass-energy equivalence. The Lorentz transformations are interpreted purely formally and are used to make a selection among possible equations. This interpretation does not allow to distinguish between Lorentz's original point of view and the entirely different point of view of Einstein. According to it Einstein achieved a very minor *formal* advance (this is the basis of Whittaker's attempt to 'debunk' Einstein). It is also very similar to what application of the double language model would yield. Still, an undesirable philosophical procedure is not improved by the support it gets from an undesirable procedure in physics. (The above comment on the contemporary attitude towards relativity was made by E. L. Hill in discussions at the Minnesota Center for the Philosophy of Science.)

[2] In about 1925 philosophers of science were bold enough to stick to their theses even in those cases where they were inconsistent with actual science. They meant to be *reformers* of science, and not *imitators*. (This point was explicitly made by Mach in his controversy with Planck. Cf. again his *Zwei Aufsaetze*.) In the meantime they have become rather tame (or beat) and are much more prepared to change their ideas in accordance with the latest discoveries of the historians, or the latest fashion of the contemporary scientific enterprise. This is very regrettable, indeed, for it considerably decreases the number of the rational critics of the scientific enterprise. And it also seems to give unwanted support to the Hegelian thesis (which is now implicitly held by many historians and philosophers of science) that what exists has a 'logic' of its own and is for that very reason reasonable.

invariance are *desirable* conditions and this quite independently of who accepts and praises them and how many Nobel prizes have been won with their help.[1] Such an investigation will be carried out in the next sections.

4. Inherent Unreasonableness of Consistency Condition

Prima facie, the case of the consistency condition can be dealt with in very few words. Consider for that purpose a theory T' that successfully describes the situation in the domain D'. From this we can infer (*a*) that T' agrees with a *finite* number of observations (let their class be F); and (*b*) that it agrees with these observations inside a margin M of error only.[2] Any alternative that contradicts T' outside F and inside M is supported by exactly the same observations and therefore acceptable if T' was acceptable (we shall assume that F are the only observations available). The consistency condition is much less tolerant. It eliminates a theory not because it is in disagreement with the *facts*; it eliminates it because it is in disagreement with *another theory*, with a theory, moreover, whose confirming instances it shares. *It thereby makes the as yet untested part of that theory a measure of validity*. The only difference between such a measure and a more recent theory is age and familiarity. Had the younger theory been there first, then the consistency condition would have worked in its favour. In this respect the effect of the consistency condition is rather similar to the effect of the more traditional methods of transcendental deduction, analysis of essences, phenomenological analysis, linguistic analysis. It contributes to the preservation of the old and familiar not because of any inherent advantage in it—for example, not because it has a better foundation in observation than has the newly suggested alternative, or because it is more elegant—but just because it is old and familiar. This is not the only instance where on closer inspection a rather surprising similarity emerges between modern empiricism and some of the school philosophies it attacks.

Now it seems to me that these brief considerations, although leading to an interesting *tactical* criticism of the consistency condition,

[1] Even the most dogmatic enterprise allows for discoveries (cf. the 'discovery' of so-called 'white Jews' among German physicists during the Nazi period). Hence, before hailing a so-called discovery, we must make sure that the system of thought which forms its background is not of a dogmatic kind.

[2] The indefinite character of all observations has been made very clear by Duhem, *La Théorie Physique: Son Objet, Sa Structure*, Chap. IX. For an alternative way of dealing with this indefiniteness, cf. S. Körner, *Conceptual Thinking*, New York, 1960.

do not yet go to the heart of the matter. They show that an alternative of the accepted point of view which shares its confirming instances cannot be *eliminated* by factual reasoning. They do not show that such an alternative is *acceptable*; and even less do they show that it *should be used*. It is bad enough, so a defender of the consistency condition might point out, that the accepted point of view does not possess full empirical support. Adding new theories *of an equally unsatisfactory character* will not improve the situation; nor is there much sense in trying to *replace* the accepted theories by some of their possible alternatives. Such replacement will be no easy matter. A new formalism may have to be learned and familiar problems may have to be calculated in a new way. Text-books must be rewritten, university curricula readjusted, experimental results reinterpreted. And what will be the result of all the effort? Another theory which, from an empirical point of view, has no advantage whatever over and above the theory it replaces. The only real improvement, so the defender of the consistency condition will continue, derives from the *addition of new facts*. Such new facts will either support the current theories, or they will force us to modify them by indicating precisely where they go wrong. In both cases they will precipitate real progress and not only arbitrary change. The proper procedure must therefore consist in the confrontation of the accepted point of view with as many relevant facts as possible. The exclusion of alternatives is then required for reasons of expediency: Their invention not only does not help, but it even hinders progress by absorbing time and manpower that could be devoted to better things. And the function of the consistency condition lies precisely in this. It eliminates such fruitless discussion and it forces the scientist to concentrate on the facts which, after all, are the only acceptable judges of a theory. This is how the practising scientist will defend his concentration on a single theory to the exclusion of all empirically possible alternatives.[1]

It is worth while repeating the reasonable core of this argument: Theories should not be changed unless there are pressing reasons for

[1]More detailed evidence for the existence of this attitude and for the way in which it influences the development of the sciences may be found in T. Kuhn's book *Structure of Scientific Revolutions* (University of Chicago Press, Chicago, 1962). The attitude is extremely common in the contemporary quantum theory. 'Let us enjoy the successful theories we possess and let us not waste our time with contemplating what *would* happen if *other* theories were used'—this seems to be the motto of almost all contemporary physicists (cf. W. Heisenberg, *Physics and Philosophy*, pp. 56, 144) and philosophers (cf. N. R. Hanson, 'Five Cautions for the Copenhagen Critics', *Philosophy of Science*, XXVI, 325–37, 1959). It may be traced back to Newton's papers and letters (to Hooke, and Pardies) on the theory of colour. See also p. 24, footnote 2;

doing so. The only pressing reason for changing a theory is disagreement with facts. Discussion of incompatible facts will therefore lead to progress. Discussion of incompatible alternatives will not. Hence, it is sound procedure to increase the number of relevant facts. It is not sound procedure to increase the number of factually adequate, but incompatible alternatives. One might wish to add that formal improvements such as increase of elegance, simplicity, generality, and coherence should not be excluded. But once these improvements have been carried out, the collection of facts for the purpose of test seems indeed to be the only thing left to the scientist.

5. Relative Autonomy of Facts

And this it is—provided these facts *exist*, *and are available independently of whether or not one considers alternatives to the theory to be tested*. This assumption on which the validity of the argument in the last section depends in a most decisive manner I shall call the assumption of the relative autonomy of facts, or the autonomy principle. It is not asserted by this principle that the discovery and description of facts is independent of *all* theorizing. But it *is* asserted that the facts which belong to the empirical content of some theory are available whether or not one considers alternatives to *this* theory. I am not aware that this very important assumption has ever been explicitly formulated as a separate postulate of the empirical method. However, it is clearly implied in almost all investigations which deal with questions of confirmation and test. All these investigations use a model in which a *single* theory is compared with a class of facts (or observation statements) which are assumed to be 'given' somehow. I submit that this is much too simple a picture of the actual situation. Facts and theories are much more intimately connected than is admitted by the autonomy principle. Not only is the description of every single fact dependent on *some* theory (which may, of course, be very different from the theory to be tested). There exist also facts which cannot be unearthed except with the help of alternatives to the theory to be tested, and which become unavailable as soon as such alternatives are excluded. This suggests that the methodological unit to which we must refer when discussing questions of test and empirical content is constituted by a *whole set of partly overlapping, factually adequate, but mutually inconsistent theories*. In the present paper only the barest outlines will be given of such a test model. However, before doing this I want to discuss an example which shows very clearly the function of alternatives in the discovery of facts.

As is well known, the Brownian particle is a perpetual motion machine of the second kind and its existence refutes the phenomenological second law. It therefore belongs to the domain of relevant facts for this law. Now, could this relation between the law and the Brownian particle have been discovered in a *direct* manner, i.e., could it have been discovered by an investigation of the observational consequences of the phenomenological theory that did not make use of an alternative account of heat? This question is readily divided into two: (1) Could the *relevance* of the Brownian particle have been discovered in this manner? (2) Could it have been demonstrated that it actually *refutes* the second law? The answer to the first question is that we do not know. It is impossible to say what would have happened had the kinetic theory not been considered by some physicists. It is my guess, however, that in this case the Brownian particle would have been regarded as an oddity much in the same way in which some of the late Professor Ehrenhaft's astounding effects[1] are regarded as an oddity, and that it would not have been given the decisive position it assumes in contemporary theory. The answer to the second question is simply—No. Consider what the discovery of the inconsistency between the Brownian particle and the second law would have required! It would have required (*a*) measurement of the exact *motion* of the particle in order to ascertain the changes of its kinetic energy plus the energy spent on overcoming the resistance of the fluid; and (*b*) it would have required precise measurements of temperature and heat transfer in the surrounding medium in order to ascertain that any loss occurring here was indeed compensated by the increase of the energy of the moving particle and the work done against the fluid. Such measurements are beyond experimental possibilities[2]. Neither is it possible to make precise measurements of the heat transfer; nor can the path of the particle be investigated with the desired precision. Hence a 'direct' refutation of the second law that considers only the phenomenological theory and the 'facts' of Brownian motion is impossible. And, as is well known, the actual refutation was brought about in a very different manner. It was brought about via the kinetic theory and Einstein's utilization of it in the calculation of the statistical properties of the Brownian

[1]Having witnessed these effects under a great variety of conditons, I am much more reluctant to regard them as mere curiosities than is the scientific community of today. Cf. also my edition of Ehrenhaft's lectures, *Einzelne Magnetische Nord- und Südpole und deren Auswirkung in den Naturwissenschaften*, Vienna, 1947.

[2]Cf. R. Fürth, *Zeitschrift für Physik*, Vol. 81, 143–62 (1933).

motion.[1] In the course of this procedure the phenomenological theory (T') was incorporated into the wider context of statistical physics (T) *in such a manner that the consistency condition was violated*; and *then* a crucial experiment was staged (investigations of Svedberg and Perrin).

It seems to me that this example is typical for the relation between fairly general theories, or points of view, and 'the facts'. Both the relevance and the refuting character of many very decisive facts can be established only with the help of other theories which, although factually adequate, are yet not in agreement with the view to be tested. This being the case, the production of such refuting facts may have to be preceded by the invention and articulation of alternatives to that view. Empiricism demands that the empirical content of whatever knowledge we possess be increased as much as possible. Hence *the invention of alternatives in addition to the view that stands in the centre of discussion constitutes an essential part of the empirical method*. Conversely, the fact that the consistency condition eliminates alternatives now shows it to be in disagreement with empiricism and not only with scientific practice. By excluding valuable tests it decreases the empirical content of the theories which are permitted to remain (and which, as we have indicated above, will usually be the theories which have been there first); and it especially decreases the number of those facts which could show their limitations. This last result of a determined application of the consistency condition is of very topical interest. It may well be that the refutation of the quantum-mechanical uncertainties presupposes just such an incorporation of the present theory into a wider context which is no longer in accordance with the idea of complementarity and

[1] For these investigations, cf. A. Einstein, *Investigations on the Theory of the Brownian Motion*, New York, 1956, which contains all the relevant papers by Einstein and an exhaustive bibliography by R. Fürth. For the experimental work, cf. J. Perrin, *Die Atome*, Leipzig, 1920. For the relation between the phenomenological theory and the kinetic theory, cf. also M. V. Smoluchowski, 'Experimentell nachwiesbare, der üblichen Thermodynamik widersprechende Molekularphaenomene', *Physikalische Zeitschrift*. (XIII, 1069–1912); and K. R. Popper, 'Irreversibility, or, Entropy since 1905', *British Journal for the Philosophy of Science*. VIII, 151 (1957). Despite Einstein's epoch-making discoveries and von Smoluchowski's splendid presentation of their effect (for the latter cf. also *Oeuvres de Marie Smoluchowski*, Cracovie, 1927, Vol. II, pp. 226 ff., 316 ff., 462 ff., and 530 ff.), the present situation in thermodynamics is extremely unclear, especially in view of the continued presence of the ideas of reduction which we criticized in the text above. To be more specific, it is frequently attempted to determine the entropy balance of a complex *statistical* process by reference to the (refuted) *phenomenological* law after which procedure fluctuations are superimposed in a most artificial fashion. For details cf. Popper, loc. cit.

which therefore suggests new and decisive experiments. And it may also be that the insistence, on the part of the majority of contemporary physicists, on the consistency condition will, if successful, for ever protect these uncertainties from refutation. This is how modern empiricism may finally lead to a situation where a certain point of view petrifies into dogma by being, in the name of experience, completely removed from any conceivable criticism.

6. The Self-Deception Involved in all Uniformity

It is worth while to examine this apparently empirical defence of a dogmatic point of view in somewhat greater detail. Assume that physicists have adopted, either consciously or unconsciously, the idea of the uniqueness of complementarity and that they therefore elaborate the orthodox point of view and refuse to consider alternatives. In the beginning such a procedure may be quite harmless. After all, a man can do only so many things at a time and it is better when he pursues a theory in which he is interested rather than a theory he finds boring. Now assume that the pursuit of the theory he chose has led to successes and that the theory has explained in a satisfactory manner circumstances that had been unintelligible for quite some time. This gives empirical support to an idea which to start with seemed to possess only this advantage: It was interesting and intriguing. The concentration upon the theory will now be reinforced, the attitude towards alternatives will become less tolerant. Now if it is true, as has been argued in the last section, that many facts become available only with the help of such alternatives, then the refusal to consider them *will result in the elimination of potentially refuting facts*. More especially, it will eliminate facts whose discovery would show the complete and irreparable inadequacy of the theory.[1] Such facts having been made inaccessible, the theory will appear to be free from blemish and it will seem that 'all the evidence points with merciless definiteness in the . . . direction . . . [that] all the processes involving . . . unknown interactions conform to the fundamental quantum law' (Rosenfeld in *Observation and Interpretation*, [referred to

[1]The quantum theory can be adapted to a great many difficulties. It is an open theory in the sense that apparent inadequacies can be accounted for in an *ad hoc* manner, by *adding* suitable operators, or elements in the Hamiltonian, rather than by recasting the whole structure. A refutation of its basic formalism (i.e., of the formalism of quantization, and of noncommuting operators in a Hilbert space or a reasonable extension of it) would therefore demand proof to the effect that *there is no conceivable adjustment of the Hamiltonian, or of the operators used* which makes the theory conform to a given fact. It is clear that such a general statement can only be provided by an *alternative theory* which of course must be detailed enough to allow for independent, and crucial tests.

in fn. 2, p. 19 above] p. 44). This will further reinforce the belief in the uniqueness of the current theory and in the complete futility of any account that proceeds in a different manner. Being now very firmly convinced that there is only one good microphysics, the physicists will try to explain even adverse facts in its terms, and they will not mind when such explanations are sometimes a little clumsy. By now the success of the theory has become public news. Popular science books (and this includes a good many books on the philosophy of science) will spread the basic postulates of the theory; applications will be made in distant fields. More than ever the theory will appear to possess tremendous empirical support. The chances for the consideration of alternatives are now very slight indeed. The final success of the fundamental assumptions of the quantum theory and of the idea of complementarity will seem to be assured.

At the same time it is evident, on the basis of the considerations in the last section, that this appearance of success *cannot in the least be regarded as a sign of truth and correspondence with nature*. Quite the contrary, the suspicion arises that the absence of major difficulties is a result of the decrease of empirical content brought about by the elimination of alternatives, and of facts that can be discovered with the help of these alternatives only. In other words, *the suspicion arises that this alleged success is due to the fact that in the process of application to new domains the theory has been turned into a metaphysical system*. Such a system will of course be very 'successful' not, however, because it agrees so well with the facts, but because no facts have been specified that would constitute a test and because some such facts have even been removed. Its 'success' *is entirely man-made*. It was decided to stick to some ideas and the result was, quite naturally, the survival of these ideas. If now the initial decision is forgotten, or made only implicitly, then the survival will seem to constitute independent support, it will reinforce the decision, or turn it into an explicit one, and in this way close the circle. This is how empirical 'evidence' may be *created* by a procedure which quotes as its justification the very same evidence it has produced in the first place.

At this point an 'empirical' theory of the kind described (and let us always remember that the basic principles of the present quantum theory and especially the idea of complementarity are uncomfortably close to forming such a theory) becomes almost indistinguishable from a myth. In order to realize this, we need only consider that on account of its all-pervasive character a myth such as the myth of witchcraft and of demonic possession will possess a high degree of confirmation on the basis of observation. Such a myth has been taught for a long time; its content is enforced by fear, prejudice, and ignorance as well as by a jealous and cruel priesthood. It penetrates the most common idiom, infects all modes of thinking and many decisions which mean a great deal in human life. It provides models for the explanation of any conceivable event, conceivable, that is, for those who have accepted it.[1] This being the case, its key terms will be fixed in an unambiguous manner and the idea (which may have led to such a procedure in the first place) that they are copies of unchanging entities and that change of meaning, if it should happen, is due to human mistake—this idea will now be very plausible. Such plausibility reinforces all the manœuvres which are used for the preservation of the myth (elimination of opponents included). The conceptual apparatus of the theory and the emotions connected with its application having penetrated all means of communication, all actions, and indeed the whole life of the community, such methods as transcendental deduction, analysis of usage, phenomenological analysis which are means for further solidifying the myth will be extremely successful (which shows, by the way, that all these methods which have been the trademark of various philosophical schools old and new, have one thing in common: They tend to *preserve* the *status quo* of the intellectual life).[2] Observational results, too, will speak in favour of the theory as they are formulated in its terms. It will seem that at last the truth has been arrived at. At the same time it is evident that all contact with the world has been lost and that the stability achieved, the semblance of absolute truth, *is nothing but the result of an absolute conformism.*[3] For how can we possibly test, or improve upon, the truth of a theory if it is built in such a manner that any conceivable event can be described, and explained, in terms of its principles? The *only* way of investigating such all-embracing

[1] For a very detailed description of a once very influential myth, cf. C. H. Lea, *Materials for a History of Witchcraft*, 3 Vols., New York, 1957, as well as *Malleus Malleficarum*, translated bv Montague Summers (who, by the way, counts it 'among the most important, wisest [sic!] and weightiest books of the world'), London, 1928.

[2] Quite clearly, analysis of usage, to take only one example, presupposes certain regularities concerning this usage. The more people differ in their fundamental ideas, the more difficult will it be to uncover such regularities. Hence, analysis of usage will work best in a closed society that is firmly held together by a powerful myth such as was the philosophy in the Oxford of about ten years ago.

[3] Schizophrenics very often hold beliefs which are as rigid, all-pervasive, and unconnected with reality, as are the best dogmatic philosophies. Only such beliefs come to them naturally whereas a professor may sometimes spend his whole life in attempting to find arguments which create a similar state of mind.

principles is to compare them with a different set of *equally all-embracing* principles—but this way has been excluded from the very beginning. The myth is therefore of no objective relevance, it continues to exist solely as the result of the effort of the community of believers and of their leaders, be these now priests or Nobel prize winners. *Its 'success' is entirely man-made*. This, I think, is the most decisive argument against any method that encourages uniformity, be it now empirical or not. Any such method is in the last resort a method of deception. It enforces an unenlightened conformism, and speaks of truth; it leads to a deterioration of intellectual capabilities, of the power of imagination, and speaks of deep insight; it destroys the most precious gift of the young, their tremendous power of imagination, and speaks of education.

To sum up: *Unanimity of opinion may be fitting for a church, for the frightened victims of some (ancient, or modern) myth, or for the weak and willing followers of some tyrant; variety of opinion is a feature necessary for objective knowledge; and a method that encourages variety is also the only method that is compatible with a humanitarian outlook*. To the extent to which the consistency condition (and, as will emerge, the condition of meaning invariance) delimits variety, it contains a theological element (which lies, of course, in the worship of 'facts' so characteristic for nearly all empiricism).

7. Inherent Unreasonableness of Meaning Invariance

What we have achieved so far has immediate application to the question whether the meaning of certain key terms should be kept unchanged in the course of the development and improvement of our knowledge. After all, the meaning of every term we use depends upon the theoretical context in which it occurs. Hence, if we consider two contexts with basic principles which either contradict each other, or which lead to inconsistent consequences in certain domains, it is to be expected that some terms of the first context will not occur in the second context with exactly the same meaning. Moreover, if our methodology demands the use of mutually inconsistent, partly overlapping, and empirically adequate theories, then it thereby also demands the use of conceptual systems which are mutually *irreducible* (their primitives cannot be connected by bridge laws which are meaningful *and* factually correct) and it demands that meanings of terms be left elastic and that no binding commitment be made to a certain set of concepts.

It is very important to realize that such a tolerant attitude towards meanings, or such a change of meaning in cases where one of the competing conceptual systems has to be abandoned, need not be the result of directly accessible observational difficulties. The law of inertia of the so-called *impetus theory* of the later Middle Ages[1] and Newton's own law of inertia are in perfect quantitative agreement: Both assert that an object that is not under the influence of any outer force will proceed along a straight line with constant speed. Yet despite this fact, the adoption of Newton's theory entails a conceptual revision that forces us to abandon the inertial law of the impetus theory, not because it is quantitatively incorrect but *because it achieves the correct predictions with the help of inadequate concepts*. The law asserts that the *impetus* of an object that is beyond the reach of outer forces remains constant.[2] The impetus is interpreted as an inner *force* which pushes the object along. Within the impetus theory such a force is quite conceivable as it is assumed here that forces determine *velocities* rather than accelerations. The concept of impetus is therefore formed in accordance with a law (forces determine velocities) and this law is inconsistent with the laws of Newton's theory and must be abandoned as soon as the latter is adopted. This is how the progress of our knowledge may lead to conceptual revisions for which no direct observational reasons are available. The occurrence of such changes quite obviously refutes the contention of some philosophers that the invariance of *usage* in the trivial and uninteresting contexts of the private lives of not too intelligent and inquisitive people indicates invariance of *meaning* and the superficiality of all scientific changes. It is also a very decisive objection against any crudely operationalistic account of both observable terms and theoretical terms.

What we have said applies even to singular statements of observation. Statements which are empirically adequate, and which are the result of observation (such as 'here is a table') may have to be reinterpreted, not because it has been found that they do not adequately express what is seen, heard, felt, but because of some changes in sometimes very remote parts of the conceptual scheme to which they belong. Witchcraft is again a very good example. Numerous eyewitnesses claim that they have actually *seen* the devil, or *experienced* demonic influence. There is no reason to suspect that

[1]For details and further references, cf. Section 6 of my 'Explanation, Reduction, and Empiricism', loc. cit.

[2]We assume here that a dynamical rather than a kinematic characterization of motion has been adopted. For a more detailed analysis cf. again the paper referred to in the previous footnote.

they were lying. Nor is there any reason to assume that they were sloppy observers, for the phenomena leading to the belief in demonic influence are so obvious that a mistake is hardly possible (possession; split personality; loss of personality; hearing voices; &c.). These phenomena are well known today.[1] In the conceptual scheme that was the one generally accepted in the fifteenth and sixteenth centuries, the only way of describing them, or at least the way that seemed to express them most adequately, was by reference to demonic influences. Large parts of this conceptual scheme were changed for philosophical reasons and also under the influence of the evidence accumulated by the sciences. Descartes's materialism played a very decisive role in discrediting the belief in spatially localizable spirits. The language of demonic influences was no part of the new conceptual scheme that was created in this manner. It was for this reason that a reformulation was needed, and a reinterpretation of even the most common 'observational' statements. Combining this example with the remarks at the beginning of the present section, we now realize that according to the method of classes of alternative theories a lenient attitude must be taken with respect to the meanings of all the terms we use. We must not attach too great an importance to 'what we mean' by a phrase, and we must be prepared to change whatever little we have said concerning this meaning as soon as the need arises. Too great concern with meanings can only lead to dogmatism and sterility. Flexibility, and even sloppiness in semantical matters is a prerequisite of scientific progress.[2]

8. Some Consequences

Three consequences of the results so far obtained deserve a more detailed discussion. The first consequence is an evaluation of *metaphysics* which differs significantly from the standard empirical attitude. As is well known, there are empiricists who demand that science start from observable facts and proceed by generalization, and who refuse the admittance of metaphysical ideas at any point of this procedure. For them, only a system of thought that has been built up in a purely inductive fashion can claim to be genuine knowledge. Theories which are partly metaphysical, or 'hypothetical', are suspect, and are best not used at all. This attitude has been formulated most

[1] For very vivid examples, cf. K. Jaspers, *Allgemeine Psychopathologie*, Berlin, 1959, pp. 75–123.

[2] Mae West is by far preferable to the precisionists: 'I ain't afraid of pushin' grammar around so long as it sounds good' (*Goodness Had Nothing to do With It*, New York, 1959, p. 19).

clearly by Newton[1] in his reply to Pardies's second letter concerning the theory of colours:

> If the possibility of hypotheses is to be the test of truth and reality of things, I see not how certainty can be obtained in any science; since numerous hypotheses may be devised, which shall seem to overcome new difficulties.

This radical position, which clearly depends on the demand for a theoretical monism, is no longer as popular as it used to be. It is now granted that metaphysical considerations may be of importance when the task is to *invent* a new physical theory; such invention, so it is admitted, is a more or less irrational act containing the most diverse components. Some of these components are, and perhaps must be, metaphysical ideas. However, it is also pointed out that, as soon as the theory has been developed in a formally satisfactory fashion and has received sufficient confirmation to be regarded as empirically successful, in the very same moment it can *and must* forget its metaphysical past; metaphysical speculation must *now* be replaced by empirical argument.

> On the one side I would like to emphasize [writes Ernst Mach on this point[2]] that *every and any* idea is admissible as a means for research, provided it is helpful; still, it must be pointed out, on the other side, that it is very necessary from time to time to free the presentation of the *results* of research from all inessential additions.

This means that empirical considerations are still given the upper hand over metaphysical reasoning. Especially in the case of an inconsistency between metaphysics and some highly confirmed empirical theory it will be decided, *as a matter of course*, that the theory or the result of observation must stay, and that the metaphysical system must go. A very simple example is the way in which materialism is being judged by some of its opponents. For a materialist the world consists of material particles moving in space, of collections of such particles. Sensations, as introspected by human beings, do not look like collections of particles, and their observed existence is therefore assumed to refute and thereby to remove the metaphysical doctrine of materialism. Another example which I have analysed in 'Problems of Microphysics' is the attempt to eliminate certain very general ideas concerning the nature of microentities on the basis of the remark that they are inconsistent 'with an immense body of

[1] I. B. Cohen, ed., *Isaac Newton's Papers and Letters on Natural Philosophy*, Harvard University Press, Cambridge, Mass., 1958, p. 106.

[2] 'Der Gegensatz zwischen der mechanischen und der phaenomenologischen Physik', *Warmelehre*, pp. 362 f.

experience' and that 'to object to a lesson of experience by appealing to metaphysical preconceptions is unscientific'.[1]

The methodology developed in the present paper leads to a very different evaluation of metaphysics. Metaphysical systems are scientific theories in their most primitive stage. If they *contradict* a well-confirmed point of view, then this indicates their usefulness as an alternative to this point of view. Alternatives are needed for the purpose of criticism. Hence, metaphysical systems which contradict observational results or well-confirmed theories *are most welcome* starting points of such criticism. Far from being misfired attempts at anticipating, or circumventing, empirical research which were deservedly exposed by a reference to experience, they are the only means at our disposal for examining those parts of our knowledge which have already become observational and which are therefore inaccessible to a criticism 'on the basis of observation.'

A second consequence is that a new attitude has to be adopted with respect to the *problem of induction*. This problem consists in the question of what justification there is for asserting the truth of a statement *S* given the truth of another statement, *S'*, whose content is smaller than the content of *S*. It may be taken for granted that those who want to justify the truth of *S* also assume that after the justification the truth of *S* will be *known*. Knowledge to the effect that *S* implies the *stability* of *S* (we must not change, remove, criticize, what we know to be true). The method we are discussing at the present moment cannot allow such stability. It follows that the problem of induction, at least in some of its formulations, is a problem whose solution leads to undesirable results. It may therefore be properly termed a pseudo problem.

The third consequence, which is more specific, is that *arguments from synonymy* (or from coextensionality), far from being that measure of adequacy as which they are usually introduced, are liable severely to impede the progress of knowledge. Arguments from synonymy judge a theory or a point of view not by its capability to mimic the world but rather by its capability to mimic the descriptive terms of another point of view which for some reason is received favourably. Thus for example, the attempt to give a materialistic, or else a purely physiological, account of human beings is criticized on the grounds that materialism, or physiology, cannot provide synonyms for 'mind', 'pain', 'seeing red', 'thinking of Vienna', in the sense

[1] L. Rosenfeld, 'Misunderstandings about the Foundations of the Quantum Theory', in *Observation and Interpretation*, p. 42.

in which these terms are used either in ordinary English (provided there is a well-established usage concerning these terms, a matter which I doubt) or in some more esoteric mentalistic idiom. Clearly, such criticism silently assumes the principle of meaning invariance, that is, it assumes that the meanings of at least some fundamental terms must remain unchanged in the course of the progress of our knowledge. It cannot therefore be accepted as valid.[1]

However, we can, and must go, still further. The ideas which we have developed above are strong enough not only to *reject* the demand for synonymy, wherever it is raised, but also to *support* the demand for irreducibility (in the sense in which this notion was used at the beginning of Section 7). The reason is that irreducibility is a presupposition of high critical ability on the part of the point of view shown to be irreducible. An outer indication of such irreducibility which is quite striking in the case of an attack upon commonly accepted ideas is the feeling of *absurdity*: We deem absurd what goes counter to well-established linguistic habits. The absence, from a newly introduced set of ideas, of synonymy relations connecting it with parts of the accepted point of view; the feeling of absurdity therefore indicate that the new ideas are fit for the purpose of criticism, i.e., that they are fit for leading either to a strong *confirmation* of the earlier theories, or else to a very revolutionary *discovery*: absence of synonymy, clash of meanings, absurdity are desirable. Presence of synonymy, intuitive appeal, agreement with customary modes of speech, far from being *the* philosophical virtue, indicates that not much progress has been made and that the business of investigating what is commonly accepted *has not even started*.

9. How To Be A Good Empiricist

The final reply to the question put in the title is therefore as follows. A good empiricist will not rest content with the theory that is in the centre of attention and with those tests of the theory which can be carried out in a direct manner. Knowing that the most fundamental and the most general criticism is the criticism produced with the help of alternatives, he will try to invent such alternatives.[2]

[1]For details concerning the mind-body problem, cf. my 'Materialism and the Mind-Body Problem', *Review of Metaphysics*, Sept. 1963.

[2]In my paper 'Realism and Instrumentalism' (in *The Critical Approach: Essays in Honor of Karl Popper*, ed. M. Bunge), I have tried to show that this is precisely the method which has brought about such spectacular advances of knowledge as the Copernican Revolution, the transition to relativity and to quantum theory.

It is, of course, impossible at once to produce a theory that is formally comparable to the main point of view and that leads to equally many predictions. His first step will therefore be the formulation of fairly general assumptions which are not yet directly connected with observations; this means that his first step will be the invention of a new *metaphysics*. This metaphysics must then be elaborated in sufficient detail in order to be able to compete with the theory to be investigated as regards generality, details of prediction, precision of formulation.[1] We may sum up both activities by saying that a good empiricist must be a critical metaphysician. Elimination of all metaphysics, far from increasing the empirical content of the remaining theories, is liable to turn these theories into dogmas. The consideration of alternatives together with the attempt to criticize each of them in the light of experience also leads to an attitude where meanings do not play a very important role and where arguments are based upon assumptions of fact rather than analysis of (archaic, although perhaps very precise) meanings. The effect of such an attitude upon the development of human capabilities should not be underestimated either. Where speculation and invention of alternatives is encouraged, bright ideas are liable to occur in great number and such ideas may then lead to a change of even the most 'fundamental' parts of our knowledge, i.e., they may lead to a change of assumptions which either are so close to observation that their truth seems to be dictated by 'the facts', or which are so close to common prejudice that they seem to be 'obvious', and their negation 'absurd'. In such a situation it will be realized that neither 'facts' nor abstract ideas can ever be used for defending certain principles come what may. Wherever facts play a role in such a dogmatic defence, we shall have to suspect foul play (see the opening quotation)—the foul play of those who try to turn good science into bad, because unchangeable, metaphysics. In the last resort, therefore, being a good empiricist means being critical, and basing one's criticism not just on an abstract principle of scepticism but upon *concrete suggestions* which indicate in every single case how the accepted point of view might be further tested and further investigated and which thereby prepare the next step in the development of our knowledge.

For support of research the author is indebted to the National Science Foundation and the Minnesota Center for the Philosophy of Science.

[1] Cf. Section 13 of my 'Realism and Instrumentalism'.

II

THE TERMS AND SENTENCES OF EMPIRICAL SCIENCE[1]

G. SCHLESINGER

I

IT has been the ambition of many philosophers in this century to construct a formal machinery through which one may mechanically sort out the meaningful from the meaningless. The earlier attempts to fulfil this ambition usually started with laying down what is meaningful in some absolute sense. Recent and more careful attempts have changed from the prescriptive to the descriptive approach and, also, instead of trying to embrace all human discourse they have been confined to the designing of criteria for determining what is meaningful discourse within empirical science. It had been hoped that a criterion could be set up that would faithfully and fully reflect what is commonly regarded as empirically significant. But the various results of these endeavours have turned out in the past to be inadequate and, consequently, the majority of philosophers have become highly critical of all such attempts. They think that the language of science is too rich and too much in a state of continual rapid change to be characterizable by any finite set of rules.

The critics are probably right.[2] Nevertheless some of the dauntless attempts to set up the desired criterion deserve close study. Not merely because of the great ingenuity they often display. But because in their failure, perhaps not less than they would have in their success, they constitute an important source of philosophical illumination. The examination of the apparatus constructed for facilitating the automatic rejection of the meaningless and the study of the factors

From *Mind*, Vol. 73 (1964), pp. 394–405. Reprinted with additional notes, by permission of the author and the editor of *Mind*.

[1] With the permission of the Editor I have added a few footnotes. These express my reactions to this paper on re-reading it after an interval of several years.

[2] Only if they claim that no criterion can be given to determine whether a sentence is significant in some absolute sense. But there seems to be no objection in principle to an attempt to construct a criterion by which it is always decidable whether a sentence is significant relative to a given theory.

preventing their proper functioning may help us to analyse the process through which meaning is acquired and forfeited by terms used in science and to gain an insight into the nature of empirical significance.

With this aim in view I propose to consider one of the best of recent efforts to set up a machinery for distinguishing between the meaningful and the meaningless, Carnap's carefully formulated criterion, which he has expounded in an essay called 'The Methodological Character of Theoretical Concepts'.[1] First I shall try to ensure that his criterion which has been subject to some wrong interpretations, is properly understood. Next I shall attempt to show how and why Carnap has failed to achieve the objectives he has set himself, in the hope that this will throw light on the nature of the terms of empirical science, in particular upon the way changes in their significance affect the meaning of the sentences in which they occur.

II

It is possible, I think, to present, without serious distortion, in a couple of sentences the essence of Carnap's thesis. As a preliminary it should be pointed out that he takes consciously into account the lesson taught by the previous failures of the attempts at setting up a criterion for sorting out the meaningful from the meaningless. All the suggested criteria in the past, says Carnap, have suffered from either of two shortcomings: they were either too strong, excluding from empirical discourse much that is valuable for science, or too weak, granting admission to what is obviously empty verbiage. Carnap sees the remedy in the departure from the old policy of inquiring into the meaningfulness of whole sentences, and proposes instead a test, by passing which, individual words may gain admission into a system of empirical theories and become terms of its language. When a word becomes a legitimate term of a language its significance relative to the other components of the same language is established.

Any language is made up of two kinds of terms, logical and descriptive terms. All logical terms like 'and', 'if then' or 'there is at least one x such that . . . ' are legitimate members of our empirical language. Adjectives like 'blue' or 'hot'; verbs like 'approaching' or 'colliding' or nouns like 'noise' or 'colour' all of which stand for

[1] *Minnesota Studies in the Philosophy of Science*, H. Feigl and M. Scriven, eds. (Minnesota), i. 38–76.

immediately observables, and are therefore called observational-descriptive terms, are also admitted into empirical discourse without ado. Our problem begins with theoretical-descriptive terms like 'temperature', 'mass' or 'electric field'. Each one of this type of terms is granted admission into our language after it has passed a certain test. The test consists essentially of the following:

We must be able to construct some proposition S_M which contains the candidate term M and which entails an observation statement S_o, that is, a statement whose truth can directly be tested. To ensure that the test is not too severe, we do not require that S_M should on its own entail S_o. It may do so with the aid of other propositions S_K (propositions, which may contain theoretical terms, but if so, these have previously passed the test and qualified as empirically significant) and in the context of a theoretical system T and a set of correspondence rules C. The system T consists of general theoretical postulates and contains no observational terms; the C-rules specify relations between theoretical terms and observation terms, e.g. 'mass' and 'heaviness'. In short we require no more than, that:

(A) S_o is logically implied by the conjunction of S_M, S_K, T and C.

On the other hand, in order to ensure that the test is not too weak we require that S_M contains M as the only descriptive term. For if it contained other terms as well, then the fact that S_M gave rise to an empirical prediction would not necessarily show the potency of M—it may have been due to the occurrence of the other terms. Another stipulation we make in order to ensure that M is a potent term is that:

(B) S_o is not logically implied by the conjunction of S_K, T and C alone.

Passing this test establishes the significance of M relative to the system T and C. It then becomes a member of the class K of terms and it may feature in an S_K with the help of which new candidate theoretical terms may be introduced into the language.

This much about the terms of the language. As to its sentences: any syntactically well formed sentence in which every term is significant, in the sense just defined, is to be regarded as meaningful relative to T and C. With the introduction of more and more M's, the number of significant terms contained in the system increases and thus the number of significant statements which can be formulated within it, increases too. Consequently, the theoretical system becomes gradually enriched and more and more interpreted.

III

If we wish to grasp more fully the import of Carnap's criterion it will be most instructive to follow an attack made on Carnap by S. F. Barker, in his *Induction and Hypothesis.*[1] Barker proposes to show that the criterion of empirical significance is ineffective and that the most obvious kind of nonsensical theory could be constructed to accord with it and thus gain Carnap's approval.

For this purpose Barker has devised a system which includes amongst its T propositions a statement like, 'The Absolute, and it alone, is such that of any two distinct things one manifests it more than does the other'. And amongst its C-rules, statements like, 'If a penny is pocketed then it is absolute, if and only if, it instantly turns into a dollar'—specifying a connexion between the theoretical 'absolute' and the observable 'turning instantly into a dollar'; and 'if x, y, z are dogs then x manifests z more than does y, if and only if, x barks louder at z than does y'—relating the theoretical predicate 'manifesting z more than . . . ' with 'barking louder at z than . . . '. Then claiming to follow Carnap's rules he defines first S_{M_1} = 'Fido manifests Rover more than does Bonzo' which, in conjunction with the given above plus S_{K_1} = 'Fido, Rover and Bonzo are dogs', entails the observation statement S_{01} = 'Fido barks louder at Rover than does Bonzo'. Thus 'manifests more than' has become a significant term. Then he defines S_{M2} = 'This penny is not absolute'. If in addition we are having S_{K2} = 'This penny is pocketed' then with the aid of S_{M2} we can make the prediction that S_{02} = 'This penny does not instantly turn into a dollar when pocketed', which makes the term 'absolute' too, empirically significant.

Wesley C. Salmon in a brief note entitled 'Barker's Theory of the Absolute'[2] points out that Barker has failed to conform to Carnap's rules on several accounts (it was stipulated for instance that M must be the only descriptive predicate in S_M, yet in S_{M_1} Barker uses 'Fido', 'Rover' and 'Bonzo' as well as 'manifests'). However, Salmon shows that without changing the import of Barker's example it is possible to reformulate it so that it should accord with Carnap's rules. Does he then agree with Barker that the inadequacy of Carnap's criteron has thus been demonstrated? No, and he concludes his paper by saying:

> There seems to be no reason for denying that Barker's theory of the Absolute is empirically meaningful. However, it would seem to have a far

[1] (Ithaca, 1957), pp. 138–42.

[2] *Philosophical Studies*, 1959, pp. 50–53.

different meaning from that (if any) of certain nineteenth-century theories of the absolute.[1]

This is supposed to be a defence of Carnap's theory, but in fact it seems to make matters worse. True enough Barker claims that his 'example suffices to suggest how a body of discourse thoroughly metaphysical' can slip through Carnap's test and Salmon points out that Barker's example bears little resemblance to genuine speculative metaphysics. But this makes his criticism only more damaging. For Barker has succeeded in constructing a theory to which no one even in his wildest metaphysical dreams would subscribe and yet we are compelled to agree that it rates as a partially interpreted empirical theory.[2]

It seems to me, however, that when correctly understood, Carnap's thesis is not damaged by Barker's counter-example. On the contrary the example may be used to bring out more clearly the significance of Carnap's criterion. Consider one of the observation statements upon which the meaningfulness of Barker's theory hinges, S_{02} = 'This penny does not instantly turn into a dollar'. Whichever penny it refers to the statement is certainly true, its truth being vouched for by some very fundamental laws about the stability of chemical substances and of physical structures. Do we acknowledge these laws of nature—the denial of which would certainly mean the abolishing most of our physics?

If Barker's answer is, yes, then his theory has failed to pass Carnap's test. When introducing the term 'absolute' he has violated rule (B): 'S_0 should not be logically implied by the conjunction S_K with T and C alone.' For in order to derive S_{02} we do not need S_{M2} (= This penny is not absolute). We can do this through theories we have already at hand. In other words, if we uphold the validity of conventional physics

[1] Ibid. p. 53.

[2] Professor Salmon in a rejoinder (published in *Mind*, July, 1967) explains that what he meant by saying that Barker's theory 'has a far different meaning, &c.' was not that it is 'further out' than standard metaphysical theories but rather 'nearer in' and of straightforward, unobjectionable, empirical significance.

But as long as Salmon concedes that Barker's terms and sentences assume significance, I cannot see that the situation has basically improved. Barker could, after all, without great difficulty endow any number of typical metaphysical terms with meaning and then *add* all the 'theories' with the aid of which he achieved this to some nineteenth-century metaphysical system positivists find particularly objectionable (since the 'theories' required consist of such few sentences, these can be so selected as not to clash with anything stated in the system) and thus lend significance to the very paradigms of meaningless assertions.

And anyway what is the point in having Carnap's test which was devised to expose the non-sensical when everything can be made to pass it as meaningful?

then S_{M2} is redundant and has not helped us to make a new prediction.

Only at the price of renouncing our physics as it is known today could Barker's theory indeed become meaningful. This shows the effectiveness of Carnap's criterion. For what we needed was a criterion to guard science against the smuggling in of pseudo-concepts, a criterion that would not allow the introduction of metaphysical theories to take their place side by side with empirical theories. This Carnap seems to have achieved. He has prevented the possibility of anyone subscribing simultaneously to the genuinely empirical and the metaphysical posing as empirical.

But an objection could still be raised. One might ask: what if S_0, which we derive through the aid of the pseudo-theory, does not happen to be an observation statement already accounted for by any known genuine theories? In this case the pseudo-theory could be proposed not as a substitute for current physics or any part of current physics but as a mere addition to it. S_{01} (= Fido barks louder at Rover than does Bonzo) may, for example, be regarded as such a statement. Which one of two dogs will bark louder at a given third dog, could, I believe, not as yet, on the basis of our present knowledge of animal psychology, always be predicted. Consequently, it could be claimed that S_{M1} (= Fido manifests Rover more than does Bonzo) has given rise to a genuine prediction. It is only a matter of a trivial modification then (i.e. the introduction of a suitable non-redundant S_{02}), and Barker's theory would be made unobjectionable and stand as a proof of the inability of Carnap's criterion to exclude non-sense from science.

The answer to this is[1] that even when it comes to statements like S_{01} we believe that it does not differ discontinuously from fully predictable statements. We know that Fido's barking louder at Rover than does Bonzo has something to do with Fido's nervous system or strength of vocal chords or at any rate with some property which is not quite strange to existing animal physiology and psychology. It may therefore be said that a statement like S_{01} is also to be regarded as predictable in principle on the basis of current theories and as our knowledge grows and these theories extend, it will become

[1]The answer actually is a much simpler one. If Barker's theory were indeed generally capable of predicting which of two dogs will bark louder at a third one, or indeed anything else not predictable by science of today, we would have to take it seriously. But it clearly cannot do so. Hence, it is a useless theory. M_1 qualified for membership nowhere but in an utterly empty theory incapable of conferring significance on its terms. A term, in order to qualify as empirical, must achieve significance relative to a theory which itself is not devoid of all empirical significance.

predictable in practice too. We are confident, going by its past record, that conventional science is a fruitful enterprise which will extend indefinitely over yet undiscovered areas. That large system of propositions commonly called 'science', looks to us capable of eventually accounting for phenomena like the one referred to by S_{01}.

Thus even if Barker had constructed a system of T and C which gave rise to S_{01} type statements alone, that is, statements not accounted for by existing science, and had wanted to incorporate his system into science or hold it concurrently with science, the S_M's of his system would still be redundant. Consequently, he would still be forced to choose between orthodox science and his theory. No rational person would choose the latter. For although Carnap himself has emphasised in the same essay (p. 62) that he has not provided a formal criterion to judge the degree of fruitfulness of theories, no matter how crude our judgement if aided by nothing but commonsense, Barker's theory looks very unpromising compared to conventional science.[1]

Thus Carnap, by making impossible the peaceful co-existence between the scientific and the pseudo-scientific, seems to have achieved his aim, which was, the prevention of the introduction into science itself of concepts and propositions devoid of empirical significance.

IV

Now we must ask ourselves the following question: is it sufficient to apply Carnap's test to a term M and thereby establish once and for all its meaningfulness relative to a given theory? Consider the statement, 'The temperature of velocity v is of t degrees'. It is obviously meaingless. But why? There is nothing in Carnap's test

[1]The mistake of Barker was to interpret the condition (B) that S_0 must not logically be implied by the conjunction of S_k, T and C alone, as referring specifically to the ones employed to introduce M, and not *any* S_K, T and C qualified as meaningful. Admittedly, Carnap is not at all explicit on this point. Yet if (B) were to be interpreted in Barker's way it would be an arbitrary, unexplained rule.

It is interesting that Rozeboom in an ingenious paper which on the surface appears to adopt a very different approach from Barker's, commits the same error (*Philosophical Studies*, April, 1960). He provides a general proof that if some rather innocuous assumptions are granted then any term will pass Carnap's test. It can easily be seen, however, that although Rozeboom does not violate (B) if the S_K mentioned in it were to refer to the one employed in introducing the new term (which in his case is the sentence symbolized as $S_L^* \supset S_{M1}$) but does violate it if it refers—as I believe it does—to any S_K qualified as significant (and in his case the sentence denoted by S_{M1} is one of these).

which says so. The sentence has been constructed according to the formation rules and it employs nothing but significant terms and ought therefore make a meaningful statement. Or to return to our previous example 'Fido manifests Rover more than does Bonzo' (S_{M1}) where we have concluded that the proposition is meaningless since Barker has failed in his attempt to endow the predicate 'manifests more than' with significance. But why is this so? The predicate as such is, after all, unquestionably significant, and it often features in perfectly meaningful propositions as in 'Fido manifests intelligence more than does Bonzo'. Thus even if Barker's theory was of no use at all, S_{M1} ought to be regarded as empirically significant simply because all the terms it contains are empirically significant and it is a well formed sentence.

The explanation of course is that although the terms 'temperature' and 'velocity' are significant in themselves, neither of them retains its significance when used to be a predicate of the other. Similarly the term 'manifests more than' may often possess meaning; however it loses it when used to designate a triadic relationship between three dogs. But does this not show the inadequacy of Carnap's rules? After all, even if these rules are fully capable of excluding all terms which are devoid of empirical significance he has achieved comparatively very little. We may sometimes be concerned with terms like 'entelechy' which in view of our acceptance of a non-vitalist biology has become one of the paradigms of a purely metaphysical term. But we have innumerably more occasions to be concerned with terms like 'temperature' which can significantly be predicated of a human body or of melting ice but not of a velocity or of a molecule. And Carnap has neglected to formulate the conditions which have to be fulfilled in order that a term that has already gained a foothold in science should remain significant—in the context of the same science—when combined with other terms.

One might want to defend Carnap's test by saying that as far as terms are concerned it accomplishes everything, for once a term has passed his test its significance is established for good. Yet we may not apply it indiscriminately as a predicate of just any subject, for certain combinations of meaningful terms constitute category mistakes. Not that the terms lose their significance; only that the sentences in which such combinations occur are not well formed sentences. But this defence in itself would not be of much use as it merely shifts the problem, which now could be restated: which combinations between terms are permissible and which are not?

What are the rules, in addition to the rules of grammar, through which we can determine whether or not a sentence is well formed? One would therefore have to explain that a sentence like 'The temperature of velocity *v* is *t* degrees' (S_{VT}) is nonsense and is not well formed, simply because it leads to no verifiable consequences, for there can be found no additional accepted hypotheses in conjunction with which it would entail observation sentences not entailed by these additional accepted hypotheses alone; or because we could not name the conditions under which a sentence like S_{VT} was used to make a true statement.

But such defence will obviously not do. To show its futility it is sufficient to point out that it leads us back to the testing of the significance of sentences. If we accept Carnap's own judgement on the matter then we are to believe that all attempts to set up a criterion for testing whole sentences are bound to end in failure. It was after all because of his realization of the impossibility of setting up such a criterion that he embarked upon the construction of a test for individual terms.

This answer in itself is effective enough to demolish hope in the possibility of defending Carnap by claiming that he has accomplished the major part of his job and that he has merely left unsolved a simple problem when he neglected to say anything more about the empirical significance of sentences than that they have to be constructed according to the rules of syntax. Yet it is important that we obtain a deeper view and appreciate that it is fundamentally wrong to think that a term once endowed with significance will retain it under all circumstances and that it is only the sentences in which it occurs which may sometimes be devoid of significance. The truth is that on the contrary it may even happen that a term should definitely lose its original meaning and yet the sentence in which it occurs expresses a meaningful proposition. Suppose that it was the convention in the scientific community that the truth of the statement 'The temperature of velocity *v* is *t* degrees' (S_{VT}) is to be tested by measuring in grams the mass of the body whose instantaneous velocity was *v* and in dynes the force acting upon it, and seeing whether the numbers so obtained satisfy the equation t = mass/force. S_{VT} would then be meaningful and in fact be equivalent to the statement, 'The velocity whose instantaneous value is *v* cm./sec. is increasing at the rate of *t* cm.²/sec.' It would, however, be perfectly obvious that when we are talking about the 'temperature of melting ice' and the 'temperature of velocity' we are only using the same word in both cases but are referring to entirely different concepts. That term 'temperature' which has acquired scientific meaning with the aid of the correspondence rule saying that when a body is of a higher temperature than the other, then upon touching it feels hotter certainly loses its meaning when combined with the term 'velocity'. This, however, could not be discovered upon examining whether S_{VT} itself lacks meaning for it so happens that another concept has also been linked to the same string of letters 'temperature' by virtue of which it makes sense to talk about the temperature of velocity.

It should be clear then, that a word which is endowed with significance and is made to stand for a given concept may lose this significance upon the change of context and cease to stand for that concept. After it has lost its original significance it may assume some new significance and stand for another concept or it may not do so. In the latter case, it becomes an empty combination of letters.

V

It would seem that the situation could be saved by claiming that we can always recognise the cases in which a basically meaningful predicate has illegitimately been applied by retracing the steps through which it has acquired meaning in the first place. When we do this for example in the case of 'temperature' we realise that it cannot apply to anything immaterial like velocity. The term 'temperature' has been endowed with significance with the help of the correspondence rule stating the connexion between temperature and the sensation of heat and the correspondence rule asserting that when the temperature of anything is *t* degrees, then if a Hg-thermometer is brought in contact with it, the top of the mercury column will be observed to coincide with a certain mark. It is taken for granted that we are fully capable of understanding these correspondence rules, that is, we understand what it is to bring a mercury containing glass in contact with something. It may therefore also be taken for granted that we realise, without the aid of any further rules, but by immediate comprehension, that velocity is not a thing to be touched by the hand nor can any other object be brought in contact with it. Hence the meaning acquired by the term 'temperature' with the help of these correspondence rules clearly does not extend to cases in which it is combined with terms like velocity.

We would, of course, have to relinquish our claim that once the significance of a term has been established it can freely be employed in any well formed sentence. We would now have to admit that a word which has already been labelled by Carnap's apparatus as part of the scientific vocabulary still has to be put to scrutiny afresh at every new instance of its combination with other terms. We have to ascertain which was the set of T, C, S_K and S_0 through which the term originally acquired its significance, inspect the set and through comprehending the very meaning of all the components of the set 'see' whether that significance can possibly extend to the case in question.

But this position cannot be maintained. Consider the statement 'The temperature at the centre of the sun is *t* degrees'. It is impossible, no matter how well shielded, to come anywhere near the sun. We are unable here, just as in the case of 'velocity', to come in contact with the thing to which we assign a temperature number, and yet it is commonly agreed that we may legitimately speak of the centre of the sun as having a temperature. The reason of course is that although the term 'temperature' in the last statement could not have acquired significance in the same way as the 'temperature' which is affixed to 'melting ice', it is not therefore deprived of meaning altogether for there is another set of propositions which render it significant. In this set among the T, C and S_K we shall find statements about: the radius of the sun; the temperature gradient along the radius of the sun; the distance of the sun from the earth; radiation laws; atmospheric absorption, &c., with the help of all which the reading recorded on a bolometer is predicted. But this 'temperature' then assumed significance in an entirely different way from the one used as a predicate of melting ice. It invoked the help of a different set of T, C and S_K, and the experience which ultimately invested it with empirical significance was other than the feeling of hot and cold or the reading sighted on a contact thermometer. Yet unlike the case of the 'temperature of velocity' we do not say that 'temperature' when applied to the centre of the sun is merely spelt and pronounced the same as when applied to melting ice but otherwise has nothing in common with it. On the contrary, we regard the two as representing essentially the same concept. The reason is that there are important correlations between them. A number of observable properties are associated both with temperatures of the order of O°C. and of the order of millions of degrees of centigrade. Despite the fact that the sets of connecting statements differ in the two cases we consider the existence of common phenomena to which both concepts of temperature are linked as of overriding significance. Also a number of purely theoretical statements (e.g. 'temperature is proportional to the average kinetic energy of the molecules') are relevant to all values of temperature. But of course there are no formal rules which determine that in spite of the great differences associated with the temperature of melting ice and of the centre of the sun the similarities are to be regarded as more decisive. It is a matter of decision based on weighing differences against the similarities and assessing their relative importance.

Thus our formal apparatus can tell us only that under specified circumstances a combination of letters stands for a given concept. We have, however, no additional machinery whereby to determine what happens when the circumstances change. Admittedly it can be claimed with good reason that we need no such apparatus to determine the cases in which as a result of the change the same string of letters altogether ceases to stand for any concept, as this can be discovered by comprehending the meaning of the components of the original set through which a concept has attached itself in the first place to the word. But when the word still represents a concept and we ask whether by using the same word under these different circumstances we are merely making a pun or are referring to essentially the same concept, we have no criteria or rules to guide us and no definite answer is available to our question.

VI

It follows from what has been said that when a term has passed Carnap's test it has only made its first step in its career as a member of the scientific vocabulary. On each occasion it is applied anew—in the context of the same theory but in a different setting—one has to re-examine that collection of propositions which originally bestowed meaning on it and see whether it is still relevant to this situation. If it is not, one has to find out whether some other set of T, C, S_K and S_o may not lend significance to it. If such a set is found then we have to probe into the question whether we ought to regard the concepts determined by the two sets as being essentially identical concepts and hence should employ the same term in both settngs. We have to compare the two groups of T, C, S_K and S_o and use our judgement to decide whether there are sufficient connecting elements between them to render the use of the same term in both cases a reasonable and useful practice.

For a moment one may have some hesitations and wonder whether we are forced to conclude that Carnap's enterprise has failed. After all why should the lack of a formal machinery for this last task worry us? We only wanted to be able to distinguish mechanically between what is empirically significant and what is totally devoid of such significance. May we not regard the determination of changes in the significance of terms as outside our scope?

But the crux of the matter is that these two tasks are wholly inseparable from one another. It should by now be possible to see perfectly clearly this most important point. Let us for a moment return to S_{VT}. We all agree that the sentence 'The temperature of velocity v is t degrees' is, relative to the current language of physics, totally lacking in any meaning. Carnap's criterion does however not really prevent you from assigning meaning to it. It will allow you, for instance, to argue like this: when a body is accelerating at different rates it is subject to stresses of different magnitudes through which its length alters to different degrees. Change in temperature also results in the altering of the lengths of a body. Temperature and acceleration have then at least one manifestation in common, or in our present terminology, there is at least one S_o which features both amongst the S_o's which determine the meaning of the term 'temperature' and amongst those determining the meaning of 'acceleration'. There are no formal rules to tell us that this is not sufficient and that the concepts of temperature and acceleration are not essentially the same and thus the terms 'temperature' and 'acceleration' are not interchangeable. Nothing, therefore, rules out formally the claim that S_{VT} should be taken to mean 'The rate of increase of the velocity is t'.[1]

It is also possible now to see clearly the basic reason for the failure of Carnap's enterprise. The trouble roots from the fact that a concept which belongs to a highly developed science is moulded by a very complex set consisting of an enormous number of T, C, S_K and S_o sentences. When a new sentence joins this set or an old one leaves it the character of the concept is altered to some degree. Its complete loss of identity comes about by a gradual process. He has not provided an apparatus which would mark the crucial point in such processes. Consequently, we are unable to cope mechanically with changing contexts and the attendant variations in the significance of terms; we cannot provide a general rule which tells us at what stage the change has been decisive enough to make us regard the term as

[1] This is not a felicitous example. But then we do not require any examples. It is only too clear that given any two terms no matter how different the concepts they stand for we shall virtually always find some aspect they share.

having completely lost its original meaning. This inability prevents us also, as we have seen, from distinguishing mechanically between empirically significant sentences and sentences completely devoid of such significance.

III
EXPLANATION IN SCIENCE AND IN HISTORY

CARL G. HEMPEL

1. Introduction

Among the divers factors that have encouraged and sustained scientific inquiry through its long history are two pervasive human concerns which provide, I think, the basic motivation for all scientific research. One of these is man's persistent desire to improve his strategic position in the world by means of dependable methods for predicting and, whenever possible, controlling the events that occur in it. The extent to which science has been able to satisfy this urge is reflected impressively in the vast and steadily widening range of its technological applications. But besides this practical concern, there is a second basic motivation for the scientific quest, namely, man's insatiable intellectual curiosity, his deep concern to *know* the world he lives in, and to *explain*, and thus to *understand*, the unending flow of phenomena it presents to him.

In times past questions as to the *what* and the *why* of the empirical world were often answered by myths; and to some extent, this is so even in our time. But gradually, the myths are displaced by the concepts, hypotheses, and theories developed in the various branches of empirical science, including the natural sciences, psychology, and sociological as well as historical inquiry. What is the general character of the understanding attainable by these means, and what is its potential scope? In this paper I will try to shed some light on these questions by examining what seem to me the two basic types of explanation offered by the natural sciences, and then comparing them with some modes of explanation and understanding that are found in historical studies.

First, then, a look at explanation in the natural sciences.

From *Frontiers of Science and Philosophy*, ed. R. G. Colodny (Allen and Unwin and University of Pittsburgh Press, 1962), pp.7–33. Reprinted by permission of the author, George Allen and Unwin Ltd., and the University of Pittsburgh Press.

2. Two Basic Types of Scientific Explanation

2.1 *Deductive-nomological explanation.* In his book, *How We Think,*[1] John Dewey describes an observation he made one day when, washing dishes, he took some glass tumblers out of the hot soap suds and put them upside down on a plate: he noticed that soap bubbles emerged from under the tumblers' rims, grew for a while, came to a standstill, and finally receded inside the tumblers. Why did this happen? The explanation Dewey outlines comes to this: In transferring a tumbler to the plate, cool air is caught in it; this air is gradually warmed by the glass, which initially has the temperature of the hot suds. The warming of the air is accompanied by an increase in its pressure, which in turn produces an expansion of the soap film between the plate and the rim. Gradually, the glass cools off, and so does the air inside, with the result that the soap bubbles recede.

This explanatory account may be regarded as an argument to the effect that the event to be explained (let me call it the explanandum-event) was to be expected by reason of certain explanatory facts. These may be divided into two groups: (i) particular facts and (ii) uniformities expressed by general laws. The first group includes facts such as these: the tumblers had been immersed, for some time, in soap suds of a temperature considerably higher than that of the surrounding air; they were put, upside down, on a plate on which a puddle of soapy water had formed, providing a connecting soap film, &c. The second group of items presupposed in the argument includes the gas laws and various other laws that have not been explicitly suggested concerning the exchange of heat between bodies of different temperature, the elastic behaviour of soap bubbles, &c. If we imagine these various presuppositions explicitly spelled out, the idea suggests itself of construing the explanation as a deductive argument of this form:

$$(D) \qquad \frac{\begin{array}{c} C_1, C_2, \ldots, C_k \\ L_1, L_2, \ldots, L_r \end{array}}{E}$$

Here, $C_1, C_2, \ldots, C_k$ are statements describing the particular facts invoked; $L_1, L_2, \ldots, L_r$ are general laws: jointly, these statements will be said to form the explanans. The conclusion E is a statement describing the explanandum-event; let me call it the explanandum-statement, and let me use the word 'explanandum' to refer to either E or to the event described by it.

The kind of explanation thus characterized I will call *deductive—*

[1]See Dewey, John, *How We Think*. Boston, New York, Chicago, 1910; Chapter VI.

nomological explanation; for it amounts to a deductive subsumption of the explanandum under principles which have the character of general laws: it answers the question '*Why* did the explanandum event occur?' by showing that the event resulted from the particular circumstances specified in C_1, C_2, . . . , C_k in accordance with the laws L_1, L_2, . . . , L_r. This conception of explanation, as exhibited in schema (D), has therefore been referred to as the covering law model, or as the deductive model, of explanation.[1]

A good many scientific explanations can be regarded as deductive-nomological in character. Consider, for example, the explanation of mirror-images, of rainbows, or of the appearance that a spoon handle is bent at the point where it emerges from a glass of water: in all these cases, the explanandum is deductively subsumed under the laws of reflection and refraction. Similarly, certain aspects of free fall and of planetary motion can be accounted for by deductive subsumption under Galileo's or Kepler's laws.

In the illustrations given so far the explanatory laws had, by and large, the character of empirical generalizations connecting different observable aspects of the phenomena under scrutiny: angle of incidence with angle of reflection or refraction, distance covered with falling time, &c. But science raises the question 'why?' also with respect to the uniformities expressed by such laws, and often answers it in basically the same manner, namely, by subsuming the uniformities under more inclusive laws, and eventually under comprehensive theories. For example, the question, 'Why do Galileo's and Kepler's laws hold?' is answered by showing that these laws are but special consequences of the Newtonian laws of motion and of gravitation; and these, in turn, may be explained by subsumption under the more comprehensive general theory of relativity. Such subsumption under broader laws or theories usually increases both the breadth and the depth of our scientific understanding. There is an increase in breadth, or

[1]For a fuller presentation of the model and for further references, see, for example, Hempel, C. G. and P. Oppenheim, 'Studies in the Logic of Explanation', *Philosophy of Science*, 15: 135–175 (1948). (Secs. 1–7 of this article, which contain all the fundamentals of the presentation, are reprinted in H. Feigl and M. Brodbeck (eds.), *Readings in the Philosophy of Science*. New York, 1953.)—The suggestive term 'covering law model' is W. Dray's; cf. his *Laws and Explanation in History*. Oxford, 1957; Chapter I. Dray characterizes this type of explanation as 'subsuming what is to be explained under a general law' (loc. cit., p. 1), and then rightly urges, in the name of methodological realism, that 'the requirement of a *single* law be dropped' (loc. cit., p. 24; italics, the author's): it should be noted, however, that, like the schema (D) above, several earlier publications on the subject (among them the article mentioned at the beginning of this note) make explicit provision for the inclusion of more laws than one in the explanans.

scope, because the new explanatory principles cover a broader range of phenomena; for example, Newton's principles govern free fall on the earth and on other celestial bodies, as well as the motions of planets, comets, and artificial satellites, the movements of pendulums, tidal changes, and various other phenomena. And the increase thus effected in the depth of our understanding is strikingly reflected in the fact that, in the light of more advanced explanatory principles, the original empirical laws are usually seen to hold only approximately, or within certain limits. For example, Newton's theory implies that the factor g in Galileo's law, $s = \frac{1}{2} gt^2$, is not strictly a constant for free fall near the surface of the earth; and that, since every planet undergoes gravitational attraction not only from the sun, but also from the other planets, the planetary orbits are not strictly ellipses, as stated in Kepler's laws.

One further point deserves brief mention here. An explanation of a particular event is often conceived as specifying its *cause*, or causes. Thus, the account outlined in our first illustration might be held to explain the growth and the recession of the soap bubbles by showing that the phenomenon was *caused* by a rise and a subsequent drop of the temperature of the air trapped in the tumblers. Clearly, however, these temperature changes provide the requisite explanation only in conjunction with certain other conditions, such as the presence of a soap film, practically constant pressure of the air surrounding the glasses, &c. Accordingly, in the context of explanation, a cause must be allowed to consist in a more or less complex set of particular circumstances; these might be described by a set of sentences: C_1, $C_2, \ldots, C_k$. And, as suggested by the principle 'Same cause, same effect', the assertion that those circumstances jointly caused a given event—described, let us say, by a sentence E—implies that whenever and wherever circumstances of the kind in question occur, an event of the kind to be explained comes about. Hence, the given causal explanation implicity claims that there are general laws—such as L_1, $L_2 \ldots, L_r$ in schema (D)—by virtue of which the occurrence of the causal antecedents mentioned in $C_1, C_2, \ldots, C_k$ is a sufficient condition for the occurrence of the event to be explained. Thus, the relation between causal factors and effect is reflected in schema (D): causal explanation is deductive-nomological in character. (However, the customary formulations of causal and other explanations often do not explicitly specify all the relevant laws and particular facts: to this point, we will return later.)

The converse does not hold: there are deductive-nomological

explanations which would not normally be counted as causal. For one thing, the subsumption of laws, such as Galileo's or Kepler's laws, under more comprehensive principles is clearly not causal in character: we speak of causes only in reference to *particular* facts or events, and not in reference to *universal facts* as expressed by general laws. But not even all deductive-nomological explanations of particular facts or events will qualify as causal; for in a causal explanation some of the explanatory circumstances will temporally precede the effect to be explained: and there are explanations of type (*D*) which lack this characteristic. For example, the pressure which a gas of specified mass possesses at a given time might be explained by reference to its temperature and its volume at the same time, in conjunction with the gas law which connects simultaneous values of the three parameters.[1]

In conclusion, let me stress once more the important role of laws in deductive-nomological explanation: the laws connect the explanandum event with the particular conditions cited in the explanans, and this is what confers upon the latter the status of explanatory (and, in some cases, causal) factors in regard to the phenomenon to be explained.

2.2. *Probabilistic explanation.* In deductive-nomological explanation as schematized in (*D*), the laws and theoretical principles involved are of *strictly universal form*: they assert that in *all* cases in which certain specified conditions are realized an occurrence of such and such a kind will result; the law that any metal, when heated under constant pressure, will increase in volume, is a typical example; Galileo's, Kepler's, Newton's, Boyle's, and Snell's laws, and many others, are of the same character.

Now let me turn next to a second basic type of scientific explanation. This kind of explanation, too, is nomological, i.e., it accounts for a given phenomenon by reference to general laws or theoretical principles; but some or all of these are of *probabilistic-statistical form*, i.e., they are, generally speaking, assertions to the effect that if certain specified conditions are realized, then an occurrence of such and such a kind will come about with such and such a statistical probability.

For example, the subsiding of a violent attack of hay fever in a given case might well be attributed to, and thus explained by reference

[1]The relevance of the covering-law model to causal explanation is examined more fully in sec. 4 of Hempel, C. G., 'Deductive-Nomological *vs.* Statistical Explanation'. In Feigl, H., et al. (eds.), *Minnesota Studies in the Philosophy of Science*, vol. III. Minneapolis, 1962.

to, the administration of 8 milligrams of chlor-trimeton. But if we wish to connect this antecedent event with the explanandum, and thus to establish its explanatory significance for the latter, we cannot invoke a universal law to the effect that the administration of 8 milligrams of that antihistamine will invariably terminate a hay fever attack: this simply is not so. What can be asserted is only a generalization to the effect that administration of the drug will be followed by relief with high statistical probability, i.e., roughly speaking, with a high relative frequency in the long run. The resulting explanans will thus be of the following type:

John Doe had a hay fever attack and took 8 milligrams of chlor-trimeton.

The probability for subsidence of a hay fever attack upon administration of 8 milligrams of chlor-trimeton is high.

Clearly, this explanans does not deductively imply the explanandum, 'John Doe's hay fever attack subsided'; the truth of the explanans makes the truth of the explanandum not certain (as it does in a deductive-nomological explanation) but only more or less likely or, perhaps 'practically' certain.

Reduced to its simplest essentials, a probabilistic explanation thus takes the following form:

$$(P) \qquad \begin{array}{c} Fi \\ p(O, F) \text{ is very high} \\ \hline\hline Oi \end{array} \qquad \text{makes very likely}$$

The explanandum, expressed by the statement '*Oi*', consists in the fact that in the particular instance under consideration, here called *i* (e.g., John Doe's allergic attack), an outcome of kind *O* (subsidence) occurred. This is explained by means of two explanans-statements. The first of these, '*Fi*', corresponds to $C_1, C_2, \ldots, C_k$ in (*D*); it states that in case *i*, the factors *F* (which may be more or less complex) were realized. The second expresses a law of probabilistic form, to the effect that the statistical probability for outcome *O* to occur in cases where *F* is realized is very high (close to 1). The double line separating explanandum from explanans is to indicate that, in contrast to the case of deductive-nomological explanation, the explanans does not logically imply the explanandum, but only confers a high likelihood upon it. The concept of likelihood here referred to must be clearly distinguished from that of statistical probability, symbolized by '*p*' in our schema. A statistical probability is, roughly speaking, the long-run relative frequency with which an occurrence of a given kind (say, *F*) is accompanied by an 'outcome' of a specified kind (say, *O*). Our likelihood, on the other hand, is a relation (capable of gradations) not between kinds of occurrences, but between statements. The likelihood referred to in (*P*) may be characterized as the strength of the inductive support, or the degree of rational credibility, which the explanans confers upon the explanandum; or, in Carnap's terminology, as the *logical*, or *inductive*, (in contrast to statistical) *probability* which the explanandum possesses relative to the explanans.

Thus, probabilistic explanation, just like explanation in the manner of schema (*D*), is nomological in that it presupposes general laws; but because these laws are of statistical rather than of strictly universal form, the resulting explanatory arguments are inductive rather than deductive in character. An inductive argument of this kind *explains* a given phenomenon by showing that, in view of certain particular events and certain statistical laws, its occurrence was to be expected with high logical, or inductive, probability.

By reason of its inductive character, probabilistic explanation differs from its deductive-nomological counterpart in several other important respects; for example, its explanans may confer upon the explanandum a more or less high degree of inductive support; in this sense, probabilistic explanation admits of degrees, whereas deductive-nomological explanation appears as an either-or affair: a given set of universal laws and particular statements either does or does not imply a given explanandum statement. A fuller examination of these differences, however, would lead us far afield and is not required for the purposes of this paper.[1]

One final point: the distinction here suggested between deductive-nomological and probabilistic explanation might be questioned on the ground that, after all, the universal laws invoked in a deductive explanation can have been established only on the basis of a finite body of evidence, which surely affords no exhaustive verification, but only more or less strong probability for it; and that, therefore, all scientific laws have to be regarded as probabilistic. This argument, however, confounds a logical issue with an epistemological one: it fails to distinguish properly between the *claim* made by a given law-statement and the *degree* of *confirmation*, or *probability*, which it possesses on the available evidence. It is quite true that statements expressing laws of either kind can be only incompletely confirmed

[1]The concept of probabilistic explanation, and some of the peculiar logical and methodological problems engendered by it, are examined in some detail in Part II of the essay cited in the previous note.

by any given finite set—however large—of data about particular facts; but law-statements of the two different types make claims of different kind, which are reflected in their logical forms: roughly, a universal law-statement of the simplest kind asserts that *all* elements of an indefinitely large reference class (e.g., copper objects) have a certain characteristic (e.g., that of being good conductors of electricity); while statistical law-statements assert that in the long run, a specified proportion of the members of the reference class have some specified property. And our distinction of two types of law and, concomitantly, of two types of scientific explanation, is based on this difference in claim as reflected in the difference of form.

The great scientific importance of probabilistic explanation is eloquently attested to by the extensive and highly successful explanatory use that has been made of fundamental laws of statistical form in genetics, statistical mechanics, and quantum theory.

3. Elliptic and Partial Explanations: Explanation Sketches

As I mentioned earlier, the conception of deductive-nomological explanation reflected in our schema (*D*) is often referred to as the covering law model, or the deductive model, of explanation: similarly, the conception underlying schema (*P*) might be called the probabilistic or the inductive-statistical, model of explanation. The term 'model' can serve as a useful reminder that the two types of explanation as characterized above constitute ideal types or theoretical idealizations and are not intended to reflect the manner in which working scientists actually formulate their explanatory accounts. Rather, they are meant to provide explications, or rational reconstructions, or theoretical models, of certain modes of scientific explanation.

In this respect our models might be compared to the concept of mathematical proof (within a given theory) as construed in meta-mathematics. This concept, too, may be regarded as a theoretical model: it is not intended to provide a descriptive account of how proofs are formulated in the writings of mathematicians: most of these actual formulations fall short of rigorous and, as it were, ideal, meta-mathematical standards. But the theoretical model has certain other functions: it exhibits the rationale of mathematical proofs by revealing the logical connections underlying the successive steps; it provides standards for a critical appraisal of any proposed proof constructed within the mathematical system to which the model refers; and it affords a basis for a precise and far-reaching theory of proof, provability, decidability, and related concepts. I think the two models of explanation can fulfil the same functions, if only on a much more modest scale. For example, the arguments presented in constructing the models give an indication of the sense in which the models exhibit the rationale and the logical structure of the explanations they are intended to represent.

I now want to add a few words concerning the second of the functions just mentioned; but I will have to forgo a discussion of the third.

When a mathematician proves a theorem, he will often omit mention of certain propositions which he presupposes in his argument and which he is in fact entitled to presuppose because, for example, they follow readily from the postulates of his system or from previously established theorems or perhaps from the hypothesis of his theorem, if the latter is in hypothetical form; he then simply assumes that his readers or listeners will be able to supply the missing items if they so desire. If judged by ideal standards, the given formulation of the proof is elliptic or incomplete; but the departure from the ideal is harmless: the gaps can readily be filled in. Similarly, explanations put forward in everyday discourse and also in scientific contexts are often *elliptically formulated*. When we explain, for example, that a lump of butter melted because it was put into a hot frying pan, or that a small rainbow appeared in the spray of the lawn sprinkler because the sunlight was reflected and refracted by the water droplets, we may be said to offer elliptic formulations of deductive-nomological explanations; an account of this kind omits mention of certain laws or particular facts which it tacitly takes for granted, and whose explicit citation would yield a complete deductive-nomological argument.

In addition to elliptic formulation, there is another, quite important, respect in which many explanatory arguments deviate from the theoretical model. It often happens that the statement actually included in the explanans, together with those which may reasonably be assumed to have been taken for granted in the context at hand, explain the given explanandum only *partially*, in a sense which I will try to indicate by an example. In his *Psychopathology of Everyday Life*, Freud offers the following explanation of a slip of the pen that occurred to him: 'On a sheet of paper containing principally short daily notes of business interest, I found, to my surprise, the incorrect date, "Thursday, October 20th", bracketed under the correct date of the month of September. It was not difficult to explain this anticipation as the expression of a wish. A few days before I had returned fresh from my vacation and felt ready for any amount of professional work, but as yet there were few patients. On my arrival I had found a letter from a patient announcing her arrival on the 20th of October. As I wrote the same date in September I may certainly have thought "X" ought to be here already; what a pity about that whole month!", and with this thought I pushed the current date a month ahead.'[1]

Clearly, the formulation of the intended explanation is *at least incomplete* in the sense considered a moment ago. In particular, it fails to mention any laws or theoretical principles in virtue of which the subconscious wish, and the other antecedent circumstances referred to, could be held to explain Freud's slip of the pen. However, the general theoretical considerations Freud presents here and elsewhere in his writings suggests strongly that his explanatory account relies on a hypothesis to the effect that when a person has a strong, though perhaps unconscious, desire, then if he commits a slip of pen, tongue, memory, or the like, the slip will take a form in which it expresses, and perhaps symbolically fulfils, the given desire.

Even this rather vague hypothesis is probably more definite than what Freud would have been willing to assert. But for the sake of the argument let us accept it and include it in the explanans, together with the particular statements that Freud did have the subconscious wish he mentions, and that he was going to commit a slip of the pen. Even then, the resulting explanans permits us to deduce only that the slip made by Freud would, *in some way or other*, express and perhaps symbolically fulfil Freud's subconscious wish. But clearly, such expression and fulfilment might have been achieved by many other kinds of slip of the pen than the one actually committed.

In other words, the explanans does not imply, and thus fully explain, that the particular slip, say s, which Freud committed on this occasion, would fall within the narrow class, say W, of acts which consist in writing the words 'Thursday, October 20th'; rather, the explanans implies only that s would fall into a wider class, say F, which includes W as a proper subclass, and which consists of all acts which would express and symbolically fulfil Freud's subconscious wish *in some way or other*.

The argument under consideration might be called a *partial explanation*: it provides complete, or conclusive, grounds for expect-

[1]Freud, S. *Psychopathology of Everyday Life*. Translated by A. A. Brill. New York (Mentor Books) 1951; p. 64.

ing *s* to be a member of *F*, and since *W* is a subclass of *F*, it thus shows that the explanandum, i.e., *s* falling within *W*, accords with, or bears out, what is to be expected in consideration of the explanans. By contrast, a deductive-nomological explanation of the form (*D*) might then be called *complete* since the explanans here does imply the explanandum.

Clearly, the question whether a given explanatory argument is complete or partial can be significantly raised only if the explanandum sentence is fully specified; only then can we ask whether the explanandum does or does not follow from the explanans. Completeness of explanation, in this sense, is relative to our explanandum sentence. Now, it might seem much more important and interesting to consider instead the notion of a complete explanation of some *concrete event*, such as the destruction of Pompeii, or the death of Adolf Hitler, or the launching of the first artificial satellite: we might want to regard a particular event as completely explained only if an explanatory account of deductive or of inductive form had been provided for all of its aspects. This notion, however, is self-defeating; for any particular event may be regarded as having infinitely many different aspects or characteristics, which cannot all be accounted for by a finite set, however large, of explanatory statements.

In some cases, what is intended as an explanatory account will depart even further from the standards reflected in the model schemata (*D*) and (*P*) above. An explanatory account, for example, which is not explicit and specific enough to be reasonably qualified as an elliptically formulated explanation or as a partial one, can often be viewed as an *explanation sketch*: it may suggest, perhaps quite vividly and persuasively, the general outlines of what, it is hoped, can eventually be supplemented so as to yield a more closely reasoned argument based on explanatory hypotheses which are indicated more fully, and which more readily permit of critical appraisal by reference to empirical evidence.

The decision whether a proposed explanatory account is to be qualified as an elliptically formulated deductive or probabilistic explanation, as a partial explanation, as an explanation sketch, or perhaps as none of these is a matter of judicious interpretation; it calls for an appraisal of the intent of the given argument and of the background assumptions that may be assumed to have been tacitly taken for granted, or at least to be available, in the given context. Unequivocal decision rules cannot be set down for this purpose any more than for determining whether a given informally stated inference which is not deductively valid by reasonably strict standards is to count nevertheless as valid but enthymematically formulated, or as fallacious, or as an instance of sound inductive reasoning, or perhaps, for lack of clarity, as none of these.

4. Nomological Explanation in History

So far, we have examined nomological explanation, both deductive and inductive, as found in the natural sciences; and we have considered certain characteristic ways in which actual explanatory accounts often depart from the ideal standards of our two basic models. Now it is time to ask what light the preceding inquiries can shed on the explanatory procedures used in historical research.

In examining this question, we will consider a number of specific explanatory arguments offered by a variety of writers. It should be understood from the beginning that we are here concerned, not to appraise the factual adequacy of these explanations, but only to attempt an explication of the claims they make and of the assumptions they presuppose.

Let us note first, then, that some historical explanations are surely nomological in character: they aim to show that the explanandum phenomenon resulted from certain antecedent, and perhaps, concomitant, conditions; and in arguing these, they rely more or less explicitly on relevant generalizations. These may concern, for example, psychological or sociological tendencies and may best be conceived as broadly probabilistic in character. This point is illustrated by the following argument, which might be called an attempt to explain Parkinson's Law by subsumption under broader psychological principles:

> As the activities of the government are enlarged, more people develop a vested interest in the continuation and expansion of governmental functions. People who have jobs do not like to lose them; those who are habituated to certain skills do not welcome change; those who have become accustomed to the exercise of a certain kind of power do not like to relinquish their control—if anything, they want to develop greater power and correspondingly greater prestige. . . . Thus, government offices and bureaus, once created, in turn institute drives, not only to fortify themselves against assault, but to enlarge the scope of their operations.[1]

The psychological generalizations here explicitly adduced will

[1]McConnell, D. W., *et al.*, *Economic Behavior*. New York, 1939; pp. 894–95.

reasonably have to be understood as expressing, not strict uniformites, but strong *tendencies*, which might be formulated by means of rough probability statements; so that the explanation here suggested is probabilistic in character.

As a rule, however, the generalizations underlying a proposed historical explanation are largely left unspecified; and most concrete explanatory accounts have to be qualified as partial explanations or as explanation sketches. Consider, for example, F. J. Turner's essay 'The Significance of the Frontier in American History,'[1] which amplifies and defends the view that 'Up to our own day American history has been in a large degree the history of the colonization of the Great West. The existence of an area of free land, its continuous recession, and the advance of American settlement westward explain American development.... The peculiarity of American institutions is the fact that they have been compelled to adapt themselves ... to the changes involved in crossing a continent, in winning a wilderness, and in developing at each area of this progress, out of the primitive economic and political conditions of the frontier, the complexity of city life.'[2] One of the phenomena Turner considers in developing his thesis is the rapid westward advance of what he calls the Indian trader's frontier. 'Why was it', Turner asks, 'that the Indian trader passed so rapidly across the continent?'; and he answers, 'The explanation of the rapidity of this advance is bound up with the effects of the trader on the Indian. The trading post left the unarmed tribes at the mercy of those that had purchased firearms—a truth which the Iroquois Indians wrote in blood, and so the remote and unvisited tribes gave eager welcome to the trader.... This accounts for the trader's power and the rapidity of his advance.'[3] There is no explicit mention here of any laws, but it is clear that this sketch of an explanation presupposes, first of all, various particular facts, such as that the remote and unvisited tribes had heard of the efficacy and availability of firearms, and that there were no culture patterns or institutions precluding their use by those tribes; but in addition, the account clearly rests also on certain assumptions as to how human beings will tend to behave in situations presenting the kinds of danger and of opportunity that Turner refers to.

[1]First published in 1893, and reprinted in several publications, among them: Edwards, Everett E. (ed.), *The Early Writings of Frederick Jackson Turner*. Madison, Wisconsin, 1938. Page references given in the present article pertain to this book.

[2]loc. cit., pp. 185–86. [3]loc. cit., pp. 200–201.

Similar comments apply to Turner's account of the westward advance of what he calls the farmer's frontier: 'Omitting those of the pioneer farmers who move from the love of adventure, the advance of the more steady farmer is easy to understand. Obviously the immigrant was attracted by the cheap lands of the frontier, and even the native farmer felt their influence strongly. Year by year the farmers who lived on soil, whose returns were diminished by unrotated crops, were offered the virgin soil of the frontier at nominal prices. Their growing families demanded more lands, and these were dear. The competition of the unexhausted, cheap, and easily tilled prairie lands compelled the farmer either to go West . . . or to adopt intensive culture.'[1] This passage is clearly intended to do more than describe a sequence of particular events: it is meant to afford an understanding of the farmers' westward advance by pointing to their interests and needs and by calling attention to the facts and the opportunities facing them. Again, this explanation takes it for granted that under such conditions normal human beings will tend to seize new opportunities in the manner in which the pioneer farmers did.

Examining the various consequences of this moving-frontier history, Turner states that 'the most important effect of the frontier has been in the promotion of democracy here and in Europe',[2] and he begins his elaboration of this theme with the remark that 'the frontier is productive of individualism. . . . The tendency is anti-social. It produces antipathy to control, and particularly to any direct control':[3] and this is, of course, a sociological generalization in a nutshell.

Similarly, any explanation that accounts for a historical phenomenon by reference to economic factors or by means of general principles of social or cultural change are nomological in import, even if not in explicit formulation.

But if this be granted there still remains another question, to which we must now turn, namely, whether, in addition to explanations of a broadly nomological character, the historian also employs certain other distinctly historical ways of explaining and understanding whose import cannot be adequately characterized by means of our two models. The question has often been answered in the affirmative, and several kinds of historical explanation have been adduced in support of this affirmation. I will now consider what

[1]loc. cit., p. 210. [2]loc. cit., p. 219. [3]loc. cit., p. 220.

seem to me two especially interesting candidates for the role of specifically historical explanation; namely first, genetic explanation, and secondly, explanation of an action in terms of its underlying rationale.

5. Genetic Explanation in History

In order to make the occurrence of a historical phenomenon intelligible, a historian will frequently offer a 'genetic explanation' aimed at exhibiting the principal stages in a sequence of events which led up to the given phenomenon.

Consider, for example, the practice of selling indulgences as it existed in Luther's time. H. Boehmer, in his work, *Luther and the Reformation*, points out that until about the end of the nineteenth century, 'the indulgence was in fact still a great unknown quantity, at sight of which the scholar would ask himself with a sigh: "Where did it come from?"'[1] An answer was provided by Adolf Gottlob,[2] who tackled the problem by asking himself what led the Popes and Bishops to offer indulgences. As a result, '. . . origin and development of the unknown quantity appeared clearly in the light, and doubts as to its original meaning came to an end. It revealed itself as a true descendant of the time of the great struggle between Christianity and Islam, and at the same time a highly characteristic product of Germanic Christianity.'[3]

In brief outline,[4] the origins of the indulgence appear to go back to the ninth century, when the popes were strongly concerned with the fight against Islam. The Mohammedan fighter was assured by the teachings of his religion that if he were to be killed in battle his soul would immediately go to heaven; but the defender of the Christian faith had to fear that he might still be lost if he had not done the regular penance for his sins. To allay these doubts, John VII, in 877, promised absolution for their sins to crusaders who should be killed in battle. 'Once the crusade was so highly thought of, it was an

[1]Boehmer, H., *Luther and the Reformation*. Translated by E. S. G. Potter. London, 1930; p. 91.

[2]Gottlob's study, *Kreuzablass und Almosenablass*, was published in 1906; cf. the references to the work of Gottlob and other investigators in Schwiebert, E. G., *Luther and His Times*. St. Louis, Missouri, 1950, notes to Chapter 10.

[3]Boehmer, loc. cit., p. 91.

[4]This outline follows the accounts given by Boehmer, loc. cit., Chapter III and by Schwiebert, loc. cit., Chapter 10.

easy transition to regard participation in a crusade as equivalent to the performance of atonement . . . and to promise remission of these penances in return for expeditions against the Church's enemies.'[1] Thus, there was introduced the indulgence of the Cross, which granted complete remission of the penitential punishment to all those who participated in a religious war. 'If it is remembered what inconveniences, what ecclesiastical and civil disadvantages the ecclesiastical penances entailed, it is easy to understand that the penitents flocked to obtain this indulgence.'[2] A further strong incentive came from the belief that whoever obtained an indulgence secured liberation not only from the ecclesiastical penances, but also from the corresponding suffering in purgatory after death. The benefits of these indulgences were next extended to those who, being physically unfit to participate in a religious war, contributed the funds required to send a soldier on a crusade: in 1199, Pope Innocent III recognized the payment of money as adequate qualification for the benefits of a crusading indulgence.

When the crusades were on the decline, new ways were explored of raising funds through indulgences. Thus, there was instituted a 'jubilee indulgence', to be celebrated every hundred years, for the benefit of pilgrims coming to Rome on that occasion. The first of these indulgences, in 1300, brought in huge sums of money; and the time interval between successive jubilee indulgences was therefore reduced to 50, 33, and even 25 years. And from 1393 on the jubilee indulgence was made available, not only in Rome, for the benefit of pilgrims, but everywhere in Europe, through special agents who were empowered to absolve the penitent of their sins upon payment of an appropriate amount. The development went even further: in 1477, a dogmatic declaration by Sixtus IV attributed to the indulgence the power of delivering even the dead from purgatory.

Undeniably, a genetic account of this kind can enhance our understanding of a historical phenomenon. But its explanatory role, far from being *sui generis*, seems to me basically nomological in character. For the successive stages singled out for consideration surely must be qualified for their function by more than the fact that they form a temporal sequence and that they all precede the final stage, which is to be explained: the mere enumeration in a yearbook of 'the year's important events' in the order of their occurrence

[1] Boehmer, loc. cit., p. 92.

[2] Boehmer, loc. cit., p. 93.

clearly is not a genetic explanation of the final event or of anything else. In a genetic explanation each stage must be shown to 'lead to' the next, and thus to be linked to its successor by virtue of some general principle which makes the occurrence of the latter at least reasonably probable, given the former. But in this sense, even successive stages in a physical phenomenon such as the free fall of a stone may be regarded as forming a genetic sequence whose different stages—characterized, let us say, by the position and the velocity of the stone at different times—are interconnected by strictly universal laws; and the successive stages in the movement of a steel ball bouncing its zigzaggy way down a Galton pegboard may be regarded as forming a genetic sequence with probabilistic connections.

The genetic accounts given by historians are not, of course, of the purely nomological kind suggested by these examples from physics. Rather, they combine a certain measure of nomological interconnecting with more or less large amounts of straight description. For consider an intermediate stage mentioned in a genetic account: some aspects of it will be presented as having evolved from the preceding stages (in virtue of connecting laws, which often will be no more than hinted at); while other aspects, which are not accounted for by information about the preceding development, will be descriptively added because they are relevant to an understanding of subsequent stages in the genetic sequence. Thus, schematically speaking, a genetic explanation will begin with a pure description of an initial stage; thence, it will proceed to an account of a second stage, part of which is nomologically linked to, and explained by, the characteristic features of the initial stage; while the balance is simply described as relevant for a nomological account of some aspects of the third stage; and so forth.[1]

In our illustration the connecting laws are hinted at in the mention made of motivating factors: the explanatory claims made for the interest of the popes in securing a fighting force and in amassing ever larger funds clearly presuppose suitable psychological generalizations as to the manner in which an intelligent individual will act, in the light of his factual beliefs, when he seeks to attain a certain objective. Similarly, general assumptions underly the reference to the fear of purgatory in explaining the eagerness with which

[1] The logic of genetic explanations in history is examined in some detail in E. Nagel's recent book. *The Structure of Science*. New York, 1961; pp. 564–568. The conception outlined in the present paper, though arrived at without any knowledge of Nagel's work on this subject, accords well with the latter's results.

indulgences were bought. And when, referring to the huge financial returns of the first jubilee indulgence, Schwiebert says 'This success only whetted the insatiable appetite of the popes. The intervening period of time was variously reduced from 100 to 50, to 33, to 25 years . . .',[1] the explanatory force here implied might be said to rest on some principle of reinforcement by rewards. As need hardly be added, even if such a principle were explicitly introduced, the resulting account would provide at most a partial explanation; it could not be expected to show, for example, why the intervening intervals should have the particular lenghts here mentioned.

In the genetic account of the indulgences, those factors which are simply described (or tacitly presupposed) rather than explained include, for example, the doctrines, the organization, and the power of the Church; the occurrence of the crusades and their eventual decline; and innumerable other factors which are not even explicitly mentioned, but which have to be understood as background conditions if the genetic survey is to serve its explanatory purpose.

The general conception here outlined of the logic of genetic explanation could also be illustrated by reference to Turner's studies of the American frontier; this will be clear even from the brief remarks made earlier on Turner's ideas.

Some analysts of historical development put special emphasis on the importance of the laws underlying a historical explanation; thus, e.g., A. Gerschenkron maintains, 'Historical research consists essentially in application to empirical material of various sets of empirically derived hypothetical generalizations and in testing the closeness of the resulting fit, in the hope that in this way certain uniformities, certain typical situations, and certain typical relationships among individual factors in these situations can be ascertained',[2] and his subsequent substantive observations include a brief genetic survey of patterns of industrial development in nineteenth-century Europe, in which some of the presumably relevant uniformities are made reasonably explicit.

6. Explanation by Motivating Reasons

Let us now turn to another kind of historical explanation that is often considered as *sui generis*, namely, the explanation of an

[1]Schwiebert, loc. cit., p. 304.

[2]Gerschenkron, A. 'Economic Backwardness in Historical Perspective', in Hoselitz B. F. (ed.), *The Progress of Underdeveloped Areas*. Chicago, 1952; pp. 3–29.

action in terms of the underlying *rationale*, which will include, in particular, the ends the agent sought to attain, and the alternative courses of action he believed to be open to him. The following passage explaining the transition from the indulgence of the Cross to the institution of the jubilee indulgence illustrates this procedure: '... in the course of the thirteenth century the idea of a crusade more and more lost its power over men's spirits. If the Popes would keep open the important source of income which the indulgence represented, they must invent new motives to attract people to the purchase of indulgences. It is the merit of Boniface VIII to have recognized this clearly. By creating the jubilee indulgence in 1300 he assured the species a further long development most welcome to the Papal finances.'[1] This passage clearly seeks to explain the establishment of the first jubilee indulgence by suggesting the reasons for which Boniface VIII took this step. If properly spelled out, these reasons would include not only Boniface's objective of ensuring a continuation of the income so far derived from the indulgence of the Cross, but also his estimate of the relevant empirical circumstances, including the different courses of action open to him, and their probable efficacy as well as potential difficulties in pursuing them and adverse consequences to which they might lead.

The kind of explanation achieved by specifying the rationale underlying a given action is widely held to be fundamentally different from nomological explanation as found in the natural sciences. Various reasons have been adduced in support of this view; but I will limit my discussion largely to the stimulating ideas on the subject that have been set forth by Dray.[2] According to Dray, there is an important type of historical explanation whose features 'make the covering law model peculiarly inept'; he calls it 'rational explanation', i.e., 'explanation which displays the *rationale* of what was done', or, more fully, 'a reconstruction of the agent's *calculation* of means to be adopted toward his chosen end in the light of the circumstances in which he found himself'. The object of rational explanation is not to subsume the explanandum under general laws, but 'to show that what was done was the thing to have done for the reasons given, rather than merely the thing that is done on such occasions, perhaps in accordance with certain laws'. Hence, a rational explanation has 'an element of *appraisal*' in it:

[1]Boehmer, loc. cit., pp. 93–94.

[2]Dray, W. *Laws and Explanation in History*. Oxford, 1957; Chapter v. All quotations are from this chapter; italics in the quoted passages are Dray's.

it 'must exhibit what was done as appropriate or justified'. Accordingly, Dray conceives a rational explanation as being based on a standard of appropriateness or of rationality of a special kind which he calls a '*principle of action*', i.e., 'a judgement of the form "When in a situation of type $C_1, C_2, \ldots C_n$ the thing to do is X."'

Dray does not give a full account of the kind of 'situation' here referred to; but to do justice to his intentions, these situations must evidently be taken to include, at least, items of the following three types: (i) the end the agent was seeking to attain; (ii) the empirical circumstances, as seen by the agent, in which he had to act; (iii) the moral standards or principles of conduct to which the agent was committed. For while this brief list requires considerable further scrutiny and elaboration, it seems clear that only if at least these items are specified does it make sense to raise the question of the appropriateness of what the agent did in the given 'situation'.

It seems fair to say, then, that according to Dray's conception a rational explanation answers a question of the form 'Why did agent A do X?' by offering an explanans of the following type (our formulation replaces the notation '$C_1, C_2 \ldots C_n$' by the simpler 'C', without, of course, precluding that the kind of situation thus referred to may be extremely complex):

(R)

A was in a situation of type C
In a situation of type C, the appropriate thing to do is X

But can an explanans of this type possibly serve to explain A's having in fact done X? It seems to me beyond dispute that in any adequate explanation of an empirical phenomenon the explanans must provide good grounds for believing or asserting that the explanandum phenomenon did in fact occur. Yet this requirement, which is necessary though not sufficient[1] for an adequate explanation, is not met by a rational explanation as conceived by Dray. For the two statements included in the contemplated explanans (*R*) provide good reasons for believing that the appropriate thing for A to do was X, but not for believing that A did in fact do X. Thus, a rational explanation in the sense in which Dray appears to understand it does not explain what it is meant to explain. Indeed, the expression 'the

[1]Empirical evidence supporting a given hypothesis may afford strong grounds for believing the latter without providing an explanation for it.

thing to do' in the standard formulation of a principle of action, 'functions as a value term', as Dray himself points out: but then, it is unclear, on purely logical grounds, how the valuational principle expressed by the second sentence in (*R*), in conjunction with the plainly empirical, non-valuational first sentence, should permit any inferences concerning empirical matters such as *A*'s action, which could not be drawn from the first sentence alone.

To explain, in the general vein here under discussion, why *A* did in fact do *X*, we have to refer to the underlying rationale not by means of a normative principle of action, but by descriptive statements to the effect that, at the time in question *A* was a rational agent, or had the dispostion to act rationally; and that a rational agent, when in circumstances of kind *C*, will always (or: with high probability) do *X*. Thus construed, the explanans takes on the following form:

(R′)

(a) *A* was in a situation of type *C*
(b) *A* was disposed to act rationally
(c) Any person who is disposed to act rationally will, when in a situation of type *C*, invariably (with high probability) do *X*

But by this explanans *A*'s having done *X* is accounted for in the manner of a deductive or of a probabilistic nomological explanation. Thus, in so far as reference to the rationale of an agent does explain his action, the explanation conforms to one of our nomological models.

An analogous diagnosis applies, incidentally, also to explanations which attribute an agent's behaviour in a given situation not to rationality and more or less explicit deliberation on his part, but to other dispositional features, such as his character and emotional make-up. The following comment on Luther illustrates this point: 'Even stranger to him than the sense of anxiety was the allied sense of fear. In 1527 and 1535, when the plague broke out in Wittenberg, he was the only professor besides Bugenhagen who remained calmly at his post to comfort and care for the sick and dying. . . . He had, indeed, so little sense as to take victims of the plague into his house and touch them with his own hand. Death, martyrdom, dishonor, contempt . . . he feared just as little as infectious disease.'[1] It may

[1]Boehmer, loc. cit., p. 234.

well be said that these observations give more than a description: that they shed some explanatory light on the particular occurrences mentioned. But in so far as they explain, they do so by presenting Luther's actions as manifestations of certain personality traits, such as fearlessness; thus, the particular acts are again subsumed under generalizations as to how a fearless person is likely to behave under certain circumstances.

It might seem that both in this case and in rational explanation as construed in (*R′*), the statements which we took to express general laws—namely, (*c*) in (*R′*), and the statement about the probable behaviour of a fearless person in our last illustration—do not have the character of empirical laws at all, but rather that of analytic statements which simply express part of what is *meant* by a rational agent, a fearless person, or the like. Thus, in contrast to nomological explanations, these accounts in terms of certain dispositional characteristics of the agent appear to presuppose no general laws at all. Now, the idea of analyticity gives rise to considerable philosophical difficulties; but let us disregard these here and take the division of statements into analytic and synthetic to be reasonably clear. Even then, the objection just outlined cannot be upheld. For dispositional concepts of the kind invoked in our explanations have to be regarded as governed by entire clusters of general statements—we might call them symptom statements—which connect the given disposition with various specific manifestations, or symptoms, of its presence (each symptom will be a particular mode of 'responding', or acting, under specified 'stimulus' conditions); and the whole cluster of these symptom statements for a given disposition will have implications which are plainly not analytic (in the intuitive sense here assumed). Under these circumstances it would be arbitrary to attribute to some of the symptom statements the analytic character of partial definitions.

The logic of this situation has a precise representation in Carnap's theory of reduction sentences.[1] Here, the connections between a given disposition and its various manifest symptoms are assumed to be expressed by a set of so-called reduction sentences (these are characterized by their logical form). Some of these state, in terms of manifest characteristics, sufficient conditions for the presence of

[1] See especially Carnap's classical essay, 'Testability and Meaning', *Philosophy of Science*, 3, 419–71 (1936) and 4, 1–40 (1937); reprinted, with some omissions, in Feigl and Brodbeck, loc. cit. On the point here under discussion, see sec. 9 and particularly sec. 10 of the original essay or sec. 7 of the reprinted version.

the given disposition; others similarly state necessary conditions. The reduction sentences for a given dispositional concept cannot, as a rule, all be qualified as analytic; for jointly they imply certain non-analytic consequences which have the status of general laws connecting exclusively the manifest characteristics; the strongest of the laws so implied is the so-called representative sentence, which 'represents, so to speak, the factual content of the set' of all the reduction sentences for the given disposition concept. This representative sentence asserts, in effect, that whenever at least one of the sufficient conditions specified by the given reduction sentences is satisfied, then so are all the necessary conditions laid down by the reduction sentences. And when *A* is one of the manifest criteria sufficient for the presence of a given disposition, and *B* is a necessary one, then the statement that whenever *A* is present so is *B* will normally turn out to be synthetic.

So far then, I have argued that Dray's construal of explanation by motivating reasons is untenable; that the normative principles of action envisaged by him have to be replaced by statements of a dispositional kind; and that, when this is done, explanations in terms of a motivating rationale, as well as those referring to other psychological factors, are seen to be basically nomological.

Let me add a few further remarks on the idea of rational explanation. First: in many cases of so-called purposive action, there is no conscious deliberation, no rational calculation that leads the agent to his decision. Dray is quite aware of this; but he holds that a rational explanation in his sense is still possible; for 'in so far as we say an action is purposive at all, no matter at what level of conscious deliberation, there is a calculation which could be constructed for it: the one the agent would have gone through if he had had time, if he had not seen what to do in a flash, if he had been called upon to account for what he did after the event, &c. And it is by eliciting some such calculation that we explain the action.'[1] But the explanatory significance of reasons or 'calculations' which are 'reconstructed' in this manner is certainly puzzling. If, to take Dray's example, an agent arrives at his decision 'in a flash' rather than by deliberation, then it would seem to be simply false to say that the decision can be accounted for by some argument which the agent might have gone through under more propitious circumstances, or which he might produce later if called upon to account for his action; for, by hypothesis, no such argument was in fact gone through by

[1]Dray, loc. cit., p. 123.

the agent at the crucial time; considerations of appropriateness or rationality played no part in shaping his decision; the rationale that Dray assumes to be adduced and appraised in the corresponding rational explanation is simply fictitious.

But, in fairness to Dray, these remarks call for a qualifying observation: in at least some of the cases Dray has in mind it might not be fictitious to ascribe the action under study to a disposition which the agent acquired through a learning process whose initial stages did involve conscious ratiocination. Consider, for example, the various complex manoeuvres of accelerating, braking, signalling, dodging jaywalkers and animals, swerving into and out of traffic lanes, estimating the changes of traffic lights, &c., which are involved in driving a car through city traffic. A beginning driver will often perform these only upon some sort of conscious deliberation or even calculation; but gradually, he learns to do the appropriate thing automatically, 'in a flash', without giving them any conscious thought. The habit pattern he has thus acquired may be viewed as consisting in a set of dispositions to react in certain appropriate ways in various situations; and a particular performance of such an appropriate action would then be explained, not by a 'constructed' calculation which actually the agent did not perform but by reference to the disposition just mentioned and thus, again, in a nomological fashion.

The method of explaining a given action by 'constructing', in Dray's sense, the agent's calculation of means faces yet another, though less fundamental, difficulty: it will frequently yield a rationalization rather than an explanation, especially when the reconstruction relies on the reasons the agent might produce when called upon to account for his action. As G. Watson remarks, 'Motivation, as presented in the perspective of history, is often too simple and straightforward, reflecting the psychology of the Age of Reason.... Psychology has come ... to recognize the enormous weight of irrational and intimately personal impulses in conduct. In history, biography, and in autobiography, especially of public characters, the tendency is strong to present "good" reasons instead of "real" reasons.'[1] Accordingly, as Watson goes on to point out, it is important, in examining the motivation of historical figures, to take into account the significance of such psychological mechanisms as reaction formation, 'the dialectic dynamic by which stinginess

[1]Watson, G. 'Clio and Psyche: Some Interrelations of Psychology and History.' In Ware, C. F. (ed.), *The Cultural Approach to History*. New York, 1940, pp. 34–47; quotation from p. 36.

cloaks itself in generosity, or rabid pacifism arises from the attempt to repress strong aggressive impulses'.[1]

These remarks have a bearing also on an idea set forth by P. Gardiner in his illuminating book on historical explanation.[2] Commenting on the notion of the 'real reason' for a man's action, Gardiner says: 'In general, it appears safe to say that by a man's "real reasons" we mean those reasons he would be prepared to give under circumstances where his confession would not entail adverse consequences to himself.' And he adds 'An exception to this is the psychoanalyst's usage of the expression where different criteria are adopted.[3] This observation might be taken to imply that the explanation of human actions in terms of underlying motives is properly aimed at exhibiting the agent's 'real reasons' in the ordinary sense of the phrase, as just described; and that, by implication, reasons in the psychoanalyst's sense require less or no consideration. But such a construal of explanation would give undue importance to considerations of ordinary language. Gardiner is entirely right when he reminds us that the 'language in which history is written is for the most part the language of ordinary speech'[4]; but the historian in search of reasons that will correctly explain human actions will obviously have to give up his reliance on the everyday conception of 'real reasons' if psychological or other investigations show that real reasons, thus understood, do not yield as adequate an account of human actions as an analysis in terms of less familiar conceptions such as, perhaps, the idea of motivating factors which are kept out of the agent's normal awareness by processes of repression and reaction formation.

I would say, then, first of all, that historical explanation cannot be bound by conceptions that might be implicit in the way in which ordinary language deals with motivating reasons. But secondly, I would doubt that Gardiner's expressly tentative characterization does justice even to what we ordinarily mean when we speak of a man's 'real reasons'. For considerations of the kind that support the idea of subconscious motives are quite familiar in our time, and we are therefore prepared to say in ordinary, non-technical discourse that the reasons given by an agent may not be the 'real reasons'

[1]Watson, ibid.

[2]Gardiner, P. *The Nature of Historical Explanation.* Oxford, 1952.

[3]Gardiner, loc. cit., p. 136.

[4]Gardiner, loc. cit., p. 63.

behind his action, even if his statement was subjectively honest, and he had no grounds to expect that it would lead to any adverse consequences for him. For no matter whether an explanation of human actions is attempted in the language of ordinary speech or in the technical terms of some theory, the overriding criterion for what-if-anything should count as a 'real', and thus explanatory, reason for a given action is surely not to be found by examining the way in which the term 'real reason' has thus far been used, but by investigating what conception of real reason would yield the most satisfactory explanation of human conduct; and ordinary usage gradually changes accordingly.

7. Concluding Remarks

We have surveyed some of the most prominent candidates for the role of characteristically historical mode of explanation; and we have found that they conform essentially to one or the other of our two basic types of scientific explanation.

This result and the arguments that led to it do not in any way imply a mechanistic view of man, of society, and of historical processes; nor, of course, do they deny the importance of ideas and ideals for human decision and action. What the preceding considerations do suggest is, rather, that the nature of understanding, in the sense in which explanation is meant to give us an understanding of empirical phenomena, is basically the same in all areas of scientific inquiry; and that the deductive and the probabilistic model of nomological explanation accommodate vastly more than just the explanatory arguments of, say, classical mechanics: in particular, they accord well also with the character of explanations that deal with the influence of rational deliberation, of conscious and subconscious motives, and of ideas and ideals on the shaping of historical events. In so doing, our schemata exhibit, I think, one important aspect of the methodological unity of all empirical science.

IV

THE STRUCTURE OF TELEOLOGICAL EXPLANATIONS

ERNEST NAGEL

(1) Is it possible to formulate in general but fairly precise terms the distinguishing structure of 'goal-directed' systems, but in such a way that the analysis is neutral with respect to assumptions concerning the existence of purposes or the dynamic operation of goals as instruments in their own realization? (2) Does the fact, if it is a fact, that teleological explanations are customarily employed only in connection with 'goal-directed' systems constitute relevant evidence for deciding the issue of whether a teleological explanation is equivalent to some nonteleological one? (3) Is it possible to explain in purely physicochemical terms—that is, exclusively in terms of the laws and theories of current physics and chemistry—the operations of biological systems? This third question will not concern us for the present, though we shall return to it later; but the other two require our immediate attention.

i. Since antiquity there have been many attempts at constructing machines and physical systems simulating the behaviour of living organisms in one respect or another. None of these attempts has been entirely successful, for it has not been possible thus far to manufacture in the workshop and out of inorganic materials any device that acts fully like a living body. Nevertheless, it has been possible to construct physical systems that are self-maintaining and self-regulating in respect to certain of their features, and which therefore resemble living organisms in at least this one important characteristic. In an age in which servo-mechanisms (governors on engines, thermostats, automatic airplane pilots, electronic calculators, radar-controlled anti-aircraft firing devices, and the like) no longer excite wonder, and in which the language of cybernetics and 'negative feedbacks' has become widely fashionable, the imputation of 'goal-directed' behaviour to purely physical systems certainly cannot be rejected

From *The Structure of Science* by Ernest Nagel (Harcourt, Brace and Routledge & Kegan Paul, 1961), pp. 409–24.

as an absurdity. Whether 'purposes' can also be imputed to such physical systems, as some expounders of cybernetics claim,[1] is perhaps doubtful, though the question is in large measure a semantic one; and in any event, this further issue is not relevant to the present context of discussion. Moreover, it is worth noting that the possibility of constructing self-regulating physical systems does not, by itself, constitute a proof that the activities of living organisms can be explained in exclusively physicochemical terms. Nevertheless, the fact that such systems have been constructed does suggest that there is no sharp demarcation setting off the teleological organizations, often assumed to be distinctive of living things, from the goal-directed organizations of many physical systems. At the minimum, that fact offers strong support for the presumption that the teleologically organized activities of living organisms and of their parts can be analysed without requiring the postulation of purposes or goals as dynamic agents.

With the homeostasis of the temperature of the human body as an exemplar, let us now state in general terms the formal structure of systems possessing a goal-directed organization.[2] The characteristic feature of such systems is that they continue to manifest a certain state or property *G* (or that they exhibit a persistence of development 'in the direction' of attaining *G*) in the face of a relatively extensive class of changes in their external environments or in some of their internal parts—changes which, if not compensated for by internal modification in the system, would result in the disappearance of *G* (or in an altered direction of development of the systems). The abstract pattern of organization of such systems can be formulated with considerable precision, although only a schematic statement of that pattern can be presented in what follows.

Let *S* be some system, *E* its external environment, and *G* some state, property, or mode of behaviour that *S* possesses or is capable of possessing under suitable conditions. Assume for the moment

[1] Cf. Arturo Rosenblueth, Norbert Wiener, Julian Bigelow, 'Behavior, Purpose and Teleology', *Philosophy of Science*, Vol. 10 (1943); Norbert Wiener, *Cybernetics*, New York, 1948; A. M. Turing, 'Computing Machines and Intelligence', *Mind*, Vol. 59 (1950); Richard Taylor, 'Comments on a Mechanistic Conception of Purposefulness', *Philosophy of Science*, Vol. 17 (1950), and the reply by Rosenblueth and Wiener with a rejoinder by Taylor in the same volume.

[2] The following discussion is heavily indebted to G. Sommerhoff, *Analytical Biology*, London, 1950. Cf. also Alfred J. Lotka, *Elements of Physical Biology*, New York, 1926, Chap. 25; W. Ross Ashby, *Design for a Brain*, London, 1953, and *An Introduction to Cybernetics*, London, 1956; and R. B. Braithwaite, *Scientific Explanation*, Cambridge, 1954, Chap. 10.

(this assumption will eventually be relaxed) that E remains constant in all relevant respects, so that its influence upon the occurrence of G in S may be ignored. Suppose also that S is analysable into a structure of parts or processes, such that the activities of a certain number (possibly all) of them are causally relevant for the occurrence of G. For the sake of simplicity, assume that there are just three such parts, each capable of being in one of several distinct conditions or states. The state of each part at any given time will be represented by the predicates 'A_x', 'B_y', and 'C_z', respectively, with numerical values of the subscripts to indicate the different particular states of the corresponding parts. Accordingly, 'A_x', 'B_y', and 'C_z', are state variables, though they are not necessarily numerical variables, since numerical measures may not be available for representing the states of the parts; and the state of S that is causally relevant to G at any given time will thus be expressed by a specialization of the matrix '$(A_xB_yC_z)$'. The state variables may, however, be quite complex in form—for example, 'A_x' may represent the state of the peripheral blood vessels in a human body at a given time—and they may be either individual or statistical co-ordinates. But in order to avoid inessential complications in exposition, we shall suppose that, whatever the nature of the state variables, in respect to the states they represent S is a deterministic system: the states of S change in such a way that, if S is in the same state at any two different moments, the corresponding states of S after equal lapses of time from those moments will also be the same.

One further important general assumption must also be made explicit. Each of the state variables can be assigned any particular 'value' to characterize a state, provided the value is compatible with the known character of the part of S whose state the variable represents. In effect, therefore, the values of 'A_x' must fall into a certain restricted class K_A; and there are similar classes K_B and K_C for the permissible values of the other two state variables. The reason for these restrictions will be clear from an example. If S is the human body, and 'A_x' states the degree of dilation of peripheral blood vessels, it is obvious that this degree cannot exceed some maximum value; for it would be absurd to suppose that the blood vessels might have a mean diameter of, say, five feet. On the other hand, the possible values of one state variable *at a given time* will be assumed to be independent of the possible values of the other state variables *at that time*. This assumption must not be misunderstood. It does not assert that the value of a variable at one time is independent of the values of the other variables at some *other* time; it merely stipulates that the value of a variable at some specified instant is not a function of the values of the other variables *at that very same instant*. The assumption is the one normally made for state variables, and is introduced in part to avoid redundant co-ordinates of state. For example, the state variables in classical mechanics are the position and the momentum co-ordinates of a particle at an instant. Although the position of a particle at one instant will in general depend on its momentum (and position) at some *previous* time, the position at a given instant is not a function of the momentum *at that given instant*. If the position were such a function of the momentum, it is clear that the state of a particle in classical mechanics could be specified by just one state variable (the momentum), so that mention of the position would be redundant. In our present discussion we are similarly assuming that none of the state variables is dispensable, so that any combination of simultaneous values of the state variables yields a permissible specialization of the matrix '$(A_x B_y C_z)$', provided that the values of the variables belong to the classes K_A, K_B, and K_C, respectively. This is tantamount to saying that, apart from the proviso, the state of S stipulated to be causally relevant to G must be so analysed that the state variables employed for describing the state at a given time are mutually independent of one another.

Suppose now that if S is in the state $(A_0 B_0 C_0)$ at some initial time, then either S has the property G, or else a sequence of changes occurs in S as a consequence of which S will possess G at some subsequent time. Let us call such an initial state of S a 'causally effective state with respect to G', or a 'G-state' for short. Not every possible state of S need be a G-state, for one of the causally relevant parts of S may be in a certain state at a given time, such that *no* combination of possible states of the other parts will yield a G-state for S. Thus, suppose that S is the human body, G the property of having an internal temperature lying in the range 97° to 99°F, A_x again the state of the peripheral blood vessels, B_y the state of the thyroid glands, and C_z the state of the adrenal glands. It may happen that B_y assumes a value (e.g., corresponding to acute hyperactivity) such that for no possible values of A_x and C_z, respectively, will G be realized. It is of course also conceivable that no possible state of S is a G-state, so that in fact G is never realized in S. For example, if S is the human body and G the property of having an internal temperature lying in the range from 150° to 160°, then there is no G-state for S. On the other hand, more than one possible state of S may be a G-state. But if there is more than one possible G-state, then (since S has been assumed to be a deterministic system) the one that is realized at a given time is uniquely determined by the actual state of S at some previous time. The case in which there is more than one such possible G-state for S is of particular relevance to the present discussion, and we must now consider it more closely.

Assume once more that at some initial time t_0, the system S is in the G-state $(A_0B_0C_0)$. Suppose, however, that a change occurs in in S so that in consequence A_0 is caused to vary, with the result that at time t_1 subsequent to t_0 the state variable 'A_x' has some other value. What value it will have at t_1 will in general depend on the particular changes that have taken place in S. We shall assume, however, that S will continue to be in a G-state at time t_1, provided that the values of 'A_x' at t_1 fall into a certain class K_A' (a subclass of K_A) containing more than one member, and provided also that certain further changes take place in the other state variables. To fix our ideas, suppose that A_1 and A_2 are the only possible members of K_A'; and assume also that neither $(A_1B_0C_0)$ nor $(A_2B_0C_0)$ is a G-state. In other words, if A_0 were changed into A_3 (a member of K_A but not of K_A') S would no longer be in a G-state; but even though the new value of 'A_x' falls into K_A', if this were the only change in S the system would also no longer be in a G-state at time t_1. Let us assume, however, S to be so constituted that if A_0 is caused to vary so that the value of 'A_x' at time t_1 falls into K_A', there will be further compensatory changes in the values of some or all of the other state variables such that S continues to be in a G-state.

These further changes are stipulated to be of the following kind. If, as a concomitant of the change in A_0, the values of 'B_y' and 'C_z' at time t_1 fall into certain classes K_B' and K_C', respectively (where of course K_B' is a subclass, though not necessarily a proper subclass, of K_B, and K_C' is a subclass of K_C), then for each value in K_A' there is a unique pair of values, one member of the pair belonging to K_B' and the other to K_C', such that for those values S continues to be in a G-state at time t_1. These pairs of values can be taken to be elements in a certain class K_{BC}'. On the other hand, were the altered values of 'B_y' and 'C_z' not accompanied by the indicated changes in the value of 'A_x', the system S would no longer be in a G-state at time t_1. In terms of the notation just introduced, accordingly, if at time t_1 the state variables of S have values such that two of them are members of a pair belonging to the class K_{BC}' while the value of the third variable is not the corresponding element in K_A', then S is not in a G-state. For example, suppose that, when A_0 changes into A_1, the initial G-state $(A_0B_0C_0)$ is changed into the G-state $(A_1B_1C_1)$, but that $(A_0B_1C_1)$ is not a G-state; and suppose also that when A_0 changes into A_2, the initial G-state is changed into the G-state $(A_2B_1C_2)$, with $(A_0B_1C_2)$ not a G-state. In this example, K_A' is the class (A_1, A_2); K_B' is the class (B_1); K_C' is the class (C_1, C_2); and K_{BC}' is the class of pairs $[(B_1, C_1), (B_1, C_2)]$, with A_1 corresponding to the pair (B_1, C_1) and A_2 to the pair (B_1, C_2).

Let us now bring together these various points, and introduce some definitions. Assume S to be a system satisfying the following conditions: (1) S can be analysed into a set of related parts or processes, a certain number of which (say three, namely A, B, and C) are causally relevant to the occurrence in S of some property or mode of behaviour G. At any time the state of S causally relevant to G can be specified by assigning values to a set of state variables 'A_x,' 'B_y,' and 'C_z.' The values of the state variables for any given time can be assigned independently of one another; but the possible values of each variable are restricted, in virtue of the nature of S, to certain classes of values K_A, K_B, and K_C, respectively. (2) If S is in a G-state at a given initial instant t_0 falling into some interval of time T, a change in any of the state variables will in general take S out of the G-state. Assume that a change is initiated in one of the state variables (say the parameters 'A'); and suppose that in fact the possible values of the parameter at time t_1 within the interval T but later than t_0 fall into a certain class K_A', with the proviso that if this were the sole change in the state of S the system would be taken out of its G-state. Let us call this initiating change a 'primary variation' in S. (3) However, the parts A, B, and C of S are so related that, when the primary variation in S occurs, the remaining parameters also vary, and in point of fact their values at time t_1 fall into certain classes K_B' and K_C', respectively. These changes induced in B and C thus yield unique pairs of values for their parameters at time t_1, the pairs being elements of a class K_{BC}'. Were these latter changes the only ones in the initial G-state of S, unaccompanied by the indicated primary variation in S, the system would not be in a G-state at time t_1. (4) As a matter of fact, however, the elements of K_A' and K_{BC}' correspond to each other in a uniquely reciprocal manner, such that, when S is in a state specified by these corresponding values of the state variables, the system is in a G-state at time t_1. Let us call the changes in the state of S induced by the primary variation and represented by the pairs of values in K_{BC}' the 'adaptive variations' of S with respect to the primary variation of S (i.e., with respect to possible values of the parameter 'A' in K_A'). Finally, when a system S satisfies all these assumptions for every pair of initial and subsequent instants in the interval T, the parts of S causally relevant to G will be said to be 'directly organized during the interval of time T with respect to G'—or, more shortly, to be 'directively organized', if the reference to G and T can be taken for granted.

This discussion of directively organized systems has been based on several simplifying assumptions. However, the analysis can be readily generalized for a system requiring the use of any number of state variables (including numerical ones), for changes in the state of a system that are initiated in more than one of the causally relevant parts of the system, and for continuous as well as discrete series of transitions from one G-state of a system to another.[1] Indeed, it is not

[1]When the state co-ordinates are assumed to be numerical, it is possible to formulate the conditions for a directively organized system as follows:

Let S be a system, G a trait of S, and 'x_1,' 'x_2,' . . . , 'x_n' the state variables for G. The variables are stipulated to be independent and continuous functions of the time; and superscripts will indicate their values at any given time t.

(a) If S is a deterministic system with respect to G, the state of S at time t is uniquely determined by the state of S at some preceding time t_0. Hence

$$x_1^t = f_1(x_1^{t_0}, \ldots, x_n^{t_0}, t - t_0)$$
$$\cdots\cdots\cdots\cdots\cdots\cdots$$
$$x_i^t = f_i(x_1^{t_0}, \ldots, x_n^{t_0}, t - t_0)$$
$$\cdots\cdots\cdots\cdots\cdots\cdots$$
$$x_n^t = f_n(x_1^{t_0}, \ldots, x_n^{t_0}, t - t_0)$$

where the f_i's are single-valued functions of their arguments. Their first derivatives with respect to the time are also single-valued functions of their arguments and of no other functions of the time.

(b) Since the special character of S imposes restrictions on the values of the state variables, the values of each variable 'x_i' will fall within an interval determined by a pair of numbers a_i and b_i. That is,

$$a_i \leq x_i \leq b_i$$

with $i \leq 1, 2, \ldots, n$, or alternately

$$x_i \epsilon \Delta x_i$$

where Δx_i is some definite interval and 'ϵ' is the usual sign for class membership.

(c) If S is in a G-state at a given time t falling into a given period of time T, the state variable must satisfy a set of conditions or equations. That S is in a G-state at time t can be expressed by requirement:

$$g_1(x_1^t, \ldots, x_n^t) = 0$$
$$\cdots\cdots\cdots\cdots\cdots$$
$$g_r(x_1^t, \ldots, x_n^t) = 0$$

where each g_j ($j = 1, 2, \ldots, r$) is a function differentiable with respect to each of the state variables, and $r < n$.

(d) The values of each state variable 'x_i^t' satisfying these equations defining a G-state of S fall into certain restricted intervals:

difficult to develop within this framework of analysis the notion of a system exhibiting self regulatory behaviours with respect to several *G*'s at the same time, alternative (and even incompatible) *G*'s at different times, a set of *G*'s constituting a hierarchy on the basis of some postulated scale of 'relative importance', or more generally a set of *G*'s whose membership changes with time and circumstance. But apart from complexity, nothing immediately relevant would be gained by such extensions of the analysis; and the schematic and incompletely general definitions that have been presented will suffice for our purposes.

It will in any case be clear from the above account that if *S* is directively organized, the persistence of *G* is in an important sense independent of the variations in any one of the causally relevant parts of *S*, provided that these variations do not exceed certain limits. For although by hypothesis the occurrence of *G* in *S* depends upon *S* being in a *G*-state, and therefore upon the state of the causally relevant parts of *S*, an alteration in the state of one of those parts may be compensated by induced changes in one or more of the other causally relevant parts, so as to preserve *S* in its assumed *G*-state. The *prima facie* distinctive character of so-called 'goal-directed' or teleological systems is thus formulated by the stated conditions for a

$$a_i \leq a_i^G \leq x_i^t \leq b_i^G \leq b_i$$

or alternately:

$$x_i^t \epsilon \Delta x_i^G$$

where Δx_i^G falls into the interval Δx_i.

(e) Assume that *S* is in a *G*-state at the initial time t_0 during the period *T*, and that a change takes place in the value of some state variable 'x_k' so that at time *t* later than t_0 in *T* its value is x_k^t. The condition that this change is a *G*-preserving change (so that $x_k^t \epsilon \Delta x_k^G$), is that for each function g_j:

$$\frac{\partial g_j}{\partial x_k^{t_0}} = \frac{\partial g_j}{\partial x_1^t} \frac{\partial x_1^t}{\partial x_k^{t_0}} + \frac{\partial g_j}{\partial x_2^t} \frac{\partial x_2^t}{\partial x_k^{t_0}} + \ldots + \frac{\partial g_j}{\partial x_n^t} \frac{\partial x_n^t}{\partial x_k^{t_0}} = 0$$

(f) The system *S* is directively organized with respect to *G* during *T* if, when such *G*-preserving changes occur in any given state variable 'x_k,' there are compensating variations in one or more of the other state variables. Accordingly, there must be at least one function g_j such that in the partial differential equations just mentioned there are at least two non-vanishing summands. That is, there are at least two summands in one or more of these equations such that

$$\frac{\partial g_j}{\partial x_i^t} \frac{\partial x_i^t}{\partial x_k^{t_0}} \neq 0$$

directively organized system. The above analysis has therefore shown that the notion of a teleological system can be explicated in a manner not requiring the adoption of teleology as a fundamental or unanalysable category. What may be called the 'degree of directive organization' of a system, or perhaps the 'degree of persistence' of some trait of a system, can also be made explicit in terms of the above analysis. For the property *G* is maintained in *S* (or *S* persists in its development, which eventuates in *G*) to the extent that the range K_A' of the possible primary variations is associated with the range of induced compensatory changes K_{BC}' (i.e., the adaptive variations) such that *S* is preserved in its *G*-state. The more inclusive the range K_A' that is associated with such compensatory changes, the more is the persistence of *G* independent of variations in the state of *S*. Accordingly, on the assumption that it is possible to specify a measure for the range K_A', the 'degree of directive organization' of *S* with respect to variations in the state parameter '*A*' could be defined as the measure of this range.

We may now relax the assumption that the external environment *E* has no influence upon *S*. But in dropping this assumption, we merely complicate the analysis, without introducing anything novel into it. For suppose that there is some factor in *E* which is causally relevant to the occurrence of *G* in *S*, and whose state at any time can be specified by some determinate form of the state variable 'F_w'. Then the state of the enlarged system *S'* (consisting of *S* together with *E*) which is causally relevant to the occurrence of *G* in *S* is specified by some determinate form of the matrix '$(A_x B_y C_z F_w)$', and the discussion proceeds as before. However, it is generally not the case that a variation in any of the internal parts of *S* produces any significant variation in the environmental factors. What usually is the case is that the environmental factors vary quite independently of the internal parts; they do not undergo changes which compensate for changes in the state of *S*; and, while a limited range of changes in them may be compensated by changes in *S* so as to preserve *S* in some *G*-state, most of the states which environmental factors are capable of assuming cannot be so compensated by changes in *S*. It is customary, therefore, to talk of the 'degree of plasticity' or the 'degree of adaptability' of organic systems in relation to their environments, and not conversely. However, it is possible to define these notions without special reference to organic systems, in a manner analogous to the definition of the 'degree of directive organization' of a system already suggested. Thus, suppose that the variations in the environmental state variable

'*F*', assumed to be compensated by further changes in *S* so as to preserve *S* in some *G*-state, all fall into the class K_F'. If an appropriate measure for the magnitude of this class could be devised, the 'degree of plasticity' of *S* with respect to the maintenance of some *G* in relation to *F* could then be defined as equal to the measure of K_F'.

This must suffice as an outline of the abstract structure of goal-directed or teleological systems. The account given deliberately leaves undiscussed the detailed mechanisms involved in the operation of particular teleological systems; and it simply assumes that all such systems can in principle be analysed into parts which are causally relevant to the maintenance of some feature in those systems, and which stand to each other and to environmental factors in determinate relations capable of being formulated as general laws. The discovery and analysis of such detailed mechanisms is the task of specialized scientific inquiry. Accordingly, since the above account deals only with what is assumed to be the common distinctive structure of teleological systems, it is also entirely neutral on such substantive issues as to whether the operations of all teleological systems can be explained in exclusively physicochemical terms. On the other hand, if the account is at least approximately adequate, it requires a positive answer to the question whether the distinguishing features of goal-directed systems can be formulated without invoking purposes and goals as dynamic agents.

There is, however, one further matter that must be briefly discussed. The definition of directively organized systems has been so stated that it can be used to characterize both biological and nonvital systems. It is in fact easy to cite illustrations for the definition from either domain. The human body with respect to homeostasis of its internal temperature is an example from biology; a building equipped with a furnace and thermostat is an example from physicochemistry. Nevertheless, although the definition is not intended to distinguish between vital and nonvital teleological systems—for the differences between such systems must be stated in terms of the specific material composition, characteristics, and activities they manifest—it *is* intended to set off systems having a prima facie 'goal-directed' character from systems usually not so characterized. The question therefore remains whether the definition does achieve this aim, or whether on the contrary it is so inclusive that almost *any* system (whether it is ordinarily judged to be goal-directed or not) satisfies it.

Now there are certainly many physicochemical systems that are not ordinarily regarded as being 'goal-directed' but that nevertheless appear to conform to the definition of directively organized systems proposed above. Thus, a pendulum at rest, an elastic solid, a steady electric current flowing through a conductor, a chemical system in thermodynamic equilibrium, are obvious examples of such systems. It seems therefore that the definition of directive organizaton—and in consequence the proposed analysis of 'goal-directed' or 'teleological' systems—fails to attain its intended objective. However, two comments are in order on the point at issue. In the first place, though we admittedly do distinguish between systems that are goal-directed and those which are not, the distinction is highly vague, and there are many systems which cannot be classified definitely as of one kind rather than another. Thus, is the child's toy sometimes known as the 'walking beetle'—which turns aside when it reaches the edge of a table and fails to fall off, because an idle wheel is then brought into play through the action of an 'antenna'—a goal-directed system or not? Is a virus such a system? Is the system consisting of members of some biological species that has undergone evolutionary development in a steady direction (e.g., the development of gigantic antlers in the male Irish elk) a goal-directed one? Moreover, some systems have been classified as 'teleological' at one time and in relation to one body of knowledge, only to be reclassified as 'nonteleological' at a later time, as knowledge concerning the physics of mechanisms improved. 'Nature does nothing in vain' was a maxim commonly accepted in pre-Newtonian physics, and on the basis of the doctrine of 'natural places' even the descent of bodies and the ascent of smoke were regarded as goal-directed. Accordingly, it is at least an open question whether the current distinction between systems that are goal-directed and those that are not invariably has an identifiable objective basis (i.e., in terms of differences between the actual organizations of such systems), and whether the *same* system may not often be classified in alternative ways depending on the perspective from which it is viewed and on the antecedent assumptions adopted for analysing its structure.

In the second place, it is by no means certain that physical systems such as the pendulum at rest, which is not usually regarded as goal-directed, really do conform to the definition of 'directively organized' systems proposed above. Consider a simple pendulum that is initially at rest and is then given a small impulse (say by a sudden gust of wind); and assume that apart from the constraints of the system and the force of gravitation the only force that acts on the bob is the friction of the air. Then on the usual physical assumptions, the pendulum will perform harmonic oscillations with decreasing amplitudes, and finally assume its initial position of rest. The system here consists of the pendulum and the various forces acting on it, while the property G is the state of the pendulum when it is at rest at the lowest point of its path of oscillation. By hypothesis, its length and the mass of the bob are fixed, and so is the force of gravitation acting on it, as well as the coefficient of damping; the variables are the impulsive force of the gust of wind, and the restoring force which operates on the bob as a consequence of the constraints of the system and of the presence of the gravitational field. However—and this is the crucial point—these two forces are *not* independent of one another. Thus, if the effective component of the former has a certain magnitude, the restoring force will have an equal magnitude with an opposite direction. Accordingly, if the state of the system at a given time were specified in terms of state variables which take these forces as values, these state variables would not satisfy one of the stipulated conditions for state variables of directively organized systems; for the value of one of them at a given time is uniquely determined by the value of the other at that same time. In short, the values of these proposed state variables at any given instant are not independent.[1] It therefore follows that the simple pendulum is not a directively organized system in the sense of the definition presented. Moreover, it is also possible to show in a similar manner that a number of other systems, generally regarded as non-teleological ones, fail to satisfy that definition. Whether one could

[1] This can be shown in greater detail by considering the usual mathematical discussion of the simple pendulum. If l is the length of the pendulum, m the mass of its bob, g the constant force of gravity, k the coefficient of damping due to air resistance, t the time as measured from some fixed instant, and s the distance of the bob along its path of oscillation from the point of initial rest, the differential equation of motion of the pendulum (on the assumption that the amplitude of vibration is small) is

$$m\frac{d^2s}{dt^2} + k\frac{ds}{dt} + \frac{mg}{l}s = 0$$

If at time t_0 the pendulum is at rest, both s_0 and v_0 $\left[=\left(\frac{ds}{dt}\right)_0\right]$ are zero, so that

$$\left(m\frac{d^2s}{dt^2}\right)_0 = 0;$$

i.e., no unbalanced forces are acting on the bob. Suppose now that at time t_1 the bob is at s_1 with a velocity v_1; the restoring force will then be

$$\left(m\frac{d^2t}{dt^2}\right)_1 = -kv_1 - \frac{mg}{l}s_1$$

But an impulsive force F_1 communicated to the bob at time t_1 uniquely determines the velocity v_1 and the position s_1 of the bob at that time. Hence the restoring force can be calculated, so that it is uniquely determined by the impulsive force.

show this for all systems currently so regarded is admittedly an open question. However, since there are at least some systems not usually characterized as teleological which must also be so characterized on the basis of the definition, the label of 'directively organized system' whose meaning the definition explicates does not apply to everything whatsoever, and it does not baptize a distinction without a difference. There are therefore some grounds for claiming that the definition achieves what it was designed to achieve, and that it formulates the abstract structure commonly held to be distinctive of 'goal-directed' systems.

ii. We can now settle quite briefly the second question on page 80, we undertook to examine, namely, whether the fact that teleological explanations are usually advanced only in connection with 'goal-directed' systems affects the claim that, in respect to its asserted content, every teleological explanation is translatable into an equivalent nonteleological one. The answer is clearly in the negative, if such systems are analysable as directively organized ones in the sense of the above definition. For on the supposition that the notion of a goal-directed system can be explicated in the proposed manner, the characteristics that ostensibly distinguish such systems from those not goal-directed can be formulated entirely in nonteleological language. In consequence, every statement about the subject matter of a teleological explanation can in principle be rendered in nonteleological language, so that such explanations together with all assertions about the contexts of their use are translatable into logically equivalent nonteleological formulations.

Why, then, does it seem odd to render physical statements such as Boyle's law in teleological form? The answer is plain, if indeed teleological statements (and in particular, teleological explanations) are normally advanced only in connection with subject matters that are assumed to be directively organized. The oddity does not stem from any difference between the explicitly asserted content of a physical law and of its purported teleologically formulated equivalent. A teleological version of Boyle's law appears strange and unaccostable because such a formulation would usually be construed as resting on the assumption that a gas enclosed in a volume is a directively organized system, in contradiction to the normally accepted assumption that a volume of gas is not such a system. In a sense, therefore, a teleological explanation does connote more than does its prima facie equivalent nonteleological translation. For the former presupposes, while the latter normally does not, that the system under consideration in the explanation is directively organized. Nevertheless, if the above analysis is generally sound, this 'surplus meaning' of teleological statements can always be expressed in nonteleological language.

(2) On the hypothesis that a teleological explanation can always be translated, with respect to what it explicitly asserts, into an equivalent nonteleological one, let us now make more explicit in what way two such explanations nevertheless do differ. The difference appears to be as follows: Teleological explanations focus attention on the culminations and products of specific processes, and in particular upon the contributions of various parts of a system to the maintenance of its global properties or modes of behaviour. They view the operations of things from the perspective of certain selected 'wholes' or integrated systems to which the things belong; and they are therefore concerned with characteristics of the parts of such wholes, only in so far as those traits of the parts are relevant to the various complex features or activities assumed to be distinctive of those wholes. Nonteleological explanations, on the other hand, direct attention primarily to the conditions under which specified processes are initiated or persist, and to the factors upon which the continued manifestations of certain inclusive traits of a system are contingent. They seek to exhibit the integrated behaviours of complex systems as the resultants of more elementary factors, frequently identified as constituent parts of those systems; and they are therefore concerned with traits of complex wholes almost exclusively to the extent that these traits are dependent on assumed characteristics of the elementary factors. In brief, the difference between teleological and nonteleological explanations, as has already been suggested, is one of emphasis and perspective in formulation.

If this account is sound, the use of teleological explanations in the study of directively organized systems is as congruent with the spirit of modern science as is the use of nonteleological ones. This conclusion is confirmed by an examination of two currently held assessments of teleological explanations, one suggesting a limit to the value of such explanations, the other objecting in principle to their use.

a. The claim has been advanced that, although teleological explanations are in general legitimate, they are useful only when the knowledge we happen to possess of directively organized systems is of a certain kind.[1] Our available information about the range of environmental changes to which such a system can make adaptive

[1]R. B. Braithwaite, *Scientific Explanation*, pp. 333ff.

responses (i.e., about what we have called the 'plasticity' of goal-directed systems) may have two sources. It may have the status simply of an extrapolation to a given system of inductive generalizations obtained from a direct experimental study of quite similar systems. For example, the knowledge we have at present concerning the plasticity of a particular human organism in maintaining its internal temperature in the face of changes in temperature of the environment is based on our familiarity with the adaptive responses of other human bodies. On the view under consideration, teleological explanations in such cases are valuable, since they enable us to predict certain future behaviours of a given system from our knowledge concerning the past of similar systems—future behaviours that would otherwise not be predictable in the assumed state of our knowledge. On the other hand, our information about the plasticity of a given system may have the status of a body of deductions from previously established causal laws concerning the mechanisms embodied in the system. In such cases, adaptive responses of a given system to environmental changes can be calculated with the help of general assumptions, and can be predicted without any familiarity with the past behaviours of similar systems. In consequence, teleological explanations in such cases are said to have little if any value.

Although the distinction between these two types of sources of available knowledge concerning the plasticity of directively organized systems is patently sound, it is nevertheless not evident why the line between valuable and useless teleological explanations should be drawn in the indicated manner. Questions about the value of an explanation are not decided by reference to the logical source of the explanatory premisses, and can be answered only by examining the effective role an explanation plays in inquiry and in the communication of ideas. It is in any event far from certain that teleological explanations for goal-directed systems concerning which we possess theoretically based knowledge are invariably or normally regarded as otiose. For there are in fact many artificial self-regulating systems (such as engines with governors regulating their speed) whose plasticity can be deduced from general theoretical assumptions. Teleological explanations for various features of such systems nevertheless continue to fill many pages in technical treatises about those systems, and there is no good reason to suppose that the explanations are commonly regarded as so much worthless lumber.

b. It is sometimes objected, however, that teleological explanations are inexcusably parochial. They are based, so it is argued, on a tacit assumption that a special set of complex systems has a privileged status; and in consequence such explanations make focal the role of things and processes in maintaining just those systems and no others. Processes have no inherent termini, the objection continues, and cannot rightly be supposed to contribute exclusively to the maintenance of some unique set of wholes. It is therefore misleading to say, for example, that *the* function of the white cells in the human blood is to defend the human body against foreign micro-organisms. This is undoubtedly *a* function of the leucocytes; and this particular activity may even be said to be *the* function of these cells from the perspective of the human body. But leucocytes are elements in other systems as well; for example, they are parts of the blood stream considered in isolation from the rest of the body, of the system composed of some virus colony together with these white cells, or of the more inclusive and complex solar system. These other systems are also capable of persisting in their 'normal' organization and activities only under definite conditions; and, from the perspective of the maintenance of these numerous other systems, the leucocytes possess other functions.

One obvious reply to this objection is in the form of a *tu quoque*. It is as legitimate to focus attention on consequences, culminations, and uses as it is on antecedents, starting points, and conditions. Processes do not have inherent termini, but neither do they have absolute beginnings. Things and processes are in general not elements engaged in maintaining some exclusively unique whole, but neither are wholes analysable into an exclusively unique set of constituents. It is nevertheless intellectually profitable in causal inquiries to focus attention on certain earlier stages in the development of a process rather than on later ones, and on one set of constituents of a system rather than on another set. Similarly, it is illuminating to select as the point of departure for the investigation of some problems certain complex wholes rather than others. Moreover, as we have seen, some things are parts of directively organized systems, but do not appear to be parts of more than one such system. The study of the unique functions of parts in such unique directively organized systems is therefore not a preoccupation that assigns without warrant a special importance to certain particular systems. On the contrary, it is an inquiry that is sensitive to fundamental and objectively identifiable differences in subject matter.

There is nevertheless a point to the objection. For the refractive influence of provincial human interests on the construction of teleological explanations is perhaps more often overlooked than it is in the case of nonteleological analyses. In consequence, certain end-products of processes and certain directions of change are frequently assumed to be inherently 'natural', 'essential', or 'proper', while all others are then labeled as 'unnatural', 'accidental', or even 'monstrous'. Thus, the development of corn seeds into corn plants is sometimes said to be natural, while their transformation into the flesh of birds or men is asserted to be merely accidental. In a given context of inquiry, and in the light of the problem which initiates it, there may be ample justification for ignoring all but one direction of possible changes and all but one system of activities to whose maintenance things and processes contribute. But such disregard of other functions that things may have, and of other wholes of which things may be parts, does not warrant the conclusion that what is ignored is less genuine or natural than what receives selective attention.

V

MEANING AND ACTION

MAY BRODBECK

"WHAT is left over if I subtract the fact that my arm goes up from the fact that I raise my arm?"[1] One may interpret Wittgenstein's question to concern the nature of human action. Recently, that question has been given a certain answer from which a moral has been drawn regarding the nature of our knowledge and understanding of man. Briefly, the something "left over" that distinguishes a mere bodily movement from an action is, according to the answer, the *meaning* of that movement. The moral drawn is that the meaningful constituents of an action make it logically impossible to explain human actions causally, in the sense in which we can causally explain physical events like bodily movements. Though the answer itself requires considerable unpacking, it is, I believe, essentially correct. But once that necessary analysis is made, the moral drawn, I shall try to show, is a *non sequitur*.

An action, as I shall use that term, is any bit of behaviour whose complete description, that is, an account of *what* is occurring, requires mention, in addition to manifest behaviour, either of such things as the person's motives, intentions, and thoughts or of such things as moral, legal, or conventional standards or rules. Strictly speaking, an explicit mention of standards is redundant, since they essentially involve thoughts or purposes. However, since these standards need not be in the mind of the person acting in accordance with a rule, as well as for other reasons that will appear as the argument unfolds, it may help to mention standards separately.

The discussions stimulated by Wittgenstein's question have revived one side of an old controversy embodied in the question, "Can there be a science of man and society?" The side now revived opposes the affirmative answer of those who stress an essential identity in method between the physical sciences and the study of man. The latter reason

From *Philosophy of Science* Vol. 30 (1963), pp. 309–24. Reprinted by permission of the author and the Editor of *Philosophy of Science*.

[1] L. Wittgenstein, *Philosophical Investigations* (Oxford, 1953), p. 161, §621.

(in part) along the following lines. Other people's mental states, their thoughts, feelings, wishes, and hopes, are not directly accessible to public inspection. Nor can we test the everyday inferences we make to them, from what we do observe, in the same way that we can independently test, for instance, the inference from an observed change in colour of a piece of litmus paper to a liquid's acidity. Though we frequently may be right in our everyday inferences to other people's mental states from their behaviour, all we have to go on is what people choose to tell us or their observable behaviour. Since there is no way of independently testing for the occurrence of these criteria and what they are criteria for, the proponents of a science of man eschew all talk about mental states. They maintain that nevertheless a complete description and causal explanation of human actions can be given *in principle* by means of terms that, like those of physical science, have reference only to objectively observable properties of material objects. The material objects of their concern are of course people's bodies, the characters, among others, are the observable behaviours of these bodies under certain conditions and in certain environments. The mentalistic terms characterizing actions, like 'purpose' and 'thought', are, on this account, all eliminable by definitions using only nonmentalistic terms. On this view, the social scientist is a spectator of the human scene, noting its observable features and the connections among them. He seeks regularities in human behaviour, just as the physicist looks for them in inanimate behaviour. His assertions being based upon observation are also refutable by it. Like those of natural science, they are at best contingent, empirical truths. This view, within psychology, is of course known as behaviourism. For a broader notion to encompass all social areas, as well as to avoid certain connotations of that term, I shall call the doctrine "objectivism".

Revived now is the negative side of the controversy, namely, the insistence upon an intrinsic difference between the study of man and of things. The objectivist programme is held to be hopelessly misguided, not merely because it is practically unfeasible but because it is radically mistaken. By the spectator methods, all that the objectivist can learn are, on this view, the external, overt features of actions. Their internal aspects, the motives, intentions, and reflections, by which overt behaviour is understood as meaningful human action elude him entirely. To understand a human action is to know its motive. Motive explanations, however, are neither a species of causal explanations nor are they replaceable by such explanations. Social concepts, like money or voting, cannot be adequately described in "neutral" nonmentalistic terms or understood by objectivist methods. We observe only manifest behaviour, like a hand going up or pulling a lever, not the internal meaning of an action, like hand-raising or voting. This meaning lies in the logical connections the action has with the complex of desires, intentions, choices, reasons, conventions, and moral rules that are all inextricably involved together in social life. As participants in a community, we have learned to use these concepts. Understanding the language, we understand the meaning of other people's overt acts by analysing the concepts appropriately applied to the situation, tracing their logical connections with the other mentalistic concepts. A matter of conceptual analysis, our understanding and knowledge of man is therefore *a priori* and necessary rather than, as with the natural sciences, *a posteriori* and contingent. The empirical science of man envisaged by the objectivist is thus *in principle*, that is, conceptually or logically, impossible.[1]

Since belief in the essential ineliminability of mentalistic terms is central to the current rejection of "objectivism", I shall call this position "mentalism". Possibly there is some incongruity in attributing "mentalism" to some among these critics who deny, or appear to deny, that terms ever have a reference to private mental states. But the mentalistic label seems to be justifiable not only historically, but also systematically, by the emphasis on the uneliminability of the mentalistic terms. The incongruity, if any, is, I suggest, not of my making.

First of all, I wish to explain some notions which, though now controversial, are nevertheless indispensable to clarity about the issues at stake.

The word 'concept' is ambiguous. In one usage, 'concept' is applied to those classes of words, either sounds or marks, that are used to refer to characters of things, either properties or relations. I shall call them terms. 'White' and '*bianco*' are two different words, but only one term. 'Concept' also has a mentalistic use, as applied to the content of a thought. I shall use 'concept' in this way for, generally, the content of any mental act, whether it be thinking, perceiving, believing, hoping, or intending. (A mental act is not, of course, an action, though they are intimately connected.) The *thought* of some-

[1]Extended statements of the position here outlined are to be found in P. Winch, *The Idea of a Social Science* (London, 1958), and R. S. Peters, *The Concept of Motivation* (London, 1958). I shall be concerned in this paper primarily, though not solely, with their formulations.

thing's being green, of a unicorn in the garden, or of rain tomorrow, are all, in this usage, concepts. Terms may be used to refer either to concepts, that is, to someone's thought of something, or to non-mentalistic things and their characters. When, in any context, we know the character or characters that a term is being used to refer to, the term has a reference or, as I shall call it, meaning_1. When, within natural science, the reference of a term, say, 'pressure', is known to be lawfully connected to other things, as the pressure of a gas is connected with its volume and temperature, then the term is also significant or "meaningful" or has what I shall call meaning_2. The meaning_1 of a term is a matter of convention; its meaning_2, if any, is a matter of fact. Only these two uses of 'meaning' are appropriately applied to scientific terms. They do not, however, exhaust the uses of 'meaning'.

Though concepts or mental states are the reference of some terms, they do not themselves refer to anything, any more than (nonlinguistic) physical states refer to anything. Yet, thoughts do "mean" other things, in a way in which nonmental or physical events do not "mean" anything. It is characteristic of mental acts generally, and of mental acts alone, that they "mean" or are directed toward something else. The thought or concept of a castle or of rain tomorrow is about a kind of material thing or event. What the thought "means" is, by a dead teleological metaphor, called its intention. Obviously, one need not adopt the metaphysics of an active Self to recognize that thoughts are about something. 'Meaning' is ambiguous even in this particular context. Sometimes the thought itself is called the "meaning", for it is that which means or intends. When used in this way, a "meaning" is what I am calling a concept. Sometimes, what the thought intends or means is called the "meaning". In this use, a meaning is often something nonmental, though, of course, we often also think about thoughts, our own and others'. I shall here use 'intentional meaning' so that intentional meaning or, briefly, meaning_3 is what a mental act intends, means, or is about. To have a thought or to think about something is one fact; what this thought intends or means_3 is a different, usually nonmental, fact.

Terms refer, concepts intend. The term 'green' means_1 the colour green, because we have chosen to use the term in this way. Meaning_1 or reference is a complex natural or descriptive relation between language users, language, and the world. A set of marks or sounds does not intrinsically refer to anything. On the other hand, it is intrinsic to mental concepts that they mean or intend something else, either in the present, past, or future. Intentionality or meaning$_3$ is characteristic of thoughts, not something we bestow upon them. However, the meaning$_3$ relation between a thought and its intention is neither a natural relation, like taller or being to the left of, nor a causal relation. The reasons it is neither are fairly obvious. For there to be a descriptive relation, both terms of that relation must exist. But we can think what is false or imagine something that does not exist. Moreover, thinking about something does not, in any relevant sense, causally affect the thing thought about. Meaning$_3$, the relation between a thought and its intention, is, in a specificable sense, a logical relation.[1]

Still another difference between concepts and terms is crucial. Two terms may refer to or mean$_1$ the same thing. Two concepts never intend or mean$_3$ the same thing. The expressions 'the square of three' and 'the sum of 7 and 2' both may be used to refer to the same thing, namely, nine. But the concept or thought-of-three-square does not intentionally mean the same as the thought-of-the-sum-of-7-and-2. We may express thoughts in various ways, by action or by speech, but to describe them we need language. The linguistic expression describing the thought is the text of that thought. Two different linguistic events may express the same facts, but are the texts of two different thoughts. The sentence, S_1, "There are seven plus two buttons in the box" referentially means the same as the sentence, S_2, "There are three-square buttons in the box", but they are the texts of two different thoughts, for the thought-that-S_1 does not intentionally mean the same as the thought-that-S_2, since one may firmly believe the former and doubt the latter. Though the *term* 'nine', means$_1$ the same as the *term* 'the square of three', the *concept* of nine does not intentionally mean$_3$ the same as the *concept* of the square of three. Even when two different expressions refer to the same thing, the concepts of which they are the texts do not have the same (intentional) meaning$_3$. Generally, in mental contexts, like Mary knows, believes, or remembers that-S, replacing the text of S with another expression having the same referential meaning need not preserve the truth of the whole statement. In fact, no two different concepts ever mean$_3$ the same, for they are different just because they have different intentional meanings. Intentional meaning of concepts is unique, while referential meaning of terms is not.

[1]For details, see Gustav Bergmann, *Meaning and Existence* (Wisconsin, 1959), pp. 3–38, 106–14; 'Acts', *Indian Journal of Philosophy*, II (1960), pp. 1–30, 96–117; and 'Purpose, Function, Scientific Explanation', *Acta Sociologica*, 5 (1962), pp. 225–38.

To think that it might snow tomorrow and to think about putting snow-tyres on the car are different thoughts, nor is either the same as actually performing that task or having a disposition to do so. Thinking about something, say, castles in Spain, is, like the dreary rain that may evoke the thought, a particular occurrence at a particular time. Generally such mental episodes are not *identical* with any behaviour or dispositions to behave that, as we significantly say, manifest them. Moreover, bodily states manifest mental ones, not tautologically, as bending "manifests" flexibility, but contingently, as exploding manifests chemical composition. Our everyday statements about minds, our own and others, are categorical. The mentalistic terms they contain have reference to states of mind that, unlike bodily states, cannot be inspected publicly. Since mentalistic terms do not either referentially or intentionally mean the same as non-mentalistic terms, they cannot be replaced "without residue" by such terms. All this I take to be common sense, that is, something we all know from our own experience. I take it also to be a commonsensical core of the mentalistic thesis, whether or not its proponents would agree with my way of putting it.

Though we cannot observe another man's conscious states, we certainly often can tell what other people are thinking or feeling. We can do so because, whether voluntarily or involuntarily, we evince our mental states by overt physical features, including behaviour, or by dispositions to exhibit such features under certain conditions. Privacy, in other words, does not entail ignorance about other people's mental states, merely that we know them differently from the way we know our own. Yet, though there are minds and bodies, there are no interacting minds. This is a piece of scientific common sense, that is, something scientists believe on the basis of their extended experience. This belief has two components. First, that there are no disembodied minds or, more precisely, whenever there is a mental state, there is always a corresponding bodily state, either neurological, physiological, behavioural, or some combination of these. The connection between mental states and such bodily states is correlational. That is how we can tell, by inference, what other people are thinking. Secondly, mental events parallel but do not interact with physical events. In other words, despite the correlation between mind and body, no mental state causally affects any material state and conversely. In a phrase, the view is that the physical world, including men's bodies, is causally closed with respect to minds. Unpacked, the phrase means that the laws used to explain and to predict physical phenomena need mention nothing nonphysical, in the broad sense of 'physical' which includes not only the terms of physics, but also overt behaviour, utterances, physiological, and environmental characters that are describable in nonmentalistic terms. To deny that minds and bodies interact is to assert that the laws permitting us scientifically to explain human behaviour need not mention anything mental. Parallelism and the belief in physical determinism form the basis for the objectivist belief that a *complete* account of human activities can be given in nonmentalistic terms.

Some philosophical problems arise because certain sets of facts, taken together, are perplexing. In the present instance, the common-sense fact, upon which the mentalists rightly insist, that mind and intelligence make a difference in the world seems to conflict with the denial of causal interaction between mind and body. Yet this denial is justified by what we know from the natural sciences. This is what makes it a piece of scientific common sense. To deny it outright is to tilt quixotically at windmills. The contemporary mentalist does not deny it outright. Instead, he denies its relevance, by asserting that scientific, that is, causal explanation and description are "inappropriate" to the explanation and description of human activities. He accepts physical determinism for physical events, agrees and even insists that both cause and effect must be physical, but, denying that human actions can be completely described in physical terms, denies that causal attribution can legitimately be made to actions. Bodies and minds neither interact nor don't interact. Rather, there is a sort of parallelism between mind and body, reflected by two different realms of discourse or "conceptual systems", one for the mental, the other for the physical. Within each realm of discourse, different sorts of explanation are appropriate. We *understand* man by mentalistic explanation, for instance, by motives; we understand body by physical explanation, that is, by causes. The attempt to replace the former by the latter is a "conceptual" error, *a priori* doomed to failure.

Even granting such a "conceptual" parallelism, an action, like signalling or buying a house, is an event taking place at a particular time. Actions are as much facts in the world as earthquakes or any natural phenomenon in which mind does not play a role. A world with actions is different from one without them. Questions about actions, therefore, cannot *merely* be linguistic, for the conceptual systems in which action-terms occur, if they are to be of any relevance, must be about actual occurrences, in exactly the same sense as conceptual systems of physics are not speculative fancies but about physical occurrences. Two kinds of questions, in particular, that may be asked regarding any event cannot arbitrarily be ruled out on linguistic grounds alone. For one, one may ask whether action-events have causes, for there is nothing in the meaning of 'cause' as that term is normally used in science, to make this question in any sense "ungrammatical". The denial of interactionism does not follow from the meaning of 'cause', but from facts and laws of the kind I mentioned. It could be false, but it is not linguistic nonsense. Moreover, since actions are events, one may also legitimately ask how we know when statements about them are true or false. The answer given, as I mentioned earlier, is that all such statements are "conceptually", hence *a priori*, true. The prima facie rationalism of this answer to questions about matters of fact may, with some justice, lead one to suspect that something has gone radically wrong. Later, I shall try to locate what has gone wrong.

On the positive side, there is at least one sense in which the mentalists are certainly right in asserting that talk about actions or, for that matter, motives cannot have the same "meaning" as talk about behaviour or, for that matter, causes. For such statements have, at the very least, different intentional meanings.[1] The objectivist must show how, eschewing mentalistic terms, he can account for this difference in (intentional) meaning$_3$. And, since actions are events, he must also show how parallelism allows him to account adequately for the presence and efficacy of mind in the world. I shall first suggest how, within his framework, the objectivist can in principle accomplish this first goal and, then, by considering certain mentalistic objections, show how he can in principle also accomplish the second.

To every mental event there corresponds one or, more likely, several material events. What occurs when Jones sees a tree? There are the mental act of seeing, certain states of his body, and, presumably, a tree in his immediate environment. When Jones says, "I see a tree", he describes directly his mental state. The objectivist scientist cannot do this, since the mentalistic term is not part of

[1]It follows that in mental-act contexts the terms 'cause' and 'motive' are not interchangeable. If Jones wants to know the motive for Smith's action, he need not also want to know its cause, even if cause and motive are one. The terms express different thoughts and, in this psychological sense, are "conceptually" distinct. But this difference in intentional meaning does not imply that motives and causes are themselves "logically" distinct.

his vocabulary. This does not mean that Jones describes the situation for him. Jones's utterance is just part of the total situation that the scientist must describe in his own language. In his language, which is in principle different from that of his subject, he introduces an inseparable complex term 'seeing-a-tree', which contains neither 'seeing' nor, for that matter, 'tree'. This term is defined dispositionally by means of terms referring to those physical states of the person (including his verbal behaviour if asked what he sees) that accompany Jones's state of consciousness when he sees a tree. Although *Jones's* term 'see' refers to a conscious state and the *scientist's* complex term 'sees-a-tree' refers to behavioural and environmental items, the latter term will be truly applicable to Jones if and only if Jones is in fact at that time seeing a tree. He knows this commonsensically, so to speak, not as a scientist. He knows it from self-examination when he applies the defined term to himself, or from what Jones tells him, though again, what Jones tells him is *data*, not description.

The investigator may of course make mistakes. But his mistakes will reveal themselves by failure of the predictions that he makes from his description. He will predict something different from Jones sees-a-tree, than from Jones sees-a-tiger. If Jones turns and runs, he may conclude that either he was wrong in applying his complex terms to Jones, or else he was wrong in defining 'seeing-a-tree' in the way he did. "Wrong" in the only way a definition can be wrong, namely, that it does not provide a significant term, that is, one that figures in confirmable laws. On the other hand, he might still be right. Jones might have a neurotic fear of trees. In that case, he has failed to take account of other operative factors. If he is right and, in principle, there is always a right physical description corresponding to the mental event, then we may speak of the former as an indirect reference to the latter. Analogously, the physicist indirectly refers to the perceptual colour red when he speaks of "the colour with the longest wave length." Seen in this way, objectivism is merely a way of talking about minds. By capturing its reflection in the material world, the behaviour scientist can indirectly speak about mind. What then is the reflection of intentional meaning?

Meaning$_1$ (reference) and meaning$_2$ (significance) are applicable to the technical terms of science. Terms and expressions have meaning for persons. When the scientist investigates this "meaning", then 'meaning' becomes one of his technical terms, call it psychological meaning or meaning$_4$. Meaning$_4$ is thus a term within science, which must itself be given meaning[1]. Certain physical patterns have meaning$_4$ for an individual. Depending upon the circumstances and manner in which it is uttered, the sound 'fire' for instance may mean$_4$ to Jones either danger or warmth. Which it means$_4$, we determine by the bodily states, behavioural and physiological, that hearing the word elicits in Jones. Generally, 'meaning$_4$' refers to, or means$_1$, certain other things, verbal or nonverbal, that a person does upon hearing sounds or seeing certain marks. Jones's awareness of the referential use, if any, of the expression he hears is an essential part of the situation to which he reacts. But an expression need not have (referential) meaning$_1$, in order for it to have (psychological) meaning$_4$ for someone. 'The Lord is my shepherd' has no meaning$_1$, but it has meaning$_4$. People use it, utter it, and behave upon hearing or uttering it in certain ways. Similarly with many expressions of religion, poetry, exclamations, commands, and so forth. Being used on certain occasions, they have meaning$_4$.

As with 'seeing', so with 'meaning'. The psychologist's technical term occurs in a hyphenated expression, say, '*S*-means-*P*-to-Jones', defined in terms of a certain dispositional relation holding between, first, the sounds *S* and Jones, he hears them, and, secondly, certain later states of Jones's body. Just as neither 'see' nor 'tree' occurs in 'seeing-a-tree', so neither '*S*' nor 'means' occurs in '*S*-means-*P*-to-Jones'. To put it differently, since *S* is a pattern of sounds and *P* a pattern of bodily states, verbal responses, and overt behaviour, no substitution can occur in the hyphenated expression.[2] Therefore, from the fact that two expressions, two patterns of sounds, may both be used to refer to the same states of affairs, it does not follow that they both mean$_4$ the same to Jones. The intentional uniqueness of concepts is reflected by their having different linguistic texts. The observable responses to two different expressions may be different. (Psychological) meaning$_4$ depends, in other words, not only upon *what* is being asserted, but also upon the linguistic form in which it is asserted. This uniqueness of meaning$_4$, objectively defined, of linguistic expressions—experimentally established, by the way—reflects the uniqueness of (intentional) meaning$_3$ of thought or concepts. The shadow, if not the substance, of intentionality can thus be captured by the objectivist.

[1]Meaning$_4$ and meaning$_2$ may both be called 'contextual meaning'; but meaning$_2$, like meaning$_1$, is *applicable to* scientific terms, including meaning$_4$.

[2]See also R. Grossmann, 'Propositional Attitudes', *Philosophical Quarterly*, 10 (1960), pp. 301–12.

Before considering certain objections to this optimistic objectivist tale, it will be helpful to sort out some uses of 'understand'. I shall indicate the various uses by subscripts. The contexts in which these subscript-terms occur will explicate their uses.

I can $understand_1$ English but not Finnish. To understand a language is to know how to use certain classes of sounds or marks to express and to convey to others our thoughts, attitudes, queries, wishes, and, among other things, information about the world. To accomplish this, I must know the conditions for applying certain expressions and not others. What is involved in $understanding_1$ varies with the kind of expression. Some I $understand_1$ only in context when they are combined with other terms. Clearly, we could not use or $understand_1$ a language if all of its terms were understood only in context by means of other terms. Armed only with a wholly Finnish dictionary, I could not $understand_1$ Finnish. Some expressions, therefore, I $understand_1$ only if I know what conditions of myself, the world, or other people they are being used to express, that is, only if I know their (referential) $meaning_1$.

I do not $understand_2$ what it meant to have been a member of the Italian Resistance. Nor do I $understand_2$ what it means to lose an only son. This sense of 'understanding' has nothing to do with language, for of course I $understand_1$ what it is that I am said not to $understand_2$. I do not $understand_2$ these things because I have not had the special feelings, emotions, or attitudes that are aroused only by having undergone certain experiences or participated in certain kinds of events. Toward those who have my empathy is limited in a way it is not limited toward people with toothaches. For I $understand_2$ what it is to have a toothache. $Understanding_2$ is a mixture of knowing $meaning_1$ and $meaning_2$. I must know to what unique feelings, of pain or of grief, the terms are being used to refer, or, as in the case of being a member of the Italian Resistance, I must know what feelings were *associated with* those underground activities referred to by the term.

I do $understand_3$ what it meant to be a member of the Resistance, just as I $understand_3$ what a golden mountain would be like. The unique phenomenological experience that is the resultant of fear, patriotism, courage, hatred of tyranny, all acting jointly, I do not $understand_2$. But, because I $understand_1$ the $meaning_1$ of the phrase 'being a member of the Italian Resistance' and because I *also* $understand_2$ the meaning of fear, patriotism, and so on, I can $understand_3$ what it meant to be a member of the Resistance. In this sense too, since

I have suffered the loss of loved ones, I can understand$_3$ what it means to have lost an only son, though I have never had a son. By understanding$_3$ one may empathize with the bereaved mother, though less completely than one who understands$_2$, that is, one who has also lost a son.

I understand$_4$ why Tom Jones left school; he wanted to make a lot of money quickly. If we know the motives and purposes of people's actions, then we understand$_4$ why people did what they did. Here we must distinguish between understanding$_1$ the action-term, that is, knowing to what the term is referring, and knowing the motive for the action. The purposes, duties, and so on, mentioned in the description of the action will, of course, be different from the purpose for which the action is performed. I shall return to this distinction presently. (Below, pp. 114–7.) For the moment, let it stand that understanding$_4$ consists in knowing motives. This may mean knowing what an action itself is or in knowing motives for it.

I understand$_5$ that increased costs of production mean an increase in selling price. The pious man understands$_5$ that regular church attendance means salvation in afterlife. The wife understood$_5$ that her husband's silence meant disapproval. The farmer understands$_5$ that a fiery red sunset means rain the next day. Generally, we understand$_5$ a kind of thing, event, or behaviour when we know or believe that there are some *other* things, events, and so on, with which it is in some way associated. In other words, we understand$_5$ the meaning of something when it does not stand isolated, so to speak, before our minds. The "meaning" that we thus understand or attribute to events is what I called significance or meaning$_2$. If we do not know the meaning$_2$ of an event, then we do not understand$_5$ the phenomenon referred to by the term expressing the occurrence. Again, I can understand$_1$ what I do not understand$_5$. Obviously, this significance or meaning$_2$ need not reflect any true connections among things. Yet, true or false, imaginary or superstitious, all of these occurrences of 'understand$_5$' are the same use, for they imply that one kind of thing is believed to be connected with something else. Understanding$_5$ thus comprehends tested generalizations of science that give their terms significance, as well as the connections, whether from common experience or fancy, that people believe certain things have with others. When these associations of one thing with another actually do reflect empirical lawful connections, then understanding$_5$ coincides with scientific explanation. There are of course other uses of 'explain'.[1]

I turn now to criticisms of the objectivist programme. The mentalist claims that "understanding of society cannot be observational and experimental"[2] because, first of all, the investigator must understand the language of the people he studies. One learns a language by sharing a mode of life. The investigator, therefore, cannot stand in the observer-observed relation to his subject matter. Moreover, the natural scientist uses external criteria to decide when two events are of the same kind. But that two actions sharing no overt features are of the "same kind", must be decided by the participant, not the spectator. The method by which we understand others is accordingly subjective, not objective. Logically, therefore, there cannot be generalizations about man and society, as there are about stones and stars. What is involved in the idea, for instance, of prayer is a *religious* not a sociological question. An idea cannot be torn out of context, for it gets its meaning from the role it plays in the system. Men's actions are intelligible when we understand their motives and the rules in accordance with which they act. But appeals to standards and to motives "rule out" appeals to causes. Mechanical, causal explanations of human actions are therefore logically inappropriate.[3] Using the distinctions drawn among the various uses of 'meaning' and of 'understanding', I should like to examine these claims.

Does the fact that the investigator must understand$_I$ the language of the people he studies vitiate the objectivist thesis? By a fairly elaborate conditioning process, a child learns, say, to call a small, furry, miaowing animal a cat, not a dog. He also learns to say "He was . . ." not "He were . . .". Pointing, obviously, is not the only method used in teaching a language. Nor can we teach the (referential) meaning$_1$ of mentalistic terms, like 'headache' or 'sorrow', by pointing. These are learned by means of their public accompaniments. It is truistic that learning a language is "rooted in a social context." Far from vitiating the objectivist thesis, the truism is a fundamental part of it. Yet undoubtedly there is a difficulty. An

[1] See also May Brodbeck, 'Explanation, Prediction, and "Imperfect" Knowledge', *Minnesota Studies in the Philosophy of Science*, Vol. III, ed. H. Feigl and G. Maxwell (Minneapolis, 1962), pp. 231–72.

[2] P. Winch, op. cit., p. 110.

[3] Cf. R. S. Peters, op. cit., pp. 4, 12, *et pass.* and P. Winch, op. cit., pp. 78, 82, *et pass.* With respect to the ineliminability of mentalistic terms and the claim that motives cannot be causes, see also A. I. Melden, *Free Action* (London, 1961).

almost infinite number of sound patterns can be used to express the same terms. Moreover, only slight oral or typographical changes create huge differences in behaviour. As the old "telegram-argument", frequently adduced by the idealists, insisted, there is an enormous difference between a telegram from a friend that says "Our son was killed" and one that reads "Your son was killed". The difference in (referential) meaning$_1$ and consequently in the reactions they arouse (meaning$_4$) is hugely disproportionate to the slight typographical differences between the marks on paper. A man presumably also reacts differently when he hears the words "I love you" than upon hearing "I love him". The considerable physical difference between 'you' and 'him' suggests how, *in principle*, the investigator could dispense with knowing a common language. And the argument on both sides is one of principle or "logic" only.

Still, the enormous difficulty of correlating slight differences in physical cues with huge differences in behaviour are obvious. In *practice*, these difficulties may well be insuperable. In practice, therefore, except when he is actually studying (psychological) meaning$_4$, the investigator simply assumes that he and the subject understand$_1$ the same language. It is not hard to tell, in purely objective ways, whether or not a person understands$_1$ what is being said to him. People behave very differently if they understand$_1$ what is being said than if they do not. If two people understand$_1$ the same language, presumably because they have both learned it in the same social context, then they can communicate with each other. There is nothing inherently subjective about the success or failure of this communication. Once we know from a prior and different investigation that a language is understood$_1$, its users may be observed. The fact that the scientist *learns* the language as a participant in the social process does not imply that he can never, so to speak, stop being a participant. To think that it does is to fall victim to the genetic fallacy. The mentalist confuses how we come to understand$_1$ a statement of, say, a belief with using that understanding$_1$, once learned, to observe that an individual has a certain belief or, at least, says he has.

Most probably, in practice subject and scientist must, as we say, speak the same language. But our saying this leads to a second confusion, namely, between the scientist's language and that which he shares with the subject. For, as I mentioned earlier, in another sense they do not "speak the same language". The language that the scientist uses to *describe* what he learns about his subject is in principle not the same language that he may use to *communicate* with him. What Jones says (and what the investigator says to him in Jones's language) is part of what is going on, which the investigator describes in his own language. In other words, everything that Jones says occurs only within quotation marks in the investigator's language. The subject's use of, say, the term 'prayer' in certain ways and under specifiable conditions is an interesting and important, because meaningful$_2$ or lawfully significant, part of the investigator's *data*. If the latter *uses* that term to describe what is going on, its "meaning" in any and all senses of 'meaning' will not be the same as the subject's term.

The subject's *concept* of prayer will of course have an (intentional) meaning$_3$ for him that it will not have for a nonreligious person and need not have for the investigator. Only in this sense of 'meaning', is it even plausible to say that only the religious man can "make sense" of religion. The sociologist may understand$_5$ religion without also understanding$_2$ it. For the participant, 'attending church services regularly' means$_{3,4}$ salvation in after-life. For the observor-scientist, the same behaviour means$_2$ something quite different, namely, certain other actions of the person and perhaps certain effects upon the community. A sociologist may call two patterns of behaviour in different cultures 'baptism', or two other patterns 'marriage', even though the Christian "would not agree" they were the same,[1] not merely because they happen to have certain overt features in common, nor yet "arbitrarily," but because they are believed to be similarly connected to other aspects of behaviour and society. To the economist, automobiles and human labour are both commodities, not because he is insensitive to human dignity, but because they have similar properties in relation to other things, such as supply and demand. In sum, the use of a common language for purposes of communication is not in itself "incompatible", as alleged, with the external observer-observed point of view.

To what are we referring when we use such terms as 'a smile', 'a salute', or 'money'? A salute, surely, had better be something observable. A smile is, according to Webster, a brightening of the eyes and upward curving of the corners of the mouth. Yet, a salute is more than a position of the hand. And to describe "writhing in pain" or "signing a contract" is indeed more than to give a description "in purely mechanical terms, using a set of space-time coordinates".[2]

[1] P. Winch, op. cit., p. 108.

[2] P. Winch, op. cit., p. 73, and R. S. Peters, op. cit., p. 13.

"Money" is more than pieces of metal, paper, or beads. But is the "something more" of actions and artifacts only describable in nonphysical terms? *One* reason for thinking so is an invidious use of 'physical' in the narrow sense of that term. Such items as muscle-twitches, glandular secretions, shape and size are, on this usage, the only "physical" properties. But a pattern of overt behaviour is also something physical, since it is certainly nonmental. A *second* reason for the belief that terms referring to actions and artifacts must mean_1 something "nonphysical" or "something more" than overt behaviour is a mistaken notion of observable reference. On this usage, only manifest or "occurrent" characters are observable. But flexibility is no less observable than bent. Our everyday statements about actions are, as I mentioned before, mentalistic and categorical. But the scientific terms corresponding to these mentalistic ones, like 'seeing-green' or 'meaning-*p*', are all dispositional. Dispositional characters merely require more complex observations than do manifest ones; they are no less observable.

Actions, in one way or another, involve a reference to thought or purposes. An objectivist definition of 'purpose', corresponding to the mental state, can be constructed. The difference between just "walking down the street" and doing so "in order to mail a letter" is not in what is presently observed, but a way of speaking about something else which we expect to occur later bringing this action to a close. Or, as with 'looking for' something, it may be a way of speaking about some past event which led to the present behaviour or, possibly, some combination of things in the past and future. All this makes 'purpose' a more complex term than 'tall', but not on that account "nonphysical." Generally, a *pattern* of behaviour observed in the past or to be observed in the future toward things and other people is the "something more" than present or manifest characters that is meant_1 by defined terms referring to actions.

Social artifacts, like money, tools, and weapons, are defined by the behaviour of people with respect to inanimate, material objects. In and of itself, a scarlet letter or a yellow arm-badge is no different in "meaning" from an iron cross or a purple heart. As material objects they are all equally "meaningless." What gives them (referential) meaning_1 as rewards or punishments is, of course, the behaviour of people toward them. A cathedral is not just a pile of stones, not even just a pile of stones arranged in a certain pattern. 'Cathedral' (referentially) means_1 a physical structure of a certain kind *and* certain ways people behave towards it, like entering it at certain intervals and performing certain activities, which *the people*, not the investigator, describe as worshipping. For the rest, the "meaning" of 'cathedral' is either the associations that people have to it, $meaning_4$ (reflecting intentional $meaning_3$), or else its $meaning_2$, that is, its connections with other aspects of the culture, such as the kind of economy or other behaviours, like being charitable. Such connections among kinds of behaviour are observable. The investigator's own past experience, aided perhaps by a class of judges, may be drawn upon to determine tentatively the identifying characteristics of, say, "friendly" behaviour. But this usable past is not part of the criteria by which he now identifies the action. The belief that it is and thus requires "participation," confuses the origins of a classification with what that category now refers to.

Not *all* of the past and future behaviours that are connected with, say, 'friendly', but not with 'hostile' actions, are part of the (referential) $meaning_1$ of the terms, only enough of them to distinguish friendly from hostile actions. How else could we assent to the proposition that a man may smile and smile, yet be a villain? It is true, even tautologically true, that "an idea gets its sense from the role it plays in a system" only if "meaning" is construed intentionally, as $meaning_3$ (reflected by the psychologist's $meaning_4$), or, for scientific terms, as significance or $meaning_2$. If I $understand_1$ another person's language, I don't necessarily also know all the "meaning" that his terms carry for him. From $understanding_1$ alone, we do not *ipso facto* learn everything that any user of that language might associate with terms. This must be discovered. Nor need I know everything about a system of religious beliefs in order to know the $meaning_1$ 'of 'baptism', any more than I need to know everything about an economic system in order to know the $meaning_1$ of 'money'. Neither to $understand_1$ a language nor to know the $meaning_1$ of its referential terms, need I know how everything is connected with everything else. I $understand_1$ the $meaning_1$ of 'sell' and of 'price', both terms with complex definitions, without also $understanding_5$ the connection between, say, selling price and cost price. Nor is the way they vary together merely a "conceptual" matter. Learning to use the word 'cost' does not entail learning all the laws of economics, any more than learning to use the word 'marriage' tells me all about marriage. Of course, to have "genuine understanding", if that means $understanding_2$, then one must *be* married. But "genuine understanding" may also mean knowing connections among things. And a bachelor sociologist's $understanding_5$ of this $meaning_2$, that is, the connections the institution of marriage has with, say, property-distribution, education, job-stability, and so on, may well exceed that of the most-often married person. Nor can he discover these things by analysing the concept of marriage. The most one can thus discover, besides the legal definition of the term, is the (psychological) meaning$_4$ it has for certain people, the gratifications and responsibilities they associate with it. For the meaning$_2$ or significance of marriage he will have to grub among the facts.

A pervasive fusion of the various meanings of 'meaning' and of 'understanding' lends a specious plausibility to the insistence upon the "total context" in order to grasp "meaning" and have "genuine understanding". What a term is used to refer to (meaning$_1$) is confused, on the one hand, with the psychological associations (meanings$_{3,4}$) we have to it and, on the other, with the lawful connections (meaning$_2$) the object of reference has with other things. An uncritical use of 'concept' blurs the distinction between our thought of something, "our idea of it", and the characteristics referred to by a term which is the text of that thought. Thoughts or concepts are sometimes also called "meanings." By spinning out these "meanings," we are said to "understand" human and social concepts, man and society. If we unpack the various uses of 'meaning' and of 'understanding', it is clear that at best such "conceptual analysis" can tell us what things (some) people think go together, not how things are actually connected.

The difference between the action of raising my arm and the movement of my arm going up is that the former is done intentionally or for a purpose. The purpose need not be conscious; an action may be performed habitually, as reaching for a cigarette, or spontaneously, as jumping to dodge a car. In other words, there need not be any mental act present when performing an action. Automatic signalling for a left turn is also an action. However, a complete description of *what* was done, of the (referential) meaning$_1$ of 'signalling', requires mention of motives or purposes that are *part* of the action. Nor need these purposes be those of the person performing the action. Many of our actions require reference to a standard for complete description. To describe what is happening when a man tips his hat to a woman acquaintance requires a set of statements that mention, besides the regularity of his behaviour, the presence in society of certain standards or norms. Norms don't exist by themselves; they ultimately involve mental acts. They may be explicated as, say, certain definite and durable expectations that people in a society have about each other's behaviour. 'Expectation', in turn, can be defined by certain dispositions, such as the imposition of penalties if certain behaviour does not occur. The new recruit's salute is not yet habitual, but may well become so. What makes it "rule-governed," while the habit of chain-smoking is not, is the recruit's membership in a hierarchically-structured institution in which such behaviour is "expected". Regularity of behaviour under certain circumstances characterizes both "rule-governed" and merely habitual behaviour. The "something more" in the former is the different way in which these regularities were acquired.

The two expressions 'raising an arm' and 'arm going up' differ in "meaning" in all four senses of 'meaning', referentially, intentionally, psychologically, and in significance. In this sense, and so far as it goes, the mentalist's answer to Wittgenstein's question is correct. There is certainly difference in "meaning." The relevant differences, however, can be objectively construed without appealing to any vitiating participant "inside knowledge." In this respect, there is nothing about such terms marking them as "logically" different from those of natural science.

Behind the rejection of so-called "mechanical" explanation seems to lie the notion that any explanation that does not use mentalistic terms in their mentalistic sense is "mechanical," that is, is about movements in space, not about intelligent, purposive behaviour. Partly, we have again the narrow use of 'physical', so that only the terms of physics and chemistry are physical or nonmental. But the definition of an action as a set of behavioural dispositions, bodily states, and environmental circumstances surely does not mention merely "movements." Nor, as I have suggested schematically in discussing 'purpose', is there any reason to believe that an objectivist account cannot be given of "intelligent" behaviour, that is, the ability to vary behaviour relative to a goal, under changing circumstances. Man of course "understands his situation", while a dog does not. This use of 'understanding' can be objectively construed by means of dispositional and occurrent factors present in and operating on the man but not the dog; for instance, his past learning of certain rules (standards and regularities) or his present awareness of them.

To be sure, explanation by causes is only one use of 'explain'. Citing a motive also explains, as does giving a detailed description, as when we explain, say, the structure of feudalism[1]. These different uses of 'explain', among others, also have their corresponding senses

[1]See May Brodbeck, 'Explanation, Prediction, and "Imperfect" Knowledge', loc. cit.

of 'understand'. They are not mutually incompatible. Which is "appropriate" depends upon what the person wants to know. Sometimes motives are causes, sometimes not. Buying a house is an action whose complete description in "neutral" or nonmentalistic terms would be quite complicated, requiring mention among other things of certain legal statutes. But an answer to why Jones bought a house might well state a motive, namely, a desire for privacy. This motive is hardly part of the (referential) meaning$_1$ of 'buying a house'. It is, though, part of its meaning$_2$, that is, living in one's own house is a way of getting privacy. Here a motive is also a cause. Doubtless other (concurrent) causes are also operative. At other times, to cite a motive is not to give a cause but to tell *what* is happening, as when explaining what a signal or salute *is*. A reference to standards and motives will occur in the descriptions of these actions. But explaining *what* an action is and explaining *why* it occurred are two different things. Each may require mention of motives, though, of course, not *the same* ones. Jumping out a window is one action, of which the desire for death might be a cause. On the other hand, we would not say that a man committed suicide because he wanted to kill himself, since this wish is part of the (referential) meaning$_1$ of suicide.

Over-attention to cases of the latter kind perhaps is the source of a basic error that unfortunately pervades Melden's temperate and frequently illuminating book. He argues that a motive can never be a cause since, on good Humean principles, the cause must be logically distinct from the effect. He interprets this to imply that a description of the cause must not contain "any reference" to the effect. But 'wanting-to-do-*X*' mentions 'doing-*X*' and, generally, a description of a desire requires reference to the object desired. Hence, Melden concludes, they are not logically independent and motives cannot be causes for actions.[1] But there is no logical *implication* between wanting-to-do-*X* and actually doing *X*. The thought-of-snow-tomorrow means$_3$ or intends snow tomorrow, but it does not logically entail that it will snow tomorrow. No more does the thought-of-doing-*X* logically entail doing-*X*. An adequate analysis of the nature of mental acts and how they are related to their intentions is indispensable. Although the relation of meaning$_3$ between a thought and its intention is a logical one, the (occurrence of) thought itself no more entails its intention than, analogously, the logical relation 'or' permits the deduction of '*q*' from '*p* or *q*'. A thought, after all, can mean$_3$ what

[1]A. I. Melden, op. cit., pp. 53, 114, 128.

does not and never will exist. *The mental act of wanting-to-do-X is one fact. Doing-X is quite another and distinct fact. The former might on some occasions cause the latter.*

In some contexts standards and motives are causes; in some other contexts, they describe the action. Those enchanted by "rule-governed" behaviour now tell us again and again that unless something is done in accordance with a rule, it is not really an action. This restriction has the odd consequence that a man may act purposively and yet not be doing anything. A married man making advances to a choirboy is not really doing anything, but instead has something "happening" to him[1]. I see no warrant either in common usage or in common sense for this restrictive use of 'action', based, at least in part, on a bad pun on "what is done" or "not done". Even granting the dubious doctrine that we only ask for a man's motives when he deviates from the "done" thing, we want the motives for his action, that is, for his purposive behaviour, not for something, like a brick falling on his head, that merely happened to him. People are often punished for doing the "not done" thing, which is hardly reasonable if, like the brick, it just "happened" to them. Freud indeed taught us how narrow is the line between what a man does and what happens to him. But it was, alas, the sphere of the latter, not that of the former, which he restricted.

The distinction between the what and the why of actions is also relevant to the notion that causal explanations are only appropriate to our "deviations from norms"[2]—(which, not quite incidentally, also may be instances of rational, purposive behaviour). Partly, this view seems to stem from the fact that when we reply to a why-question by stating a norm, we often are explaining what is occurring, that being all the person wants to know. By definition, such an answer could not be given for "deviant" behaviour. Even more fundamental is a pervasive equivocation between different uses of 'rule', once as a descriptive regularity and once as a prescriptive standard or norm. We do indeed consider that an insane man, incapable of judging between alternative courses of action, thus deviating from descriptively regular or normal human behaviour, has things "happen" to him that a normal man "does". A man who deviates from a prescriptive norm, however, is not necessarily insane. He may be the only sane one among us.

[1]R. S. Peters, op. cit., p. 10.

[2]Ibid.

On this possibly frivolous note, I conclude that the objectivist programme emerges unscathed from the barrage of criticisms recently directed against it. Yet, some uneasiness about the objectivist thesis remains to be allayed. When all is said and done, is the objectivist talking about the "same facts" as we describe in everyday mentalistic language? *Can* talk about causes replace, without residue, talk about motives? Can the scientist's non-interactionist account be made to accord with our common-sense (and clinical) belief that mind and body do affect each other? As a final therapeutic step, it may pay to be explicit by distinguishing three uses of the phrase "same fact" that are relevant to this discussion.

(1) Two statements may describe different states of affairs, yet be such that one of them is true (false) if and only if the other is also true (false). Such (synthetically) extensional equivalences may be said to express the same_1 fact. In particular, if to any given statement about a person's motives or other mental states, there is another containing only physiological, behavioural, and environmental terms that is extensionally equivalent to the first, then they express the same_1 fact. They do not mean the same either intentionally or referentially. The scientist's description, containing no terms referring to conscious states, thus "leaves out" minds. Talk about overt behaviour and other physical items does not replace "without residue" talk about motives. On the other hand, since they express the same_1 fact, whenever the objectivist description is true of anyone, a corresponding mentalistic account will also be true.

(2) We can strengthen, beyond mere extensional equivalence, the use of "same fact". The term 'red', for instance, directly refers to a colour. Light waves cause but are not colours. However, the descriptive phrase 'the colour with the longest wave length' is a way of indirectly referring to the colour red. 'The colour of this book is red' and 'The colour of this book is the colour with the longest wave length' express the same_2 fact. Similarly, a mentalistic term, like 'thinking-about-Italy_m' directly describes a state of consciousness, while its objectivist parallel 'thinking-about-Italy_0' indirectly refers to this state. Generally, two different statements express the same_2 fact, if the terms in which they differ are related to each other as direct and indirect descriptions or ways of referring. Since corresponding mentalistic and objectivist statements in this twofold way express the $\text{same}_{1,2}$ facts, their "sameness" is stronger than the mere extensional equivalence of, say, 'Roses are red' and 'Sugar is sweet'.

We say that mental anguish, for instance, anxiety, causes ulcers or that a bodily wound causes pain. Our common language is interactionist through and through. Extensional equivalence and direct *versus* indirect reference permit us to fit scientific parallelism with this piece of interactionist common sense. On the objectivist account, a mental state can affect the body only through its corresponding physical state. But the objectivist term 'anxiety_0' is an indirect description of the mentalistic 'anxiety_m'. They may thus each be used to express the same_2 fact. In particular, if it is true that anxiety_0 causes ulcers, we may also truly say that anxiety_m causes ulcers. The two causal attributions, the everyday interactionist one and that of the objectivist, are extensionally equivalent and express the same_1 fact. Since they also express the same_2 fact, there is more than mere extensional equivalence. We can thus make sense both of our common-sense interactionism as well as of its scientific denial. This is as it should be for, as we know, philosophy leaves everything as it is.

(3) The statement-form '*P* or *Q*' is logically equivalent to "not both not-*P* and not-*Q*'. By virtue of this tautology, 'Either Jones has a daughter or he has a son' expresses the same_3 fact as 'It is not the case that Jones has neither a daughter nor a son'. Generally, two statements may be said to express the same_2 fact, if they are logically, that is, tautologically equivalent, or, to say the same thing differently, if the statement of their equivalence is analytic. Statements containing terms directly referring to mental states are not *tautologically* equivalent to statements containing their corresponding indirectly-referring objectivist terms. They do not therefore express the same_3 facts. However, most if not all action and other social terms must be explicated, that is, given "real definitions" of their (referential) meaning_1, whether in everyday speech or in science. Given such explications of usage, the terms, like 'owning property' or even 'behaving according to a standard', serve as abbreviatory expressions for the more complex ones. Statements containing the abbreviatory terms are then analytically equivalent to statements containing, in their place, the longer explicating expressions. They thus express the same_3 fact. But even in such cases, the two expressions, the short and the long ones, would not have the same (intentional or associational) $\text{meanings}_{3,4}$. Two expressions that are "logically" different in a use of 'logical' that encompasses and conflates several different ways that an expression can mean may yet be logically the same in a different and precise sense of 'logical'.

The crucial terms in this controversy are 'meaning' and 'understanding'. Often in philosophical controversy, once several uses of certain crucial terms have been distinguished, little remains to argue about. Doubtless this happy outcome is too much to hope for now, though I hope that some contribution has at least been made to clarity about the issues at stake. I hazard the diagnosis that a vast irresolution about the status of mind lies at the root of the revived attempt to resolve empirical matters of fact "logically" or "conceptually". Unwilling to grant ontological status to mind, what properly belongs to mind, our thoughts or concepts, is projected on to the world. This is the road, not trodden for the first time, that leads to anthropomorphic rationalism.

VI

SAFETY, STRENGTH, SIMPLICITY

NELSON GOODMAN

WHEN the evidence leaves us with a choice among hypotheses of unequal strength, how is the choice to be made?

Caution would counsel us to choose the weakest, the hypothesis that asserts the least, since it is the least likely to fail us later. But the principle of maximum safety quickly reduces to absurdity; for it always dictates the choice of a hypothesis that does not go beyond the evidence at all.

The very opposite proposal has often been advanced: that the strongest hypothesis not falsified by the evidence should be preferred. But for every hypothesis strong enough to go beyond the evidence, there is an equally strong conflicting hypothesis based upon the same evidence. This is easily shown. Suppose our evidence tells us just that every examined *A* is a *B*, and suppose hypothesis H_1 affirms in addition that every (or even some one) other *A* is a *B*. Then hypothesis H_2, affirming that every examined *A* is a *B* and that every (or the particular one) other *A* is *not* a *B*, likewise conforms to the stated evidence. Hence strength is indifferent as between any projection and its opposite. And to exclude every hypothesis that conflicts with another equally strong one unviolated by the evidence would be, once more, to exclude every hypothesis that goes beyond the evidence at all.

Thus although both safety and strength are desirable features of a theory, they are by themselves incompetent criteria for choice. Another and controlling factor, simplicity, must be taken into account. Simplicity has sometimes been mistakenly identified with safety or with strength, but is readily shown to be distinct from both. Suppose we have examined many and widely distributed specimens of maple trees and found them all to be deciduous, and suppose this constitutes our entire evidence. Since we still will not have examined specimens from every small locality, our evidence may then leave us with a choice between the following two hypotheses:

From *Philosophy of Science*, Vol. 28 (1961), pp. 150–1. Reprinted by permission of the author and the Editor of *Philosophy of Science*.

(1) All maples, except perhaps those in Eagleville, are deciduous.

(2) All maples are deciduous.

The second is clearly both the stronger and the simpler. We would incorporate (2) in our theory, and retreat to (1) only if further evidence indicated that (2) is false. Insertion of the *ad hoc* exceptive clause both weakens and complicates the hypothesis. Cases like this, where the preferable hypothesis is the simpler and stronger one, give plausibility to the view that strength is the measure of simplicity and is the cardinal principle of choice. But exactly comparable cases point to the opposite conclusion. The stated evidence also leaves unfalsified the hypothesis:

(3) All maples whatsoever, and all sassafras trees in Eagleville, are deciduous.

Now (3) is stronger than (2) but is less simple and acceptable. The expansion made in (3) is as unwelcome as the exception made in (1). Hypothesis (2), although it lies between (1) and (3) in safety and strength, is simpler than and preferable to either.

This shows that neither safety nor strength is the measure of simplicity, and that simplicity takes precedence over both as a factor in the choice of hypotheses. The delicate problem of balancing safety and strength against each other is significant only as between hypotheses of equal simplicity.

If neither safety nor strength determines simplicity, what does? Formulation of general standards for comparing the simplicity of hypotheses is a difficult and neglected task. Here brevity is no reliable test; for since we can always, by a calculated selection of vocabulary, translate any hypothesis into one of minimal length, the simplicity of the vocabulary must also be appraised. I am inclined to think that the standards of simplicity for hypotheses derive from our classificatory habits as disclosed in our language, and that the relative entrenchment of predicates underlies our judgement of relative simplicity; but spelling this out takes some pains. Merely to reject unfamiliar predicates wholesale in favour of familiar ones would be to disallow the introduction of needed new terms into scientific language. Furthermore, we must ordinarily decide not merely which of two hypotheses is the simpler but which one makes for the simpler total theory. I have discussed these matters in *Fact, Fiction, and Forecast*[1]; and the criterion of projectibility I have outlined there in

[1] 2nd edition. Bobbs-Merrill Co., Inc., Indianapolis, 1965 and O.U.P., London, 1967; see especially Chapter IV.

terms of entrenchment is perhaps essentially a simplicity criterion. But the whole matter wants more study. What is evident is that adequate canons of induction must incorporate criteria of simplicity that cannot be given solely in terms of strength or safety.[2]

[2] [In addition to the three items cited in the Bibliography, the following are among N. Goodman's other writings on simplicity: *The Structure of Appearance*, 2nd. ed., Bobbs-Merrill, New York, 1966, pp. 66–117; 'Condensation and simplification', *Theoria*, 27 (1961), pp. 47–48; 'Science and simplicity' in *Philosophy of Science Today*, ed. S. Morgenbesser, Basic Books, New York, 1967; 'Uniformity and simplicity', *75th Anniversary Lecture*, Geological Society of America (1963) (forthcoming). Ed.]

VII

INDUCTIVE SIMPLICITY

ROBERT ACKERMANN

THE fact that simplicity has been linked with induction by many philosophers of science, some of whom have proposed or supported criteria of 'inductive simplicity', means that the problem must be given some serious attention. I take 'inductive simplicity' as a title, however, only by way of concession to these historical treatments, since it is precisely the burden of my paper to show that there is no such thing. So much for the conclusion. I shall spend the remainder of my time arguing for it.

A particular problem of induction, which may appropriately be called the 'curve-fitting' problem, has been isolated for attention by those who claim that some rule of simplicity is an integral part of the inductive process. The problem is usually introduced by allowing experimental observations to be represented by points on a real plane, but the alternative hypotheses invoked to explain those observations to be represented by curves drawn through the plane. In this simple model a satisfactory hypothesis is represented by a curve passing through, or very near to, each designated point in the plane. It is at once obvious that many curves can be drawn so as to satisfy this intuitive criterion. But science, so it is said, can only accept one. We may solve that problem, according to the tradition that I am referring to, by drawing *the* simplest curve through the points and accepting that as representing the hypothesis that science accepts. This is, however, but the description of a solution that can be no better than the notion of simplicity involved. It is not likely that all of the problems usually associated with induction could be dissolved by an adequate solution to the curve-fitting problem. On the other hand, it will be assumed here that an adequate account of inductive inference would have to provide a solution to this laboratory paradigm. Induction and curve-fitting, then, are related areas for any adequate philosophy of science, and we shall examine the latter here

From *Philosophy of Science*, Vol. 28 (1961), pp. 152–61. Reprinted by permission of the author and the Editor of *Philosophy of Science*.

because specific proposals for inductive rules of simplicity do exist for the curve-fitting problem.

It would only be fair to examine in detail some of the specific proposals extant in the literature. This procedure, in view of the nature of this symposium, would not be optimum strategy. I would merely call your attention to the passages on simplicity in Harold Jeffreys's *Scientific Inference,*[1] Karl Popper's *The Logic of Scientific Discovery,*[2] and John Kemeny's 'The Use of Simplicity in Induction'[3] as representative of attempts to propose some workable rule of simplicity as a criterion for making inductive inferences. In spite of the differences in notation and approach taken in these articles, they exhibit a remarkable similarity in overall strategy. It is obviously the case that a scientist can, by means of ordinary algebraic manipulations, find a curve representing a suitable hypothesis that will pass through all of the observation points. The remarkable fact to these writers is that often the curve accepted is quite different from the curve that algebraic methods would produce. For example, restricting ourselves to polynomials, often a quadratic equation might be taken as representing the acceptable hypothesis where an algebraic technique fitting all of the points would result in a polynomial of high degree. Obviously the problem is to find some compromise between simplicity and fit of the data, since the simple curve accepted does not necessarily pass through every observation point. There is no need to seek rigour here; simple laws of mechanics are not taken to be disconfirmed by the experiments conducted in sophomore lab sections, where experience quickly confirms that few sophomore experimenters ever produce observational data that coincides with what the already accepted theories of physics predict.

The approach of the authors that I have referred to is quite natural. They attempt to find a simplicity ordering of all possible scientific hypotheses which the scientist is bid to work through until he finds the simplest hypothesis in the ordering that is in some sense compatible with his data. The notion of compatibility with the data is not sufficiently clarified in any of these accounts, but that need not concern us here. It can be shown independently of that difficulty that a simplicity ordering of the kind envisaged has not been satisfactorily accomplished. Both Jeffreys and Popper take the simplicity ordering to be in terms of the number of parameters in the equations being considered as possible hypotheses with respect to some such set of

[1] Cambridge, 1957.

[2] New York, 1959.

[3] *Philosophical Review*, LVII (1953), pp. 391–408.

data, and in general, the scientist considers those equations with one parameter first, then those with two parameters, and so on.[1] I believe that it can be shown of both of these orderings that they are not well defined, and that they entail the difficulty that they are hardly practical, since Galileo, for example, under one construal of these proposals, would still be leafing through a book of equations without having come to the appropriate solution to some of his specific problems. Practicality is not essential, unless a philosopher of science wishes to propose inductive rules that are to be of use to the scientist, and that is just the kind of rule that the simplicity ordering is taken to be. Kemeny is more sophisticated in his approach than either Popper or Jeffreys, and escapes some of the direct problems with their ordering by proposing, not an overall ordering of all possible candidates for scientific hypotheses, but an ordering relativized to specific experimental situations. Unfortunately, however, his proposals amount to descriptions of measure functions which would yield the ordering but which do not, as they stand, enable the scientist to find the ordering in any particular case. The only concrete examples involve functions which are ordered once again according to the number of their parameters, or similar intuitive orderings in one case of more complex functions than polynomials. Kemeny explicitly points out that he intends his article only to prepare the ground for an adequate treatment of the problem, but his own formulation contains the patent and irresolved problem that while *1/3* is earlier in one simplicity ordering than *1/10*, the order of these numbers is reversed when their equivalents in terms of decimal expansions are considered. Kemeny attempts to avoid this by the obscure claim that '$f(x) = .25$' and '$f(x) = 1/4$' express different hypotheses with respect to the same problem.[2] We thus reach the point where it becomes obvious that the traditional accounts of inductive simplicity in terms of a simplicity ordering have failed to solve the problem, or at least I believe we would reach that point if we had the time to give each of these authors a careful treatment.

There is another source for information on the curve-fitting problem in the laboratory handbooks and treatises on practical analysis. But these books will not solve our problem. The scientist is greeted in their pages with something like the following:[3]

[1]Harold Jeffreys, *Scientific Inference*, p. 39, and Karl Popper, *The Logic of Scientific Discovery*, p. 142.

[2]'The Use of Simplicity in Induction', loc. cit., p. 403.

[3]Joseph Lipka, *Graphical and Mechanical Computation*, London, 1921.

The nature of the experiment may give us a hint as to the form of the equation which will best represent the data. Otherwise the problem is more indeterminate.

Actually, these laboratory manuals are designed to answer the following question: 'Given a set of data points, and a curve form, what is the best curve of that form that can be drawn through the data within a desired degree of accuracy?' Clearly, this is not the problem of simplicity with respect to induction with which we started. For that reason, the discussion of this kind of literature will terminate at this point. Experimental design may enable us to discriminate between hypotheses which have already been proposed, but that discrimination is on the basis of evidential fit, and not on the basis of simplicity. Let us tentatively conclude that none of the laboratory handbooks solves the problems surrounding inductive simplicity.

The observation which appears to be most damaging to optimism in connection with the problem of curve-fitting is the observation that the unsatisfactory results of previous investigations appear to have occurred in a context where certain assumptions have implicitly been made that severely restrict the potential difficulties with curve-fitting. Most of the authors concerned with the problem have proposed solutions which would completely collapse under the removal of these restrictions. Since the assumptions do not appear to be warrantable in general, their removal in an adequate philosophy of science seems imperative. In particular, three such assumptions will be mentioned at the present time: the assumption of continuity of functions, the assumption of the adequacy of measurement, and the assumption of non-statistical assumptions.

What is here called the assumption of continuity refers to the tendency among philosophers of science to limit the functions available to the scientist in some *a priori* fashion. Certain historical accidents may account for this, such as the fact that many philosophers of science have taken classical mechanics as their paradigm case of a well-developed science. The difficulty is the following: If the results of experimentation are taken quite simply to be points in a plane, there does not appear to be any reason why the curve drawn through them should be continuous, except that most scientific laws to the present have, as a matter of fact, been continuous where they might be represented as curves through data. That continuity has been assumed in the treatments appears obvious from the measure of complexity which is taken to be related to the number of parameters in the accounts of Jeffreys and Popper. The manner in which these authors have spoken seems to indicate that they were thinking of polynomials in their treatments to the virtual exclusion of other kinds of functions. Polynomials, of course, are continuous curves, and attention to them exclusively seems to promise hope for an application of the intuitive notion of drawing the 'smoothest' curve through a set of points as a possible explication of inductive simplicity. It is equally obvious that not all functions requisite to the purposes of science are polynomials. For example, the importance of transcendental functions to scientific investigation is not accounted for in any of the treatments so far discussed. Consider the simple transcendental functions '$y = \sin(x)$,' '$y = \log(x)$,' and '$y = e^x$'. None of the simplicity orderings referred to discuss the position of these functions in a simplicity ordering. It is possible, of course, to get an approximation to them by means of power series, but that would result in taking them to be extremely complex, which is counter-intuitive. On the other hand, lumping them with the simplest functions causes the embarrassment to Galileo that I suggested earlier in that the early part of the ordering is so dense that it would not be practical to work through it with respect to some given scientific problem.

When the possibility of discontinuous functions is admitted, the situation becomes vastly more complicated than any extant treatment has even intimated. Even if a solution of curve-fitting that yields a unique continuous curve could be found, it seems too severe to put an *a priori* limit on scientific hypotheses to the set of equations representing continuous functions. In any given problem, it would not be known necessarily whether discontinuous functions were a possible solution, and hence there might often be no warrant for using the technique for continuous functions already described. And, of course, recent developments in science include discontinuous functions which appear as deductions from theories which are at least tentatively accepted. In an experiment to test such a theory, discontinuous curves would have to be mapped on to the laboratory data, so that at least in principle the curve-fitting problem cannot be restricted to continous curves in an adequate philosophy of science.

By the assumption of the adequacy of measurement is meant what seems to be the supposition that enough data should, in principle, eliminate an infinite number of hypotheses, leaving only a finite number from which choice might be made by means of a modified simplicity ordering. Lurking behind this notion seems to be the old fallacy that subtraction of an infinite set from an infinite set must leave a finite set. In the case of curve-fitting, it is not enough to show, for example, that the scientist begins with an enumerable set of hypotheses and can eliminate an enumerable set of them by experiment. There can still be an enumerable set of hypotheses left to consider.

But this is only a digression: the assumption of the adequacy of measurement can be shown to have undesirable consequences on other grounds. The use of empirical measurement can only justify use of rational numbers in describing experimental results. Any theory of curve-fitting which results in the notion that a hypothesis must fit the data is not sufficient to explain why certain hypotheses with real numbers in their expressions are an integral part of science. The occurrence of π and of e, for example, cannot be easily explained on the basis of extrapolation from observational data. This obvious point in connection with the application of mathematics to scientific experiment is so well known that it is difficult to believe that philosophers who have examined the problem could have taken the position that experimental fit will rule out all but a finite number of hypotheses in conjunction with some rule of simplicity. After any number of observations, an infinite number of real-valued functions will still be compatible with the experimental results. Hence, to put it mildly, it is somewhat hasty to suppose that parameters may be decisively evaluated by a little work in the lab. This difficulty is in fact crucial, and it seems to hold the key to a fundamental error in supposing that curve-fitting may be done in terms of a simplicity ordering.

The assumption which was referred to as the assumption of non-statistical hypotheses suggests that most accounts have had a tendency to underestimate the importance of statistical data in curve-fitting. Accounts of curve-fitting in the philosophical literature have often tacitly assumed that a scientist has one set of points through which he desires to draw a curve with as little error as possible. The difficulty which arises over the point of repeated experiment, by the same scientist or other scientists, is not touched upon. Now a law, which is what these discussions have assumed the curve through the data to represent ultimately, is expected to remain the same for every such experiment. The criteria given, however, do not allow the scientist to make a very clear choice when more than one set of data confronts him, that is, when conflicting data are gathered on more than one experiment. It might be supposed that the conflict can be resolved by further experiment. But what is to be done as the result of the experiment is not at all clear. Should apparently 'strange' results which have only been taken once be thrown out? This kind of abandonment of data has caused some embarrassment in scientific history, and it is a moot and extremely difficult point as to whether data incongruity should be resolved by abandoning apparently bad observations, or when the hypothesis should be made more complex to account for the apparent oddities in the data. These problems are important to any curve-fitting problem, since in practice a scientist is likely not to consider the results of experiment as points on a page, but as observations which he may have the right to interpret and juggle with before determining the result. It is true that sometimes such juggling, in the hands of an expert, results in a scientific advance. The view of the previously considered philosophers of science appears perilously close to taking the data of an experiment to be *just* a collection of points on a page, and it is not an adequate explication of scientific practice.

One objection should probably be dispelled at this point. It might be supposed that in a sense *all* data are statistical. For example, it might be claimed that statements thought to be tautologous can only be shown to be so by some operation, like the truth-table technique. It might be further claimed, on statistical grounds, that some statement commonly taken to be tautologous is in fact not, on the grounds that everyone constructing the truth table has always made the same mistake. This is a not uninteresting problem, but it does not have immediate application to our difficulty with inductive simplicity. Someone might claim that in principle scientific determinations could become as accurate as truth-table determinations, due to refinement in measure techniques. If this were to happen, then the simplicity orderings suggested might receive a new importance, and the only talk of statistical evidence would reduce to the kind of perplexity referred to in the example of the incorrect truth table. This line of argument will not do. It can be shown, or perhaps better, described, how a truth table is constructed in an accurate manner. Each entry, for example, is either *t* or *f*. Perhaps no one has accomplished the right truth table for some given expression, but it certainly exists. This is not true of all scientific determinations. To go back to an earlier point, no experiment can discriminate between two hypotheses one of which contains a real value in its expression and the other a rational value in the same place which is arbitrarily close to the real value. It would thus appear that the problem of discriminating between analytic functions and polynomials, say, of an appropriate sort, represents an inherent limitation on curve-fitting which is not analogous to any difficulty in certain other disciplines, such as logic.

What follows from the isolation of these three assumptions as implicit limitations on the solution to the curve-fitting problem? It would appear that they have no justification within a philosophy of science, and dropping them seems to damage severely hopes for any notion of inductive simplicity along the lines of finding a simplicity ordering for the possible hypotheses of science.

There are difficulties, moreover, with the notion of inductive simplicity even should the programme be completed in spite of dropping the assumptions. For example, supposing a well-ordering of scientific hypotheses is discovered along the lines that have already been suggested, and indeed, I have no *proof* that such a well-ordering could not be found, only the difficulties that I have mentioned. Given such a well-ordering, two serious problems would still confront us: the notion of simplicity invoked to justify the ordering, and the problem of its mesh with a total philosophy of science.

We have seen that some of the authors who have treated inductive simplicity have taken an ordering of polynomials in term of increasing numbers of parameters. This, however, is far from justifying the ordering in terms of some explicit notion of simplicity. In other words, the ordering is said to be in terms of simplicity; but it is questionable what notion of simplicity is really important here. We might say to a scientist that the proper method to use when searching for a hypothesis to fit his data is to start at one end of the ordering and work to the other until some hypothesis is met which is reasonably well in accord with the data (defining 'reasonably' in some fairly precise fashion, if possible). This would amount to a rather mechanical procedure designed to facilitate a planned examination of all possible laws. Any well-ordering of scientific hypotheses would serve this purpose. The question is then whether any clear notion of simplicity can be invoked to justify the ordering as a simplicity ordering. It is a reasonable contention that no such notion has been adequately discussed by the philosophers treating inductive simplicity in the past, and that no such notion is really available. If that is the case, it would appear that the use of simplicity in this connection is entirely gratuitous.

For any practical purpose, the suggestion that the scientist must work laboriously through an infinite number of hypotheses in a simplicity ordering sounds more like the temporary solution to a philosophical impasse than an adequate description of what scientists have done even in rigorous moments. It is this which leads to the suggestion that inductive simplicity does not mesh well with what would often be taken to be an adequate philosophy of science. To summarize, what is available in the way of information about the ways in which scientists actually work appears to suggest that scientists are able to work efficiently while only considering some small number of hypotheses. Scientific practice, in fact, is often concerned with the evaluation of only two or three alternate hypotheses. It would appear, therefore, that the curve-fitting problem as it is usually presented is not an adequate explication of the problem of choosing between rival hypotheses in day-to-day scientific practice.

Several observations may account for this discrepancy, but the most important one is concerned with what the scientist does when he experiments. The proposals for curve-fitting seemed to suppose that the scientist was only concerned with observing data without bias which he would later use to construct a hypothesis or hypotheses. As a matter of fact, the scientist rarely appears to engage in this sort of activity. More usually some hypothesis has been suggested, perhaps from some general theory by deductive inference, or even by a hunch on the part of the investigator. The experiment may then be undertaken to see whether the data predicted by the hypothesis is in close agreement with observation. An analogy to mathematics may be useful. Mathematical theorems may be found either by deduction from previously established theories, or by the subsequent discovery of some proof for a theorem which is originally considered merely as a proposal or conjecture, which, if proved, would prove interesting in some way. Part of the difficulty with the inductive approach to curve-fitting that we have been considering is that it tends to make experiment determine the theoretical structure of science to an extent which minimizes or ignores the important way in which previously considered theories and hypotheses determine experiment, and experimental interpretations in science.[1] The scientist is often not dealing with an infinite number of hypotheses in considering

[1]This is a familiar notion in the philosophy of science. See discussions in Pierre Duhem, *The Aim and Structure of Physical Theory*, Princeton, 1954, and Richard B. Braithwaite, *Scientific Explanation*, Cambridge, 1953.

the results of an experiment, but with a finite number determined by the theoretical structure available to him in constructing the experiment. Experiment can thus appear to be a justification of an already conceived state of affairs rather than the basis of some type of inductive inference. It should be noted here that hypotheses to be confirmed by an experiment may occur at a number of levels. For example, a scientist may wish to determine whether a hypothesis stating that X and Y are related by a linear function is confirmable by experiment. Here any observed linear relationship would confirm the hypothesis. It is not convenient to think of the scientist as considering every linear relationship as a prior possibility, since any observed relationship of that kind will suffice to confirm, or partially confirm, the *one* hypothesis that he has in mind.

It might immediately be objected that we have just crossed to the other extreme, and that this view of the experimental situation is equally false to scientific practice. Many experiments are certainly run to *determine* a previously unknown quantity in some scientific statement. For example, theory may not suggest a value for x in the singular statement 'The coefficient of expansion of this particular piece of iron is x'. An experiment may be designed to find such a coefficient by observation. Such a determination, however, seems really to be the result of temporary ignorance as to some desired explanation of a wide range of events. Most such determinations, without auxiliary theory, do not suffice to permit prediction, and are consequently defective as candidates for scientific hypotheses. An extrapolation to a scientific hypothesis from data is always taken as more unsatisfactory by scientists than the confirmation in the laboratory of a hypothesis deduced from some useful theoretical structure.

One difficulty in the preceding proposals appears to be that it is implicitly assumed that 'acceptance' of a hypothesis by scientists is a well defined notion, when as a matter of fact it is not very clear at all. Certainly *science* accepts nothing, in the sense that human beings do, and we are forced to search for some explanation in terms of what scientists do. Now the body of scientists would be a very difficult group to define in order to conform to an intuitive notion that acceptance by all scientists would constitute acceptance by science as an institution. This problem, obviously, needs attention.

Falling back on the familiar figure of speech as though it were meaningful, however, we still have problems with the notion of acceptance. It seems to be assumed in most of the traditional discussions of the philosophy of science that a given hypothesis is either accepted or not accepted by science. The advantages of such a view are numerous, but it is questionable whether these advantages are compatible with an adequate analysis. It would appear that the coefficient of expansion of iron as determined by experiment is not accepted by scientists in the same way as, say, the theory of relativity. A complete study of this problem might well show that the figure for the coefficient is always taken to be approximate, and subject to revision, while the theory of relativity may represent in scientists' minds a complete, and *simple*, explanation of all relevant cosmological data. Although this is not likely to remain a permanent view, if we regard the mortality rate of theories in the history of science, it does seem that the theory of relativity is accepted in a 'different spirit' than the coefficient of expansion of iron as extrapolated from a series of experiments. Some explanation of this may be found in the way that the theory of relativity functions as a fundamental law, from which many familiar and tentatively accepted law-like statements can be deduced, while the fundamental law or laws from which coefficients of expansion can be deduced is still a desideratum for physics. Until such laws are discovered, the approximate determinations of the laboratory appear to be an *ad hoc* blemish on the theoretical structure of physics.

Any simplicity ordering of the kind envisioned by the proponents of inductive simplicity thus appears to be an arbitrary device for selecting one extrapolation out of an infinite number of alternative hypotheses compatible with the experimental data. It would thus appear that curve-fitting treatments leave untouched a great many important and crucial experiments in science by leaving unexplained the relationship of theory to the hypotheses being tested by experiment, while they do deal only with experiments which yield provisional determinations of quantities until such time that they can be incorporated into science as deductions from higher-level hypotheses.

The conclusions to this probe of inductive simplicity are thus rather negative. Taking the special problem of curve-fitting, it has been suggested that no simplicity ordering of the kind desired has been developed, and that there are strong arguments, although not a proof, militating against the completion of any such proposal. It would further seem that the notion of inductive simplicity along the lines explored in connection with the curve-fitting problem accounts for only a small portion of actual scientific practice, and that it fails to account satisfactorily for experiment designed to confirm a hypothesis or to choose among a finite set of already proposed hypotheses. Indeed, the difficulties with the notion of inductive simplicity force attention to the notions of simplicity as related to scientific systems, where experiments are designed to test the deductive consequences of these systems. Simplicity of systems, which has been explored by Nelson Goodman among others, has received fairly precise explication, and it seems that hopes for a clear and useful notion of simplicity may well lie in that direction.[1]

[1] Goodman's notion is developed in his 'Axiomatic Measure of Simplicity', *Journal of Philosophy*, LII (1955), pp. 709–22; 'Recent Developments in the Theory of Simplicity', *Philosophy and Phenomenological Research*, XIX (1959), pp. 429–46; and *The Structure of Appearance*, Cambridge, 1951. References to other proposals are to be found in 'Recent Developments in the Theory of Simplicity'.

VIII

SELF-SUPPORTING INDUCTIVE ARGUMENTS

MAX BLACK

THE use of inductive rules has often led to true conclusions about matters of fact. Common sense regards this as a good reason for trusting inductive rules in the future, if due precautions are taken against error. Yet an argument from success in the past to probable success in the future itself uses an inductive rule, and therefore seems circular. Nothing would be accomplished by any argument that needed to assume the reliability of an inductive rule in order to establish that rule's reliability.

Suppose that inferences governed by some inductive rule have usually resulted in true conclusions; and let an inference from this fact to the probable reliability of the rule in the future be called a *second-order* inference. So long as the rule by which the second-order inference is governed differs from the rule whose reliability is to be affirmed, there will be no appearance of circularity. But if the second-order inference is governed by the very same rule of inference whose reliability is affirmed in the conclusion, the vicious circularity seems blatant.

Must we, then, reject forthwith every second-order inductive argument purporting to support the very rule of inference by which the argument itself is governed? Contrary to general opinion, a plausible case can be made for saying, No.[1] Properly constructed and interpreted, such 'self-supporting' inferences, as I shall continue to call them, can satisfy all the conditions for legitimate inductive inference: when an inductive rule has been reliable (has generated true conclusions from true premisses more often than not) in the past, a second-order inductive inference governed by the same rule can show that the rule deserves to be trusted in its next application.

The reasons I have given for this contention have recently been

From the *Journal of Philosophy*, Vol. 55 (1958), pp. 718–25. Reprinted by permission of the author and the *Journal of Philosophy*.

[1] See Max Black, *Problems of Analysis* (Ithaca, N.Y., 1954), chapter 11, and R. B. Braithwaite, *Scientific Explanation* (Cambridge, 1953), chapter 8.

sharply criticized by Professor Wesley C. Salmon.[1] In trying to answer his precisely worded objections, I hope to make clearer the view I have been defending and to dispel some lingering misapprehensions.

My original example of a legitimate self-supporting inductive argument was the following:[2]

(a) In most instances of the use of *R* in arguments with true premisses examined in a wide variety of conditions, *R* has been successful.

Hence (probably):

In the next instance to be encountered of the use of *R* in an argument with a true premiss, *R* will be successful. The rule of inductive inference mentioned in the premiss and the conclusion of the above argument is:

R: To argue from *Most instances of A's examined in a wide variety of conditions have been B* to (probably) *The next A to be encountered will be B.* Thus the second-order argument (a) uses the rule *R* in showing that the same rule will be 'successful' (will generate a true conclusion from a true premiss[3]) in the next encountered instance of its use.

The rule, *R*, stated above is not intended to be a 'supreme rule' of induction, from which all other inductive rules can be derived; nor is it claimed that *R*, as it stands, is a wholly acceptable rule for inductive inference. The unsolved problem of a satisfactory formulation of canons of inductive inference will arise only incidentally in the present discussion. The rule *R* and the associated argument (a) are to serve merely to illustrate the logical problems that arise in connection with self-supporting arguments: the considerations to be adduced in defence of (a) could be adapted to fit many other self-supporting arguments.

The proposed exculpation of the self-supporting argument (a) from the charge of vicious circularity is linked to a feature of the corresponding rule *R* that must be carefully noted. Inductive

[1]See Wesley C. Salmon, 'Should We Attempt to Justify Induction?' *Philosophical Studies*, Vol VIII No. 3 (April, 1957), pp. 45–47.

[2]See *Problems*, page 197, where the argument is called '(a_2)' and the rule by which it is governed 'R_2'. At that place, I also presented another self-supporting argument with a more sweeping conclusion of the *general* reliability of the corresponding rule. But since I was unable to accept the premiss of that argument, or the reliability of the rule it employed, I shall follow Salmon in discussing only the argument presented above.

[3]Here and throughout this discussion, I assume for simplicity that all the premisses of any argument or inference considered have been conjoined into a single statement.

arguments governed by *R* vary in 'strength'[1] according to the number and variety of the favourable instances reported in the premiss. So, although *R* permits us to assert a certain conclusion categorically, it is to be understood throughout that the strength of the assertion fluctuates with the character of the evidence. If only a small number of instances have been examined and the relative frequency of favourable instances (*A*'s that are *B*) is little better than a half, the strength of the argument may be close to zero; while a vast predominance of favourable instances in a very large sample of observations justifies a conclusion affirmed with nearly maximal strength. The presence of the word 'probably' in the original formulation of *R* indicates the variability of strength of the corresponding argument; in more refined substitutes for *R*, provision might be made for some precise measure of the associated degree of strength.

Variability in strength is an important respect in which inductive arguments differ sharply from deductive ones. If a deductive argument is not valid, it must be *in*valid, no intermediate cases being conceivable; but a legitimate inductive argument, whose conclusion may properly be affirmed on the evidence supplied, may still be very weak. Appraisal of an inductive argument admits of degrees.

Similar remarks apply to inductive rules, as contrasted with deductive ones. A deductive rule is either valid or invalid—*tertium non datur*; but at any time in the history of the employment of an inductive rule, it has what may be called a *degree of reliability* depending upon its ratio of successes in previous applications. A legitimate or correct inductive rule may still be a weak one: appraisal of an inductive rule admits of degrees.

Now in claiming that the second-order argument (a) *supports* the rule *R*, I am claiming that the argument raises the degree of reliability of the rule, and hence the strength of the arguments in which it will be used; I have no intention of claiming that the self-supporting argument can definitively establish or demonstrate that the rule is correct. Indeed, I do not know what an outright demonstration of the correctness or legitimacy of an inductive rule would be like. My attempted rebuttal of Salmon's objections will turn upon the possibility of raising the degree of reliability of an inductive rule, as already explained.

[1]In *Problems*, page 193, I spoke, with the same intention, of the 'degree of support' given to the conclusion by the premiss. If the latter has the form m/n *A's examined in a wide variety of conditions have been B*, it is natural to suppose that the strength of the argument increases as m increases, and also as m/n increases. A plausible formula for the 'strength' of the argument might be $(1 - e^{-m})(2m/n - 1)$.

The contribution made by the second-order argument (a) to strengthening the rule R by which it is governed can be made plain by a hypothetical illustration. Suppose evidence is available that $\frac{4}{5}$ of the A's so far examined have been B, and it is proposed, by an application of the rule R, to draw the inference that the next A to be encountered will be B. For the sake of simplicity the proposed argument may be taken to have a strength of $\frac{4}{5}$.[1] Before accepting the conclusion about the next A, we may wish to consider the available evidence about past successes of the rule R. Suppose, for the sake of argument, that we know R to have been successful in $\frac{9}{10}$ of the cases in which it has been previously used. If so, the second-order argument affirms with strength $\frac{9}{10}$ that R will be successful in the next $\frac{9}{10}$ instance of its use. But the 'next instance' is before us, as the argument whose premiss is that $\frac{4}{5}$ of the A's have been B. For R to be "successful" in this instance is for the conclusion of the first-order argument to be true; the strength of the second-order argument is therefore immediately transferred to the first-order argument. Before invoking the second-order argument, we were entitled to affirm the conclusion of the first-order argument with a strength of no better than $\frac{4}{5}$, but we are now able to raise the strength to $\frac{9}{10}$. Conversely, if the second-order argument had shown R to have been unsuccessful in less than $\frac{4}{5}$ of its previous uses, our confidence in the proposed conclusion of the first-order argument would have been diminished.

There is no mystery about the transfer of strength from the second-order argument to the first-order argument: the evidence cited in the former amplifies the evidence immediately relevant to the latter. Evidence concerning the proportion of A's found to have been B permits the direct inference, with strength $\frac{4}{5}$, that the next A to be encountered will be B. It is, however, permissible to view the situation in another aspect as concerned with the extrapolation of an already observed statistical association between true premisses of a certain sort and a corresponding conclusion. The evidence takes the form: In 9 cases out of 10, the truth of a statement of the form *m/n X's have been found to be Y's* has been found associated in a wide variety of cases with the truth of the statement *The next X to be encountered was Y.*[2] This is better evidence than that cited in the

[1]This means taking m/n as the measure of strength, rather than some more complicated formula like the one suggested in footnote 1, p. 138. The argument does not depend upon the exact form of the measure of strength.

[2]We might wish to restrict the second-order argument to cases in which the ratio m/n was close to $\frac{4}{5}$. Other refinements readily suggest themselves.

premiss of the original first-order argument: it is therefore to be expected that the strength of the conclusion shall be raised.

It should be noticed that the evidence cited in the second-order argument is not merely greater in amount than the evidence cited in the first-order argument. If *R* has been successfully used for drawing conclusions about fish, neutrons, planets, etc. (the "wide variety of conditions" mentioned in the premiss of the second-order argument), it would be illegitimate to coalesce such heterogeneous kinds of objects into a single class for the sake of a more extensive *first-order* argument. Proceeding to 'second-order' considerations allows us to combine the results of previous inductive inquiries in a way which would not otherwise be possible.

Nothing in this conception of inductive method requires us to remain satisfied with the second-order argument. If circumstances warrant, and suitable evidence can be found, we might be led to formulate third- or even higher-order arguments. These might conceivably result in lowering the measures of strength we at present attach to certain arguments in which *R* is used. But if this were to happen, we would not have been shown to have been mistaken in previously attaching these measures of strength. Nor is it required that a first-order argument be checked against a corresponding second-order argument before the former can properly be used. If we have no reason to think that *R* is unsuccessful most of the time, or is objectionable on some logical grounds, that is enough to make our employment of it so far reasonable. The function of higher-order arguments in the tangled web of inductive method is to permit us to progress from relatively imprecise and uncritical methods to methods whose degrees of reliability and limits of applicability have themselves been checked by inductive investigations. It is in this way that inductive method becomes self-regulating and, if all goes well, self-supporting.

Salmon's objections to the foregoing conception are summarized by him as follows:

> The so-called self-supporting arguments are . . . circular in the following precise sense: the conclusiveness of the argument cannot be established without assuming the truth of the conclusion. It happens, in this case, that the assumption of the truth of the conclusion is required to establish the correctness of the rules of inference used rather than the truth of the premises, but that makes the argument no less viciously circular. The circularity lies in regarding the facts stated in the premises as *evidence* for the conclusion, rather than as evidence against the conclusion or as no

evidence either positive or negative. To regard the facts in the premises as evidence for the conclusion is to assume that the rule of inference used in the argument is a correct one. And this is precisely what is to be proved. If the conclusion is denied, then the facts stated in the premises are no longer evidence for the conclusion.[1]

Comments: (1) Salmon's reference to 'conclusiveness' smacks too much of the appraisal of deductive argument. An inductive argument is not required to be 'conclusive' if that means that its conclusion is entailed or logically implied by its premisses; it is, of course, required to be correct or legitimate, but that means only that the rule of inductive inference shall be reliable—shall usually lead from true premisses to true conclusions. The correctness of an inductive argument could only depend upon the truth of its conclusion if the latter asserted the reliability of the rule by which the argument was governed. But this was not the case in our argument (a). The conclusion there was that *R* would be successful in the next instance of its use: this might very well prove to be false without impugning the reliability of *R*. Salmon was plainly mistaken if he thought that the falsity of (a)'s conclusion entails the incorrectness of the rule by which (a) is governed.[2]

(2) Can the *correctness* of argument (a) be 'established without assuming the truth of the conclusion' of (a)? Well, if 'established' means the same as 'proved by a deductive argument', the answer must be that the correctness of (a) cannot be established at all. But again, a correct inductive argument in support of the rule governing (a) can certainly be constructed without assuming (a)'s conclusion. We do not have to assume that *R* will be successful in the next instance in order to argue correctly that the available evidence supports the reliability of *R*.

(3) Salmon says: 'To regard the facts in the premises as evidence for the conclusion is to assume that the rule of inference used in the argument is a correct one'. In using the rule of inference we certainly *treat* it as correct: we would not use it if we had good reasons for suspecting it to be unreliable. If this is what Salmon means, what he says is right, but not damaging to the correctness of (a). But he

[1] Salmon, loc. cit., p. 47.

[2] I conjecture that Salmon was led into making this mistake by forgetting the conclusion of the argument that he correctly reproduces at the foot of page 45 of his article. It is a sheer blunder to say 'A given inductive rule can be established by a self-supporting argument, according to Black' (p. 45)—if 'established' means the same as 'proved reliable'. The self-supporting argument can *strengthen* the rule, and in this way '*support*' it.

would be plainly wrong if he maintained that an assertion of the correctness of (a) was an additional premiss required by (a), or that an argument to the effect that (a) was correct must precede the legitimate use of (a). For if this last demand were pressed, it would render deductive inference no less than inductive inference logically impossible. If we were never entitled to *use* a correct rule of inference before we had formally argued in support of that rule, the process of inference could never get started.

I shall end by considering an ingenious counter-example provided by Salmon. He asks us to consider the following argument:

(a′): In most instances of the use of *R′* in arguments with true premisses in a wide variety of conditions, *R′* has been unsuccessful.

Hence (probably)

In the next instance to be encountered of the use of *R′* in an argument with a true premiss, *R′* will be successful.

The relevant rule is the 'counter-inductive' one:

R′: To argue from *Most instances of A's examined in a wide variety of conditions have not been B* to (probably) *The next A to be encountered will be B*.

Salmon says that while (a′) must be regarded as a self-supporting argument by my criteria, the rule here supported, *R′*, is in conflict with *R*. From the same premisses the two rules 'will almost always produce contrary conclusions'.[2] This must be granted. But Salmon apparently overlooks an important respect in which the 'counter-inductive' rule *R′* must be regarded as illegitimate.

In calling an inductive rule 'correct', so that it meets the canons of legitimacy of *inductive* rules of inference, we claim at least that the rule is reliable, in the sense of usually leading from true premisses to true conclusions. That is part of what we *mean* by a 'correct inductive rule'. It can easily be shown that *R′* must fail to meet this condition.

Suppose we were using *R′* to predict the terms of a series of 1's and 0's, of which the first three terms were known to be 1's. Then our first two predictions might be as follows (shown by underlining):

$$1\ 1\ 1\ \underline{0}\ \underline{0}$$

At this point, suppose *R′* has been used successfully in each of the two predictions, so that the series is in fact now observed to be

[1]Salmon, loc. cit., p. 46.

1 1 1 0 0. Since 1's still predominate, direct application of the rule calls for 0 to be predicted next. On the other hand, the second-order argument shows that R' has been successful each time and therefore demands that it not be trusted next time, i.e., calls for the prediction of 1. So the very definition of R' renders it impossible for the rule to be successful without being *incoherent*.[1] The suggested second-order argument in support of R' could be formulated only if R' were known to be unreliable, and would therefore be worthless. So we have an *a priori* reason for preferring R to its competitor R'. But it is easy to produce any number of alternative rules of inductive inference, none of which suffers from the fatal defect of R'. The choice between such rules, I suggest, has to be made in the light of experience of their use. I have tried to show in outline how such experience can properly be invoked without logical circularity.

[1]A parallel situation would arise in the use of R in predicting the members of the 1–0 series only if R were to be predominantly *un*successful. But then we would have the best of reasons for assigning R zero strength, and the second-order argument would be pointless.

IX

THE CIRCULARITY OF A SELF-SUPPORTING INDUCTIVE ARGUMENT

PETER ACHINSTEIN

1. MANY philosophers regard as circular, and hence illegitimate, any justification of a principle of induction which makes reference to the success of that principle in the past. Taking issue with this position, Max Black has defended the thesis that the appeal to the past performance of an inductive rule in order to provide support for its future success need involve no circularity whatever, and may indeed constitute a legitimate argument in favour of the rule.[1] As an example, he considers the following inductive rule of inference:

R: To argue from *Most instances of As examined under a wide variety of conditions have been B* to (probably) *The next A to be encountered will be B*.

In defence of R, Black proposes the following 'self-supporting' argument which he claims to be free from circularity:

(a): In most instances of the use of R in arguments with true premisses examined in a wide variety of conditions, R has been successful.

Hence (probably):

In the next instance to be encountered of the use of R in an argument with a true premiss, R will be successful.

Argument (a) uses R as its rule of inference and purports to support the use of R in the next instance of its application by citing the fact that R has been successful in the past. As Black points out, the premiss of (a) is neither identical with the conclusion nor the conclusion in different words, nor is the conclusion a premiss of any argument used to support the premiss of argument (a). Hence, he emphasises, one cannot attribute circularity to (a) on grounds such as these.

From *Analysis*, Vol. 22 (1962), pp. 138–41. Reprinted by permission of the author, *Analysis*, and Basil Blackwell.

[1] Max Black, *Problems of Analysis* (London, 1954), ch. 11.

Despite Black's attempts to defend (a),[1] it has been maintained by Wesley Salmon that the argument is circular.[2] Salmon attributes its circularity to the fact that in proposing (a) one must '. . . assume that the rule of inference [R] used in the argument is a correct one. And this is precisely what is to be proved'. Undaunted by such criticism, Black offers a detailed reply to the charge of circularity.[3] Because I do not find Salmon's formulation sufficient to expose the circularity, nor Black's attempt to defend argument (a) successful, I wish to open the issue once more by considering the cogency of a 'self-supporting' argument such as (a).

2. When any argument is proposed for the purpose of showing that a certain proposition is probable, the correctness or validity of the argument, and hence of the rule of inference which governs the argument, is obviously assumed. Now to claim that a non-deductive rule of inference is correct or valid is to imply, at least for one thing, that the rule will generally be successful, and in particular, that it will probably be successful in the next instance of its use, i.e., that in the next argument with a true premiss the rule will afford an inference to a conclusion that is probably true. This is part of the concept of a correct or valid non-deductive rule of inference. Black, indeed, would seem committed to the latter point when he writes: 'In order for an inductive argument to be correct the rule to which it conforms must be *reliable*. A rule is reliable if it yields true conclusions in *most* cases in which it governs arguments having true premisses'.[4] (If a rule leads to success in most cases—and Black here is speaking of future as well as past successes—then I take it to be an analytic consequence that it is probable that it will be successful in its next application.)

It should be noted that although the claim that a non-deductive rule of inference is correct or valid does not entail that it will definitely be successful in its next application, it does entail that it will probably be so. This means that if the next application of the rule turns out to be unsuccessful, the rule is not thereby shown to be incorrect. (Although, of course, too many such failures certainly would affect its claim to correctness.)

What follows from these considerations is this. The assumption

[1]See ibid, pp. 198–206.

[2]Wesley C. Salmon, 'Should We Attempt to Justify Induction?', *Philosophical Studies*, 8 (1957), 33–48.

[3]Black, 'Self-Supporting Inductive Arguments' [pp. 136–143 above].

[4]*Problems of Analysis*, p. 194.

that argument (a) is correct logically involves the assumption that the rule of inference R which sanctions (a) will probably be successful in its next application. This means that the assumption that (a) is correct involves the assumption that (a)'s conclusion (which is that R will be successful in its next application) is probable. Now, as we observed earlier, in using an argument to show that a proposition is probable the correctness of the argument must be assumed. It follows, therefore, that in using (a) to show that the proposition 'R will be successful in its next application' is probable it must already be assumed probable that R will be successful in its next application. And it is precisely this fact which renders (a) circular.

3. By way of defending and further expounding the present charge, it will be helpful to consider how Black defends argument (a) against the type of criticism offered by Salmon.

In his first two rebuttals Black complains—with some justification—that when Salmon writes 'The conclusiveness of argument (a) cannot be established without assuming the truth of its conclusion', he seems to be treating (a) as if it were a deductive argument, and furthermore he is mistaken in maintaining that (a)'s conclusion must be assumed to be true when the argument is proposed. Thus, Black emphasizes, the validity of (a) does not depend upon the truth of its conclusion, since the conclusion of (a) could turn out false and not impugn the validity of the rule of inference involved.

However, while Salmon was incorrect in suggesting that the validity of (a) depends upon the truth of (a)'s conclusion, it is nevertheless the case, as we observed earlier, that the assumption that (a) is valid (an assumption which is made in proposing (a)) does involve the claim that (a)'s conclusion is *probable*. It is this assumption which suffices to render (a) circular, since (a) purports to show that its conclusion is probable. And the claim that (a)'s conclusion is probable would not be shown to be unfounded if (a)'s conclusion turned out false.

It is Black's third reply to the charge of circularity which seems centrally important in his defence of argument (a): Here Black agrees that in using rule R we assume that it is correct ('treat it as correct'); but, he argues, this does not suffice to expose circularity in (a). For to assume that R is correct is not to assume its correctness as a premiss of the argument itself, nor as a premiss of any argument used to establish the premiss of (a). That is, Black seems to be maintaining, the only assumptions which could justify a charge of circularity in (a) would have to be assumptions expressed actually as premisses of (a) or as premisses of other arguments whose conclusions are used to support the premisses of (a). It is this claim that merits closer examination.

When one proposes an argument in support of a certain proposition one makes at least two kinds of assumptions; those expressed as premisses of the argument (or as premisses of other arguments used to establish these premisses), and those involving the claim of the correctness or validity of the rule of inference which sanctions the argument. As Black rightly remarks, assumptions of the latter sort cannot be expressed as premisses of the argument itself, on pain of infinite regress. Nevertheless, an assumption of the correctness of the rule of inference governing an argument is made by one who claims that the argument supports or establishes a certain conclusion. Suppose, now, that a proposition *p*, as well as being required to be assumed by one who proposes a certain argument, constitutes also the conclusion of that argument. Then the proponent of the argument must assume *p* (assume that *p* is probable) in order to establish *p* (or show that *p* is probable). And this is what is essentially involved in circular reasoning, whether or not *p* is actually a premiss of the argument.

The fact that an argument whose conclusion neither appears as, nor is presupposed by, a premiss can nevertheless be circular will become even more patent if we consider the following (non-valid) *deductive* rule D and the corresponding 'self-supporting' argument (b) in its favour:

D: To argue from *No F if G* and *Some G is H* to *All F is H*.

The 'self-supporting' argument (b) can now be formulated as follows:

(b): No argument using D as its rule of inference is an argument which contains a premiss beginning with the term 'All'. Some arguments containing premisses beginning with the term 'All' are valid.

Therefore:

All arguments using D as their rule of inference are valid.

Argument (b), each of whose premisses is true, uses D as its rule of inference and purports in its conclusion to demonstrate the validity of D. Furthermore, the conclusion of (b) is not the same as its premisses, nor is it presupposed by them. According to Black's reasoning, then, (b) could legitimately be employed to demonstrate the validity of the unacceptable rule D. However, the circularity, and hence illegitimacy, of (b) lies in the fact that the validity of D must be assumed when one uses (b) in trying to demonstrate the validity of D.

Black, then, would seem to be mistaken in his claim that circularity can only be imputed to arguments whose conclusions are included in their premisses, or whose conclusions must be the premisses of other arguments which are used to establish the premisses of the arguments in question. Any defence of argument (a) which rests on such a claim must be considered unsatisfactory.

Accordingly, in his replies to the charge of circularity, Black does not appear to succeed in demonstrating the logical cogency of a 'self-supporting' argument such as (a).

X

ON THE NEW RIDDLE OF INDUCTION

S. F. BARKER AND PETER ACHINSTEIN

I

IN HIS *Fact, Fiction, and Forecast* Nelson Goodman formulates a striking puzzle which he calls 'the new riddle of induction'.[1] He reminds us of how we are willing to 'project' a predicate like 'green': since all the emeralds we have so far observed have been green, we adopt the hypothesis that all future emeralds probably are going to be green also. But then he asks us to consider a predicate such as 'grue', which is to be understood as applying to a thing at a given time if and only if either the thing is then green and the time is prior to time *t*, or the thing is then blue and the time not prior to *t*.[2] Let us take *t* as a time in the future, say, the year 2000 A.D. Now, all emeralds observed in the past have been green, and therefore they have been grue. Thus the hypothesis that all emeralds are grue has as much inductive support as the hypothesis that all emeralds are green, for we have equal numbers of positive instances in favour of each hypothesis and no negative instances. But the two hypotheses yield incompatible predictions regarding emeralds in the future, since a grue emerald after the year 2000 A.D. will be blue. We cannot accept both these conflicting hypotheses, yet they seem equally to have good inductive support. Why ought one predicate to be 'projected' rather than the other? This is the 'new riddle of induction'.

One answer which has been suggested to the riddle is this: predicates not involving any sort of reference to time ought to be projected in preference to ones that do involve such reference. 'Grue' and 'bleen' (where 'bleen' is a predicate which is to be understood

From *Philosophical Review*, Vol. 69 (1960), pp. 511–22. Reprinted by permission of the authors and the *Philosophical Review*.

[1] Nelson Goodman, *Fact, Fiction, and Forecast* (Cambridge, Mass., 1955), Ch. III. The authors are indebted to Professor Goodman for valuable criticism; he does not accept the conclusions, however.

[2] This appears to be what Goodman means when he explains 'grue' as applying to 'all things examined before *t* just in case they are green but to other things just in case they are blue' (ibid., p. 74).

as applying to a thing at a given time if and only if either the thing is then blue and the time is prior to *t*, or the thing is then green and the time is not prior to *t*) are predicates which do involve reference to time whereas 'green' and 'blue' are not. For this reason 'blue' and 'green' ought to be projected in preference to 'grue' and 'bleen'.[1]

But this answer will not satisfy Goodman. In his most scathing tone he will ask, 'And what, pray, is it for a predicate to be a predicate involving reference to time?' It is true that a person brought up to speak the language of green and blue will not understand 'grue' and 'bleen' unless these latter are defined for him in terms of green and blue and time. But, Goodman will insist, a person brought up to speak the language of grue and bleen will define 'green' and 'blue' in an exactly symmetrical manner: that is, he will not understand 'green' and 'blue' until their uses are explained for him in terms of 'grue' and 'bleen' and time; he will employ the definition that 'green' applies to all and only those things which are grue prior to the year 2000 or bleen thereafter, and the definition that 'blue' applies to all and only those things which are bleen prior to the year 2000 or grue thereafter. Goodman will maintain that 'grue' is not intrinsically a more nontemporal predicate than is 'green'; the situation is perfectly symmetrical, he will say. For the speaker of the green-blue language, 'grue' and 'bleen' appear to be temporal predicates; but for the speaker of the grue-bleen language, 'green' and 'blue' appear to be temporal predicates. Which predicate seems temporal to you and which one not will all depend on which predicate happens to have got more deeply entrenched in the language that you are accustomed to speaking.

Goodman's way of rejecting this proposed solution to his riddle of induction is acute. But does he not go too far? Does he not exaggerate the extent to which the grue-bleen language and the green-blue language are symmetrical in nature? To see whether he does, we must consider just what claims he makes.

In maintaining that there exists so much symmetry between these two languages, Goodman implicitly is making two especially important claims. (1) He is claiming that people brought up to use 'grue' understand their predicate in such a way that it applies to all

[1]This claim was advanced by Carnap. 'On the Application of Inductive Logic,' *Philosophy and Phenomenological Research* VIII (1947), 133–147; he put it in a stronger form, implying that it is a necessary condition for projectability of a predicate that it be nontemporal.

and only those objects of all kinds to which speakers of the green-blue language would apply the phrase 'green if the date is prior to the year 2000 or blue if the date is thereafter'. And this surely means that such people must understand not only what it is for actual objects to be grue but also what it means for fictional objects, imaginary objects, or objects in pictures to be grue. A grue-bleen speaker, on this assumption, when confronted with pictures of Robin Hood in Sherwood Forest, would be able to tell that the foliage of the forest in the picture is grue, not bleen. And (2) Goodman is claiming that the predicate 'grue' is for the speaker of the grue-bleen language a nontemporal predicate, in that such a speaker does not need to ascertain the date of an object before being able to tell whether the object is grue or not. On the other hand, if we, who speak the green-blue language, were asked to determine whether an object in a painting satisfies the condition of being either green if the date is before A.D. 2000 or blue if the date is thereafter, we would have to ascertain the date of the scene in the picture. If the picture contained people or buildings, for example, we might determine the date of the scene by noticing the style of the people's costumes or the style of the architecture, and dating this style through historical research if it is a past style, or through careful prediction if it is a future style. Our use of these procedures indicates that the predicate 'green if the date is prior to 2000 or blue if the date is thereafter' is for us a temporal predicate, that is, one which we know how to apply to a thing only after we have ascertained the date of the thing. But Goodman's speaker of the grue-bleen language (whom we shall call Mr. Grue) must not need to go through such procedures in determining whether or not something is grue; for if he did, 'grue' would be for him a temporal predicate. Nor is it enough to say that Mr. Grue must be able to use 'grue' without explicitly consulting history books and looking at calendars; he must be able to use 'grue' without even implicitly basing his judgement upon observable temporal clues, such as styles of costumes or of architecture.

Goodman must take for granted these two suppositions about speakers of the grue-bleen language. But what would it be like for there to be such people? Is there not some difficulty latent in this conception?

II

Mr. Grue and Mr. Green (a speaker of the green-blue language) both will often be using their colour predicates in discussions of other things besides actual objects. For instance, they will sometimes want to talk about objects in pictures. Let us consider their respective conceptions of what it is for ordinary, straightforwardly representational pictures to picture coloured objects.

With regard to his favourite colour, Mr. Green of course will have the notion that (excluding special subtleties of painting) an object in a picture is green if and only if the pigment used in representing the object is green pigment. This rule belongs to his conception of what it is for an object in a picture to be coloured.

But what of Mr. Grue? His case is a bit more complicated. With regard to his favourite colour, there would seem to be two different possibilities about what his notion of pictorial representation will be. (A) Perhaps he calls an object in a picture 'grue' when and only when the pigment used in representing it is grue pigment. Or (B) perhaps he calls an object in a picture 'grue' when and only when either the pigment used in representing it is green and the date in the picture is prior to 2000, or the pigment used is blue and the date in the picture 2000 or later.

But we see that (A) and (B) are not equally possible, if we look back at Goodman's assumption (1) that Mr. Grue's term 'grue' is to be applicable to all and only those objects to which Mr. Green's phrase 'green if the date is prior to 2000 or blue if the date is thereafter' correctly applies. Mr. Grue, if he is to satisfy assumption (1), cannot classify in accordance with notion (A); for (A) and (1) directly conflict. To see that this is so, consider a painting done this year, which depicts a pastoral scene of the year 2001; in this painting green pigment is used in representing the grass. What colour is the grass in the picture? If (A) were the case then Mr. Grue would have to regard the grass in the picture as grue, since it is represented by means of grue pigment. But Mr. Green will hold that the grass in the picture is green and that therefore the phrase 'green if the date is prior to 2000 or blue if the date is thereafter' does not properly apply to it, since the date in the picture is after 2000. Of course Mr. Green is willing to apply the phrase 'green if the date is prior to 2000 or blue if the date is thereafter' to the pigment used to represent the grass; but he will not apply it to the grass itself. Thus if (A) were the case, assumption (1) would be violated. Since we have assumed that Mr. Grue does satisfy assumption (1), we must suppose that his notion of pictorial representation is in accordance with (B) rather than (A).

In the light of this, let us proceed to see whether we can detect any difficulties latent in Goodman's formulation of his new riddle of induction.

III

A person who spoke the grue-bleen language, who was able to tell whether a thing is grue at a given time without first needing to ascertain what the date is at that time, and who applied the predicate 'grue' to all and only those objects to which speakers of the green-blue language apply the phrase 'green if the date is prior to the year 2000 or blue if the date is thereafter' would be a person of remarkable powers.

Suppose that we present Mr. Grue with two black-and-white drawings of plots of grass, drawings which we carefully construct so that he cannot tell them apart. Now we prepare two larger drawings of Commencement in the Harvard Yard, into one of which we incorporate one of our drawings of grass, into the other of which we incorporate the other of our drawings of grass. These two larger drawings of the Harvard Yard are not alike, however; one represents the Yard as it is nowadays, the other shows the Yard not as it is but as it will be. In the first drawing the buildings all have their familiar present-day aspect, and an alumni procession is straggling past, those at the very rear bearing a placard announcing themselves as the Class of '58. The second drawing has an altered aspect, for the fifty-story Boylston Street Apartments tower in the distance, the air is filled with flying saucers, and the rear of the procession is brought up by a group whose placard proclaims them to be the Class of' 00. Suppose that we now confront Mr. Grue with these two large drawings; we do not, however, let him see either of them entire, for we cleverly screen off most of the area of each drawing from the gaze of Mr. Grue, forcing him to peer at each drawing through a small opening in a screen, so that in each case all that he is allowed to see is the area of grass which he saw previously, before it was incorporated into the larger drawing. We now provide him with a palette and put to him the question, 'What paint should be used in order to colour these two pictures in such a way that the grass in the pictures will be grue?'

Now, according to Goodman's supposition, Mr. Grue is a person who is able to tell whether a thing is grue just by looking at it, without first needing to ascertain its date. So presumably in this case he will be able to tell, just by looking at the grass, what sort of look it needs to be given in order to be grue. Presumably he will correctly respond to our query and will answer that one kind of paint (which we call green) needs to be used for the first picture while another kind of paint (which we call blue) needs to be used for the second. But if Mr. Grue chooses the appropriate paints, green for the pre-2000 picture and blue for the other, then he must be recognizing a difference between the pictures, a difference which makes necessary this difference in pigments. And he must recognize that the two pictures are different even though what he sensuously perceives is the same in both cases, even though the light reaching his eye and stimulating his retina is just the same in both cases. How should we describe Mr. Grue's power? It is clear that the power which he possesses is a type of extrasensory perception.

Thus, one curious consequence of Goodman's set of suppositions is that the speaker of the grue-bleen language must possess a faculty of extrasensory perception not possessed by people such as ourselves who are speakers of the green-blue language.

IV

Suppose we were to grant that there is nothing logically absurd about the idea that Mr. Grue possesses this queer faculty of extrasensory perception. Still, is it really the case that the predicate 'grue' as he uses it is a nontemporal predicate, whose applicability he can determine without needing to ascertain the date?

Let us suppose that Mr. Grue knows how to apply temporal terms such as 'now', 'before A.D. 2000', and 'after A.D. 2000'; or, if he does not know how to do this, let us teach him how. Now we present him with a single black-and-white sketch of the Harvard Yard, just showing the Holden Chapel with its tympanum which is so well maintained that its colour never changes. We first say to Mr. Grue, 'This sketch is a picture of the Holden Chapel in 1959. But black-and-white pictures are dull, aren't they? The tympanum in the picture is bleen, of course. Just colour it in for us, won't you?' And we give Mr. Grue a palette of paints. He will reach for the paint that we call blue. But next we tell Mr. Grue that we wish to have a picture of the Holden Chapel in the year 2001; and we explain to him that the Holden Chapel is so carefully maintained that it never changes in appearance. We now ask Mr. Grue to give us his advice; we say, 'Please show us what paint should be used if we are now to paint the tympanum in a picture which will show the Holden Chapel in the year 2001'. If Mr. Grue is the type of person Goodman supposes him to be, he will of course be able to answer this question. He will point out the paint which we call green.

In this case we see that Mr. Grue uses two different paints in order to colour the two pictures bleen; but the difference between the two pictures is solely a temporal difference. Thus his knowledge of the temporal difference is here sufficient to affect his choice of the paint needed in order to make the object in the picture look bleen. Moreover, knowledge of the temporal difference is necessary in order to enable him to decide what paint is needed. For if we were simply to say to him, 'What paint should be used now in order to colour a picture of the bleen tympanum of the Holden Chapel? We are not saying what the date of the scene in the picture is to be', then he will be unable to reply. He will be unable under these circumstances to tell us which paint is the correct one.

Thus it is clear here that the predicates 'grue' and 'bleen' cannot be used successfully by Mr. Grue unless he is somehow apprised of the date of the object to which the predicates are to be applied. In this sense, whether he himself is aware of it or not, these predicates are for Mr. Grue temporal predicates.

V

What about the predicates 'green' and 'blue', on the other hand? Mr. Grue might try to argue that as he understands the term 'green' it is for him a temporal predicate. He may try to argue that he cannot tell whether an object in a picture is green or not, unless he knows whether the object is grue before A.D. 2000 or bleen thereafter; and he may claim that he cannot ascertain this unless he knows the date of the object in the picture. He may say that it is only when there is some indication of the date of the scene in the picture, as, for example, the presence of Robin Hood and his men, that he can tell that the foliage in the picture is green. If we presented him with two black-and-white pictures of the Harvard Yard of no definite date which he could not tell apart, and if we now used grue paint to paint the grass in one and bleen paint to paint the grass in the other, he might claim that this would not be enough to enable him to tell the pictured scenes apart as regards their greenness. According to Mr. Grue, then, 'green' and 'blue' are temporal predicates.

His claim is misleading, however. We should point out to Mr. Grue how even he is really capable of detecting whether an object in a picture is green or not without having to ascertain what date the picture represents. First, we ask Mr. Grue always to notice whether or not the paint on the canvas is grue in colour. This, of course, Mr. Grue can do. We then tell him that nowadays whenever the paint on a certain area of the canvas is grue, then the object being portrayed at that area of the canvas is green, and whenever the paint is bleen, the object represented is blue. These instructions are sufficient for the present, and if he uses the terms 'green' and 'blue' according to these instructions he will be able to tell whether the object in the picture is green or blue without having to ascertain its date; for recognizing whether the paint used at that spot on the canvas is grue or not does not entail ascertaining the date of the object which the paint is being used to portray.

Mr. Grue cannot point out for Mr. Green's benefit an analogous device for recognizing grue objects in pictures without noticing their dates. Mr. Grue cannot tell Mr. Green, for example, that whenever the paint on the canvas is green then the object in that area of the canvas is grue, nowadays; for a picture of a post-2000 scene painted with green paint is bleen nowadays and not grue. And this reinforces the claim that the predicates 'green' and 'grue' are asymmetrical in their logical character.

VI

So far, we have seen that there are reasons for believing that Goodman's set of suppositions about Mr. Grue contains latent difficulties. Not only would Mr. Grue have to possess extrasensory perception, but what is worse, his use of the predicate 'grue' would logically involve prior ascertaining of the date, and in this sense 'grue' could not be for him a nontemporal predicate. On the other hand, 'green' is a nontemporal predicate for him.

It is possible, however, that Goodman might seek to reply in the following vein. He might maintain that the situation is nevertheless symmetrical as between the grue-bleen language and the green-blue language; that is, granting the aptness of the description which we have so far given of Mr. Grue, Goodman might nevertheless wish to argue that if we were to frame a description of Mr. Green it would be necessary from the point of view of Mr. Grue to describe Mr. Green as possessing a faculty of extrasensory perception and as using his predicate 'green' in a way which involves essential reference to the date. But would this counterargument be sound?

What kind of experiment might we consider in hope of showing that Mr. Green possesses a faculty of extrasensory perception? Suppose we were to conduct with Mr. Green an experiment analogous to the one which demonstrated Mr. Grue's occult power. Here we would show Mr. Green two black-and-white drawings of plots of grass carefully constructed so that he cannot tell them apart. Then we prepare two larger drawings of the Harvard Yard into which we incorporate these smaller drawings of grass. One of the larger drawings represents the Commencement of 1959, the other that of 2001. We confront Mr. Green with these two large drawings, preventing him however from seeing them entire; he is allowed only to view the portions of grass which he has previously seen. We now ask him which paint should be used in order now to colour these two drawings in such a way that the grass in the pictures will be green. What will be his response? Here of course Mr. Green will use the same paint in both cases. Thus the outcome of this experiment gives no reason whatever for imputing to Mr. Green any faculty of extrasensory perception, not even from Mr. Grue's point of view.

We might try to alter the experiment, however, so that Mr. Green will have to give different reactions instead of the same one. Instead of telling Mr. Green to paint the grass green in both pictures, we tell him that we would like to have the grass in the first picture green and that in the second picture blue. In this case, Mr. Green will reach for different paints. Mr. Grue might be inclined to say that Mr. Green is recognizing a difference between the two pictures, a difference which requires that he use one kind of paint on the first picture and another kind on the second. This difference, Mr. Grue may be inclined to say, is a difference that is not sensuously perceptible; hence, Mr. Green possesses a faculty of extrasensory perception. But of course this inference on the part of Mr. Grue would be mistaken. Even in this experiment no evidence has been given of any occult power being possessed by Mr. Green. The fact that Mr. Green reaches for two different kinds of paint reflects only the fact that he was given different instructions with respect to the different pictures.

Thus it seems impossible to demonstrate that Mr. Green possesses any faculty of extrasensory perception. But are predicates such as 'green' and 'blue' temporal predicates for Mr. Green?

Suppose again that we were to say to Mr. Green that we want to colour a sketch of the Holden Chapel in the Harvard Yard; we tell him that we want the tympanum of the Chapel in the picture to be blue, but we do not tell him what the date of the pictured scene is to be. Unlike Mr. Grue in the analogous experiment, Mr. Green here will be able to decide which paint to reach for in order to carry out these instructions, even if we tell him nothing about the date of the scene represented in the picture. And if we do tell him that the picture represents the Chapel in 1959 rather than in 2001, this information will not at all affect Mr. Green as he decides what paint to use in order to colour the picture. Thus there is no basis here for saying that Mr. Green is using 'blue' as a temporal predicate; knowledge of the date is irrelevant for him to the application of 'blue'.

Thus this possible counterargument fails.

VII

Another kind of objection which might be raised is this. Someone might suppose that Mr. Grue can never tell what kind of paint to use to paint an object in a picture grue or bleen; he might suppose that Mr. Grue's peculiar ability lies only in the fact that, once it is painted, he can tell whether or not the object in the picture is grue, but not until then. So Mr. Grue, if presented with two black-and-white sketches of the Harvard Yard, one pre-2000 and the other post-2000, and if allowed to see only a plot of grass in each, might not be able to tell us how he would paint the pictures so that they would both be pictures of grue grass. He might have to experiment with all the paints on the palette before the grue colour would emerge for him, as a gestalt quality, in each picture. How can we say, then, that because Mr. Grue reaches for different paints to paint both sketches grue he therefore recognizes a difference in the two black-and-white sketches? For, according to this supposition, the fact that he does not know what paints to use would be a good indication that he recognizes no difference between the two sketches.

This type of objection is directed against all the earlier examples which were intended to show that Mr. Grue must have a kind of extra-sensory perception in order to be able to use 'grue' and 'bleen' and which were intended to show that these predicates are temporal predicates. According to this objection, there is no sense in asking Mr. Grue what paints he will use in painting a certain picture grue (as we did in our examples), for he will not know.

This supposition is very strange indeed, for it implies that 'grue' is hardly a colour predicate at all, so peculiar is its status. However, even if Mr. Grue were this type of person, the earlier points can still be made, if the examples are altered. Suppose we show Mr. Grue a picture in colour of the Harvard Yard at Commencement time, but this is to be an idealized picture representing Harvard at no definite time; for example we see a procession with placards of classes ranging from 1640 to 2500, and there are some buildings of the eighteenth century and some of the twenty-sixth century (the picture is entitled 'Harvard through the Ages'). But we screen off most of this picture, allowing Mr. Grue to see only one small plot of grass. If we now ask him to tell us the colour of the grass in the picture, then, of course, he cannot do so, for it is not grass of any given date. Now, without his being aware of it, we cleverly change the concealed portion of the picture so that it will be a picture of the Harvard Yard at Commencement time in 1959. Now we ask him the colour of the grass. This time, on the assumption that he needs no observable temporal clues from the object itself in order to be able to identify grue objects, he will tell us that the grass in the picture is grue. But he is receiving no more sensory stimulation now than he was before, and yet he is cognizant of a change. For this reason, we attribute to him a faculty of extrasensory perception.

In order to show that this Mr. Grue is using 'grue' as a temporal predicate, we can change the previous experiment in the following way. We allow Mr. Grue to see entire both pictures of the Commencement scenes. In the first case, he cannot tell us the colour of the grass because it is not part of a scene of Harvard at any definite time. When we now change the picture so that it represents the Commencement of 1959, he can tell us that the grass in the picture is indeed grue. Here Mr. Grue is perceptually aware of the change which, in effect, is merely a temporal one. In the first case, when he was aware of no definite date of the objects in the picture, he could not tell whether to apply the term 'grue'. But when the picture is changed so that he becomes aware of a definite date for the scene in question, then he can correctly identify the grass in the scene as grue. Thus Mr. Grue is using 'grue' as a temporal predicate, for he must be cognizant of the data of the object in the picture in order to be able to tell whether it is grue.

VIII

The suggestion that nontemporal predicates are more legitimately projectable than temporal ones was put forward as an answer to the new riddle of induction. The conclusion which seems to emerge here is that one ought not to dismiss this suggestion in the brusque way in which Goodman has been inclined to do. It is not the case that there is no difference (except as regards their entrenchment in our language) between predicates such as 'green' and 'grue'; it is not the case that there exists a thorough symmetry between the grue-bleen language and the green-blue language. On the contrary, if the examples discussed above are appropriate, they seem to show that a logically important difference does exist between 'grue' and 'green', a difference sufficiently important to help us to see why it is that we rightly regard 'green' as more projectable than 'grue'.

In formulating his 'new riddle of induction' Goodman of course had in mind a wide range of puzzling predicates in addition to 'grue' and 'bleen'. For instance, one might consider the predicate 'condulates electricity', a predicate true of a thing at a given time if and only if the thing then conducts electricity and the time is prior to A.D. 2000 or the thing is then an electrical insulator and the time is not prior to A.D. 2000; and one might ask why we judge that things made of copper are going to conduct electricity rather than judge that they are going to condulate electricity. An unlimited array of similarly puzzling predicates could be constructed. But whatever these new predicates might be, it would seem that what has been said with regard to 'grue' suffices to provide a clue for dealing with each of them.

Thus, for example, we could bring out that 'condulates electricity', like 'grue', is a temporal predicate in a sense in which 'green' and 'conducts electricity' are not. Suppose we were to make a picture clearly showing an object properly connected to a battery and ammeter, with the ammeter giving a high reading; but suppose that the background of the picture is concealed from the observer's view, so that nothing is visible to indicate whether the date in the picture is prior to A.D. 2000 or not. An observer then can readily tell that the object in the picture is a conductor of electricity; for that, he does not require clues as to the date in the picture. But a person not possessing extrasensory perception of the background will be wholly unable to tell whether the object in the picture is a condulator of electricity. The point is that it is the temporal clues contained in the picture which are essential to telling whether the object in the picture is a condulator of electricity; while if the background is such as to show that the date in the picture is not prior to A.D. 2000, then the object in the picture is not a condulator of electricity. And if even the background of the picture contains no clues as to the date in the picture, then the object in the picture neither is nor is not a condulator of electricity, although it is a conductor. This brings out the sense in which determining whether an object condulates electricity at a given time essentially involves prior ascertaining of what the date is at that time.

Hence it would seem that we may be able in any case we meet to explain the difference between the nontemporal and legitimately projectable predicate and its temporal and less legitimately projectable competitors.

XI

POSITIONALITY AND PICTURES

NELSON GOODMAN

LUCKILY we need not bother with the artistic *dramatis personae*, the talk of extrasensory perception, or the other embellishments of the preceding paper by Barker and Achinstein.[1] The only serious question is whether the authors succeed in defining the distinction between positional and non-positional predicates. In substance, the formulation they propose is this: a single picture or representation can be given for all instances of application of a non-positional predicate, while at least two different representations are needed to cover all instances of application of a positional predicate. For example, a single present patch of green paint will represent the colour of all green things irrespective of their dates; but two present patches will be needed to represent all grue things: a green one for cases up to time *t* and a blue one for cases thereafter.

The limitations upon what can represent what are far from obvious. We often see black-and-white diagrams in which different colours are represented by different shadings: say green by cross-hatching, blue by dotting, and so forth. Plainly symbols like these can equally well be used for grue. Vertical shading, say, for what is green up to time *t* or blue thereafter is as legitimate a representation of grue as the other symbols are of green and blue. Presumably Barker and Achinstein will reject such diagramming as not the natural representation they have in mind. Just what, then, constitutes representation within their meaning? To stipulate that a colour must be represented by a sample of it will not do; for a present patch of paint that is a sample of green is also a sample of grue. And if we deny that grue is a single colour we are in effect merely saying that grue is positional, and so begging the question. Does representation perhaps require, then, that the colour of an

From *Philosophical Review*, Vol. 69 (1960), pp. 523–5. Reprinted by permission of the author and the *Philosophical Review*.

[1] I am indebted to the authors for showing me their manuscript before publication.

object be represented by another object that is indiscriminable from, or matches, the first in colour? This will not work either; for then a patch of green paint, since it matches very few green things, cannot represent the colour of all green things.[1]

At this point Barker and Achinstein may say that while precise definition of what they mean by representation is difficult, all they have in mind is ordinary, everyday, realistic representation, and that this notion is clear enough without definition. They are saying, then, that so long as only accustomed modes of representation—only common and familiar representational devices—are used, a non-positional predicate is one such that there is a single time-indifferent representation for all its instances of application. But if one is willing to put the matter thus, relying upon restriction to a familiar representational vocabulary, representation need not be brought in at all. 'Grue' can be classed as positional on the ground that in terms of ordinary, familiar language, no one term describes the colour of all grue objects; two different ordinary words, 'green' and 'blue', are needed. This, however, depends entirely upon 'green' and 'blue' rather than 'grue' happening to belong to ordinary language; that is, it depends entirely upon the facts of habit or entrenchment. In resting their definition of positionality upon restriction to the most accustomed means of representation, Barker and Achinstein are making much the same appeal to entrenchment but in a more roundabout and covert way. They are not offering a new alternative.

Furthermore, the line between natural and artificial representation can hardly be so drawn as to support the use these authors want to make of it. This becomes glaringly apparent in the final paragraphs of their paper. As a time-indifferent representation for 'conducts electricity', they suggest a picture showing a battery connected by wires to an ammeter with its pointer indicating a flow of current. That this is clearly a representation for 'conducts electricity' rather than for 'is a closed circuit' or 'is a live battery' or 'is an operating meter', or the like is highly implausible. Even aside from that, unless the word 'ammeter' or some equivalent expression is included in the picture,

[1] 'Grue' might be classed as positional on the ground that its instances of application before *t* cannot match those after *t* in colour, while this does not hold for 'green'. Noam Chomsky pointed this out to me a couple of years ago, but did not publish it because it is too *ad hoc* to be of much interest. Other clearly non-projectible colour predicates that are not positional by this criterion are easily constructed; and the criterion is inapplicable where, as in the case of 'conducts electricity', matching is irrelevant. Barker and Achinstein, in correspondence, reject this possible formulation of their proposal.

by what means is the meter pictured shown to be an ammeter rather than a thermometer or a meter registering the remaining hours of life in the battery or the loss of current in transmission? But if verbal inscriptions are admissible in a picture, we can construct a representation for 'condulates electricity' simply by labelling the pictured meter 'b-meter' for an easily made instrument whose pointer rests elsewhere than at zero up to time *t* when a current passes through and thereafter when no current passes through (or we can replace 'b-meter' by the description in familiar terms just given). Any claim that this is a less natural or admissible representation for 'condulates electricity' than the original picture is for 'conducts electricity' would be rather absurd. Perhaps with enough ingenuity an unambiguous representation of an ammeter could be achieved without the use of a word or even of dial figures; but such ingenuity would hardly falter at representing a b-meter without use of words or figures, especially after one had been produced.

Accordingly, it seems to me that the authors succeed neither in defining positionality nor in showing that anything in *Fact, Fiction, and Forecast* needs modification.

XII

THE PARADOX OF CONFIRMATION

J. L. MACKIE

THE paradox of confirmation, also known as the paradox of the ravens, has been much discussed.[1] But the sound points that have been made, I believe, by all the contributors are in danger of being lost in the controversy, and particularly in the mutual misunderstanding and charges of misunderstanding. I shall, therefore, try to place in order some of the main points that should emerge from the discussion and also to develop some further considerations.

The paradox is constituted by the three propositions:

(1) Observations of black ravens confirm 'All ravens are black'.

(2) Observations of black shoes, white swans, &c., are neutral to (i.e., do not confirm) 'All ravens are black'.

(3) If observations confirm one formulation of a hypothesis they confirm any logically equivalent formulation.

These three propositions all seem plausible, but they are incompatible; for an observation of a white swan is an observation of a non-black non-raven, this is related to 'All non-black are non-ravens' in the same way that the observation of a black raven is to 'All ravens are black', and these two universal propositions are equivalent. Since no-one will reject (3) or deny the equivalence of the two universals, the paradox can be solved only by rejecting or qualifying (1) or (2) or both. Professor Hempel rejects (2); Mr Watkins qualifies both (1) and (2), and uses the difficulties he sees in Hempel's solution as a support for Professor Popper's theory of confirmation.

For simplicity I shall exclude, for a time, the complications involved in the use of such terms as 'white', 'shoes', 'swans', &c., and take it

From *British Journal for the Philosophy of Science*, Vol. 13 (1963), pp. 265–77. Reprinted by permission of the author and Cambridge University Press.

[1]See, for example: Janina Hosiasson-Lindenbaum, *Journal of Symbolic Logic*, 1940, **5**, 133–148; Carl G. Hempel, *Mind*, 1945, **54**, 1–26 and 97–121, also *Philosophy*, 1958, **33**, 342–348; J. W. N. Watkins, *Philosophy*, 1957, **32**, 112–131 and 1958, **33**, 349–355, also this *Journal* [*British Journal for the Philosophy of Science*], 1960, **10**, 318–320, also *Australasian Journal of Philosophy*, 1959, **37**, 240–241 and 1960, **38**, 54–58; D. C. Stove, *Australasian Journal of Philosophy*, 1959, **37**, 149–151 and 1960, **38**, 51–54; H. G. Alexander, this *Journal*, 1958, **9**, 227–233 and 1959, **10**, 229–234; J. Agassi, this *Journal*, 1959, **9**, 311–317; I. J. Good, this *Journal*, 1960, **11**, 145–149 and 1961, **12**, 63–64.

that (2) asserts that observations of black non-ravens and non-black non-ravens are neutral to the hypothesis (*h*) that all ravens are black.

I

If we consider this problem in the setting in which Hempel proposed it, namely, without reference to any additional knowledge, then we must say that if the observation of a black raven confirms *h* then an observation of a non-black non-raven equally confirms *h*. But in a setting as bare as this there could be no better confirmation of *h* than the observation of black ravens. So if we are to define confirmation in such a way that it can occur in relation to a context of this sort, we must accept (1) and therefore reject (2). And we can do so, because in this context the rejection of (2) is not counter-intuitive; we simply have no intuitions in favour of (2) that are relevant to a setting as bare as this. Thus Hempel's solution of the paradox is adequate for its context; the paradox is not a difficulty for his definition of confirmation in its original setting, and he is justified in using the paradox to reject Nicod's definition according to which a black raven would confirm *h* but a non-black non-raven would not.

But whether we can plausibly speak of confirmation in a setting as bare as this, or, what comes to the same thing, whether any definition of confirmation that gives positive results in this setting can be carried over to ordinary contexts or will even throw light on confirmation in ordinary contexts, is a further question.

II

If we take account of the additional information that there are far more non-black things than ravens, then we can solve the paradox in another way. That is, we can still deny (2), but argue that the observation of non-black non-ravens is not nearly so good a confirmation of *h* as the observation of black ravens, and that, being intuitively aware of the relative weakness of the former confirmation, we mistake it for a complete failure to confirm, and so we have, in this context, a mistaken intuition in favour of (2).[1]

This explanation applies generally, for although it is only if there are far more non-ψ's than ϕ's that the observation of something that is both ϕ and ψ is really a much better confirmation of

[1]Hosiasson-Lindenbaum, Alexander, and Good all develop variants of this way of solving the paradox, though they also make other points.

$(x)\ [\phi x \supset \psi x]$ than the observation of something that is both non-ϕ and non-ψ, we are so used to giving affirmative terms to minority classes (if ϕ is an affirmative term, there are nearly always far more non-ϕ's than ϕ's) that we can understand how a mistaken intuition in favour of the generalisation of (2) could arise.

It is important to see, however, that to develop this solution we have to appeal to what I shall call the *Inverse Principle*, that a hypothesis h is confirmed by an observation-report b in relation to background knowledge k if and only if the observation-report is made more probable by the adding of the hypothesis to the background knowledge, that is, if the probability of b in relation to the conjunction of k and h is greater than the probability of b in relation to k alone—in symbols, if $p(b, k\ .\ h) > p(b, k)$—and that b confirms h the better the more the adding of h to k raises the probability of b.

For example, in one of Alexander's accounts of this solution, we assume this principle and assign probabilities in accordance with the relative size of the classes 'ravens', 'non-ravens', &c. Thus if we take it as known that the ratio of ravens to non-ravens is x to $1 - x$, and that of black things to non-black things y to $1 - y$, where $x < y < \frac{1}{2}$, then the probabilities of each of the four sorts of observation-report b_1 ('This is a black raven'), b_2 ('This is a non-black raven'), b_3 ('This is a black non-raven'), and b_4 ('This is a non-black non-raven'), in relation (i) to our background knowledge k alone, and (ii) to the conjunction of k with h, are as set out below:

	b_1	b_2	b_3	b_4
(i)	xy	$x(1 - y)$	$y(1 - x)$	$(1 - x)(1 - y)$
(ii)	x	0	$y - x$	$1 - y$

Then clearly reports of the form b_1 have their probability raised by the adding of h far more than those of the form b_4, and so b_1 reports confirm h far better than b_4 ones do, while a b_3 report is actually made less probable by the adding of h to the k assumed here and thus, in relation to *this* background knowledge, disconfirms h, though only slightly.[1]

In this setting also, then, we can solve the paradox by denying (2) and explaining away our intuitions in favour of it. It follows that the paradox cannot be used against an account of confirmation of this

[1] I have followed one of Alexander's accounts, but his other account, and the more elaborate accounts of Hosiasson-Lindenbaum and Good, all rest upon theories which involve the Inverse Principle and the assigning of probabilities in accordance with the distribution of characteristics.

sort—an account which does not equate confirming with satisfying a hypothesis, but which bases it on the Inverse Principle and an assignment of probabilities in accordance with a taken-as-known distribution of characteristics. But it is still a further question whether confirmation defined thus, for a context of still very severely limited knowledge, has much to do with confirmation in ordinary contexts. But this qualification works in two directions. If we accept this account in its proper context, we cannot go on and apply it unhesitatingly in other contexts. But equally we should not use difficulties in its application to other contexts to throw doubt on the account itself.

Thus this account of confirmation does not imply that observations of black ravens, however numerous, in ordinary contexts will provide a worthwile confirmation of *h*, still less that such observations of non-black non-ravens will do so, or even that they will confirm *h* at all, especially if they are actually observations of white swans, &c., which involve further terms which may possibly be related to *h* in other ways.[1] But for this very reason our commonsense doubts whether observations of non-black non-ravens in ordinary contexts could confirm *h* do not reflect adversely upon this account of confirmation or upon this solution of the paradox in its own context.

Thus to deny (2) in this still restricted context does not commit us to any absurd practical policies of investigation, such as trying to confirm *h* by cheaply scoring up enormous numbers of non-black non-ravens, and the absurdity of this policy in no way tells against the denial of (2) in this context.[2] Nor does it commit us to a policy of trying to support currently-accepted hypotheses as opposed to a policy of trying to overthrow them. And even if we wanted to support a certain hypothesis, the fact that a certain kind of observation would, in relation to severely limited background knowledge, confirm that hypothesis, does not imply that a sensible way of supporting it would be to *try* to make observations of that kind; for *trying* to make a certain kind of observation alters our background knowledge, and (as I shall show in section 4 below) may alter it in such a way that observations of that kind now confirm the hypothesis much less, or perhaps not at all.

[1] Cf. Good's distinction between 'stoogian' and 'non-stoogian' observations.

[2] Watkins and Agassi repeatedly use this improper extension to discredit the 'instantial theory'. See, e.g. Watkins in *Philosophy*, 1958, **32**, 118, and Agassi in *British Journal for the Philosophy of Science*, 1959, **9**, 315.

III

It would seem, then, that Hempel-type solutions of the paradox, denying only proposition (2), can be defended, at any rate within some limited contexts. But Mr Watkins has a strong argument in favour of the view that both (1) and (2) should be qualified,[1] which I would restate as follows.

Suppose that there is an observation-procedure which could turn out in just one of only two possible ways. For example, we inspect an object already known to be black, to see whether it is a raven or not; the outcome must be either that it is a raven or that it is not. Both the alternative outcomes cannot confirm the same hypothesis: if the observation's having turned out one way confirms the hypothesis, its having turned out the other way would not have confirmed it. This, which I shall call the *Alternative Outcome Principle*, is obvious enough in its own right; it is also provable as a consequence of the Inverse Principle. For in relation to a *k* which includes the fact that a procedure with just these alternative outcomes has been followed, the denial of one outcome is equivalent to the assertion of the other; so if *b* confirms *h*, then adding *h* to *k* makes *b* more likely, and therefore makes not-*b* less likely, and so the alternative outcome, not-*b*, would not confirm *h* but disconfirm it.

From this it follows that if we inspect an object already known to be black, its turning out to be a raven and its turning out to be a non-raven cannot both confirm *h*, though both are compatible with or satisfy the hypothesis; to confirm a hypothesis, then, an observation must do something more than satisfy it.

This seems to show that b_1 and b_3 observations, since they could be such alternative outcomes, cannot both confirm *h*, and it suggests the following further conclusions. If we inspect an object already known to be a raven and it turns out to be black, this confirms *h*, for the procedure might have turned out the other way and falsified *h*; but if we inspect an object already known to be black and it turns out to be a raven, this does not confirm *h*. Similarly, if we inspect an object already known to be non-black and it turns out to be a non-raven, this

[1] *Philosophy*, 1957, 32, 119–120, and *British Journal for the Philosophy of Science*, 1960, 10, 319. Watkins has not always made it clear that his conclusion is that both (1) and (2) should be qualified. On p. 116 of the article in *Philosophy* he describes his way out as being to 'deny the instantiation theory of confirmation implicit in proposition (1)', and one might be forgiven for supposing that he was denying or modifying (1) only. But subsequent discussion has brought it out that his account qualifies (2) also, saying that *h may* be confirmed by a b_4 observation if it is made in a *test* of *h*.

confirms *h*, for the alternative outcome would have falsified *h*, but if we inspect an object already known to be a non-raven and it turns out to be a non-black, this does not confirm *h*. And on this view there is no order of inspection by which the observation of a black non-raven could confirm *h*. Thus both (1) and (2) should be qualified.

But these further conclusions are paradoxical. If we adopt in this sense the view that to confirm a hypothesis a procedure must first endanger it, we make confirmation depend not on what we observe but on the order in which we notice characteristics. A black raven observed in one way ('Look, a raven—and it's black') confirms *h*, but observed in another way ('Look, something black—why, it's a raven') it does not. And this must be wrong. We might concede that the way in which an observation is made could affect its confirmatory power, but only if the 'way' involved more significant differences than this. The mere order in which characteristics are spotted must be an irrelevant difference. If confirmation is to be an objective relation, and not a psychological one, the total observation of a black raven must have the same confirmatory value in whichever order its components are put together. In other words, the 'further conclusions' suggested by the Alternative Outcome Principle fall foul of a *Principle of Relevance*.

Part of this difficulty is removed if we distinguish carefully the various 'procedures' and 'outcomes'. The procedure of inspecting something already known to be a raven, with the alternative outcomes that it is, or is not, black, is only the second stage of the observation of a black raven; before it there was another procedure, in which a previously uncharacterised object turned out to be a raven, but might have turned out to be a non-raven. The observation of a black raven can be regarded as being made up of two stages, then, in either of the following ways:

1. (1.1) This (previously uncharacterised object) is a raven, and (1.2) This raven is black.
2. (2.1) This (previously uncharacterised object) is black, and (2.2) This black thing is a raven.

Similarly, the observations of a black non-raven and of a non-black non-raven can be divided into stages as follows:

3. (3.1) This is black, and (3.2) This black thing is a non-raven.
4. (4.1) This is a non-raven, and (4.2) This non-raven is black.
5. (5.1) This is a non-raven, and (5.2) This non-raven is non-black.
6. (6.1) This is non-black, and (6.2) This non-black thing is a non-raven.

This analysis makes a solution at least formally possible, for our 'further conclusions' from the Alternative Outcome Principle have stressed differences in the confirming effect of the various second stages, such as 1.2 and 2.2, but the Principle of Relevance requires only that 1 as a whole, the combination of 1.1 and 1.2, should have the same confirming effect as 2 as a whole, the combination of 2.1 and 2.2. Clearly, 2 as a whole could be as good a confirmation as 1 as a whole, even if 1.2 was superior to 2.2, provided that 2.1 was correspondingly superior to 1.1.

We cannot, however, save the extreme view expressed in our 'further conclusions' in this manner. For if 2.2 did not confirm *h* at all, we should have to say that 2.1 alone confirms *h* as well as 1 as a whole does, which is absurd, especially as the reason given for saying that 2.2 does not confirm *h* at all, that the alternative outcome would not falsify *h*, would equally tell against 2.1.

This extreme view, then, must be rejected, and it can be rejected without regret since it is not required by the Alternative Outcome Principle. That principle tells us only that one outcome can confirm only if the other outcome would disconfirm, not that the other outcome would have to falsify.[1] But a more moderate view can be worked out as follows.

1.2 is in general a better confirmation of *h* than 2.2, but 2.1 is in general correspondingly better than 1.1, so that 1 as a whole and 2 as a whole are, as the Principle of Relevance requires, equally good.[2] Similarly, while 2.2 and 3.2, being alternative outcomes of the same procedure, cannot both confirm *h*, it is none the less possible that 2 as a whole and 3 as a whole should both do so, though not equally, if the confirming by 3.1 outweighs the disconfirming by 3.2; and likewise it is possible that 4 as a whole and 5 as a whole should both confirm *h*, though not equally.

In other words, although the finding that something, already known to be black, is a raven, is not in itself as good a confirmation of *h*

[1]As Watkins suggests in *British Journal for the Philosophy of Science*, 1960, 10, 319: '. . . *could not possibly* lead to its falsification and hence that the results of such an investigation, whatever they might be, could not confirm it according to a testability theory of confirmation.'

[2]An artificial example may be sufficient to illustrate this. Suppose that our background knowledge tells us that 10 per cent of objects are ravens and that 10 per cent of non-ravens are black. Then the probable distributions in relation to (i) this knowledge alone (ii) this knowledge plus *h*, are as follows:

	black ravens	non-black ravens	black non-ravens	non-black non-ravens
(i)	1/100	9/100	9/100	81/100
(ii)	1/10	0	9/100	81/100

as the finding that something, already known to be a raven, is black, yet the total observation of a black raven confirms *h* equally well in whichever order the characteristics are noticed. For we have to take account also of the *first* stage in each case, the finding that this previously uncharacterised object is black, and the finding that this previously uncharacterised object is a raven, and these first stages will also have some confirmatory effect, and a different effect from one another, in relation to whatever background knowledge we assume. In the same way, it is true that if finding that something, already known to be black, is a raven, confirms *h*, then finding that something, already known to be black, is a non-raven, cannot confirm *h* but must disconfirm it; but it may be true none the less, when we take account of the confirmatory effect of the common first stage, the finding that this previously uncharacterised object is black, that the total observation of a black non-raven confirms *h*, though not so well as the total observation of a black raven.

The Alternative Outcome Principle, then, is itself sound, and its legitimate consequences can be reconciled with the Principle of Relevance. But the extreme view, that only those procedures can confirm a hypothesis which endanger it in the strong sense that one of their possible outcomes is a falsification, must be rejected. It is not required by the Alternative Outcome Principle, and it conflicts with the Principle of Relevance. Indeed we can decisively refute this extreme view by comparing our procedures 1 and 2. Here we have two procedures whose total effects are equivalent; but one of them contains a first stage which does not endanger *h* and a second stage which does endanger *h*, whereas the other contains two stages neither of which endangers *h*. Two procedures, then, which must be equivalent in confirmatory power, may fail to contain the same element of endangering; it follows that endangering, in this strong sense, cannot be essential to confirmation.

Consequently the reports in stages, 1.1, 1.2, 2.1, and 2.2 will have the following probabilities relatively to *k* and *k.h* respectively

	1.1	1.2	21.	2.2
(i)	1/10	1/9	1/10	1/9
(ii)	1/10	1	19/100	10/19

Thus the addition of *h* raises the probability of 1.2 in the ratio 9:1, while it raises the probability of 2.2 only in the ratio 90:19, but it raises the probability of 2.1 in the ratio 19:10, while it leaves the probability of 1.1 unchanged. Multiplying the ratios 1.1 and 2.1, and again for 2.1 and 2.2, we find that the total probabilities of 1 and 2 are raised equally in the ratio 9:1. Of course, when the probabilities are thus based on numerical distributions the answer has to come out right. But the example shows how this can be combined with a marked superiority of 1.2 to 2.2.

IV

I have said that the fact that a certain kind of observation would, relatively to limited background knowledge, confirm a certain hypothesis, does not imply that a sensible way of supporting it would be to try to make observations of that kind. I want to develop this hint and to link it with the claim constantly made by Professor Popper and his followers that a hypothesis is confirmed by a (favourable) observation only if that is made in a *test* of the hypothesis, in an attempt to falsify it.

This concept of testing, of attempting to falsify, must not be a psychological one, or this claim would fall foul of the Principle of Relevance. When challenged (by Mr Stove) to state an objective, non-psychological criterion of a *test* Mr Watkins referred to what I have been calling the Inverse Principle, saying that b is a genuine test of h if $p(b, k \,.\, h) > p(b, k)$; a test is a procedure in which a certain outcome is less probable without the hypothesis than with it. This is, I think, a fair general criterion for what is relevant to confirmation, but it lets in far more than the procedures that anyone would ordinarily count as tests or attempts to falsify in actual scientific practice. As we saw in section 2 above, this criterion would allow casual observations of black ravens—and even (to a slight degree) of non-black non-ravens—to count as tests of h in relation to the kind of background knowledge assumed in Alexander's solution of the paradox. But we can give a narrower (but still objective) account of a *test*. We may start from the concept of *looking for* or *trying to find* something. Ordinarily, no doubt, this concept is partly psychological, but it is not wholly so. It has an objective part, which can be considered on its own; in this respect to look for, say, a lost golf ball is to adopt a procedure which *raises our chances* of coming upon the ball as compared with the procedure of, say, sitting still or wandering aimlessly about. Similarly, to look for black ravens is to adopt a procedure which raises our chances of coming upon black ravens (if there are any) as compared with the procedure of, say, observing anything and everything that happens along. To test a hypothesis, I suggest, in the sense that we require, is analoguously to look for a falsification of it, to adopt a procedure which raises our chances of falsifying it, if it is false. Let us see how *tests* and *looking for* various things, thus objectively defined, may affect confirmation.

Suppose, first, that we add, to the background knowledge assumed in Alexander's solution in section 2 above, the fact that we are looking for black ravens. Then this will raise the probability of b_1 reports above the previously assigned value *xy*. It will also raise the probability of b_1 reports in relation to *k* plus *h* above its previously assigned value *x*, but not in as high a ratio. Therefore the effect of adding to *k* the fact that we are looking for black ravens is to reduce the degree in which the adding of *h* increases the probability of b_1 reports, and hence to make such reports confirm *h* less well. And the more efficiently we look, the more is this so. In other words, as Popper's supporters (among others) have always said, if we try to confirm a hypothesis the favourable observations confirm it less well. This would be nonsense if 'try to confirm' had here a purely psychological meaning, but it makes very good sense if it means 'adopt a procedure which raises the chance of a favourable observation'.

The obverse policy, of not looking for falsifications, has an even more blatant effect. If we very efficiently do not look for non-black ravens, we may reduce to zero our chance of observing a non-black raven, even if there are some. And then the probabilities of reports of the forms b_1, b_2, b_3, b_4, given this policy and Alexander's background knowledge, will be x, 0, y—x, and 1—y respectively, that is, exactly the same values as when we add the hypothesis *h*. It follows that, given this policy, *h* does not raise the probability of any form of observation, and so no observation can confirm *h* if this policy is pursued with perfect efficiency.

On the other hand, if we (in this sense) try to falsify *h*, and look for non-black ravens, then we are adopting a policy which in relation to *k* alone raises our chances of observing non-black ravens, and therefore reduces the probabilities of the three other forms of observation, but which in relation to *k.h* makes no difference, since if there are no non-black ravens our chances of finding one cannot be raised, however hard we look. Thus by trying to falsify the hypothesis we create conditions in which the addition of *h* increases the probability of favourable observation-reports more than it would otherwise; we create conditions in which the observation of a black raven is a better confirmation of *h* than it would otherwise be.

Although we cannot give numerical measures to these probabilities, it is plausible to say that in ordinary contexts the probability of a certain sort of observation, and hence the degree of confirmation of a hypothesis by an observation of that sort, will be radically affected by the observer's policy, by what he is looking for. Hence, if we restrict the notion of a genuine test more narrowly than Watkins (as quoted above) did, so that we count as tests only procedures which raise considerably the chance of falsifying the hypothesis if it is false, we may well be right in saying that in ordinary contexts worthwhile confirmations come only from genuine tests. On the other hand it will not be true that observations not made in tests do not confirm at all; this is true only if 'test' is given the wider definition that Watkins suggests, when it is simply a re-statement of the Inverse Principle.

This discussion supports Popper's doctrine with regard to actual investigation in ordinary contexts, but at the same time it shows that this does not conflict with something like an instantiation theory of confirmation in restricted contexts. The view that instances of black ravens confirm *h* in relation to severely limited background knowledge does not imply that we can confirm *h* by *looking for and finding* such instances (for such looking takes us beyond the limits set), and so it does not imply that it would be sensible to try to confirm *h* by looking for black ravens. And since this is so, we cannot argue from the fact that this is (obviously) not sensible to the rejection of that view.

V

The paradox of the ravens, then, is to be solved in different ways in different contexts.

(i) Given no additional knowledge, it is to be solved in Hempel's way; in this context, proposition (2) in the set that constitutes the paradox can be denied without qualms.

(ii) Given only the information that ravens are less numerous than non-ravens, and black things than non-black things (and therefore that ravens are less numerous than non-black things), the paradox is to be solved in Alexander's way (or Hosiasson-Lindenbaum's, or Good's); proposition (2) can be denied, but its plausibility is explained by the fact that we mistake a relatively poor confirmation for no confirmation at all.

(iii) Given unrestricted admission of relevant information of kinds that we commonly have, while proposition (1) is in general true and proposition (2) is in general false, they are so only if we take account of all confirmations, including quite weak ones, and it is more to the point to replace both (1) and (2) with (1′) and (2′) as follows:

(1′) Observations of black ravens confirm 'All ravens are black' to a worthwhile degree only if they are made in genuine tests of this hypothesis (as defined in section 4).

(2′) Observations of black non-ravens never confirm 'All ravens are black' to a worthwhile degree, and observations of non-black non-ravens confirm 'All ravens are black' to a worthwhile degree only if they are made in genuine tests of this hypothesis.

It is clear that (1′) and (2′) are together compatible with (3).

This does not mean, however, that we cannot have a single theory of confirmation which applies in contexts of all sorts. In developing solutions of type (ii) we appeal to some theory that involves the Inverse Principle, and this principle is at least the basic idea of Popper's theory of confirmation, which gives us a solution of type (iii). The difference between these types of solution lies not in the fundamental principle that is used, but in the range of information called upon to supply the probabilities from which that principle generates confirmations. Type (ii) solutions draw their probabilities from relative distributions of characteristics, type (iii) solutions draw theirs from relevant information of all sorts, and the probabilities to which they refer can therefore be radically affected by the policies of the investigator himself. If there is a break in continuity, then, it comes not between solutions of types (ii) and (iii), but between those of types (i) and (ii).

But even a type (i) solution can be related to the Inverse Principle. For we might say that in an absolutely bare setting, to which this solution applies, reports of all the four kinds b_1, b_2, b_3, and b_4 are initially equally probable. Adding *h* in this context merely rules out the possibility of b_2 reports, and therefore increases equally the probabilities of reports of the other three kinds, that is, of all reports which are consistent with or satisfy *h*. Thus Hempel's satisfaction criterion of confirmation can be understood as the consequence of applying the Inverse Principle to the only probabilities available in a setting as bare as this.

I conclude, then, that a theory of confirmation based on the Inverse Principle can do justice to what the rival schools of thought have said about this paradox. The conflicts between these schools, on issues so far raised, can be resolved. They have arisen partly because the 'rival' theories and 'rival' solutions of the paradox have been interpreted as applying beyond their proper contexts, and partly because the Alternative Outcome Principle has been used over-enthusiastically and without a sufficiently precise specification of procedures and outcomes. The only legitimate dispute, if the Inverse Principle is itself accepted, would be about the probabilities to which it is applied; for clearly a confirmation in terms of this principle can be no more objective than the probabilities from which it is generated.

NOTES ON THE CONTRIBUTORS

P. K. FEYERABEND is a member of the Department of Philosophy at the University of California in Berkeley. He has published many papers on the philosophy of science, and he edited with Grover Maxwell *Mind, Matter, and Method*, a collection of essays in honour of Herbert Feigl, published in 1966.

G. SCHLESINGER is a Senior Lecturer in Philosophy at the Australian National University, Canberra, His *Method in the Physical Sciences* appeared in 1963.

CARL G. HEMPEL is Stuart Professor of Philosophy at Princeton University. His *Aspects of Scientific Explanation* appeared in 1965, and he has written many influential papers in the philosophy of science.

ERNEST NAGEL is a Professor at Columbia University. Among his writings are *Godel's Proof* (with J. R. Newman, 1959) and *The Structure of Science* (1961).

MAY BRODBECK is a member of the Department of Philosophy at the University of Minnesota. She is a member of the editorial board of *Philosophy of Science*, and edited, with Herbert Feigl, *Readings in the Philosophy of Science* (1953).

NELSON GOODMAN is now a Professor at Brandeis University. Among his writings are *Fact, Fiction and Forecast* (1954) and *The Structure of Appearance* (1951).

ROBERT ACKERMANN is a member of the Department of Philosophy at Washington State University, St. Louis, Missouri. His *Nondeductive Inference* appeared in 1966.

MAX BLACK is a Professor at Cornell University. Among his writings are *Problems of Analysis* (1954), *Models and Metaphors* (1962), and *A Companion to Wittgenstein's Tractatus* (1964).

PETER ACHINSTEIN is a member of the Department of Philosophy at Johns Hopkins University.

S. F. BARKER is a member of the Department of Philosophy at Johns Hopkins University. His *Induction and Hypothesis* appeared in 1957, and *The Philosophy of Mathematics* in 1964.

J. L. MACKIE has held appointments in the Universities of Sydney and York, and is now a Fellow of University College, Oxford.

BIBLIOGRAPHY

This Bibliography contains a selected list of books and papers in English published since 1950; for earlier works, cf. Feigl and Brodbeck [29]. No separate mention is made of papers to be found in the anthologies or symposia volumes, or in other books (e.g. Hempel [46], Sellars [75]), which are referred to below. An asterisk accompanying a book title indicates the inclusion of an extensive bibliography.

1. ACHINSTEIN, P., 'Circularity and induction', *Analysis*, 23 (1963), 123–127.
2. ACKERMANN, R. J., *Nondeductive Inference** (Routledge & Kegan Paul, London, 1966).
3. AGASSI, J., 'Towards an Historiography of Science', *History and Theory, Studies in the Philosophy of History*), Beiheft 2, 1963.
4. ALEXANDER, P., 'Theory-construction and theory-testing', *British Journal for the Philosophy of Science*, 9 (1958), 29–38.
5. BARBOUR, I. G., *Issues in Science and Religion* (Prentice-Hall, New York, and S.C.M. Press, London, 1966).
6. BARKER, S. F., *Induction and Hypothesis* (Cornell University Press, Ithaca, 1957).
7. BARTLEY, III, W. W., 'Achilles, the tortoise, and explanation in science and history', *British Journal for the Philosophy of Science*, 13 (1962), 15–33.
8. BAUMRIN, B. (editor), *Philosophy of Science, The Delaware Seminar*, 2 volumes (Interscience, New York, 1963).
9. BLACK, M., 'Self-support and circularity: a reply to Mr. Achinstein', *Analysis*, 23 (1962), 43–44.
10. BRAITHWAITE, R. B., *Scientific Explanation* (Cambridge University Press, London, 1953).
11. BRODBECK, M., 'Philosophy of the social sciences', *Philosophy of Science*, 21 (1954), 140–156.
12. BUNGE, M., *Causality: The Place of the Causal Principle in Modern Science** (Harvard University Press, Cambridge, Mass. 1959).
13. BUNGE, M. (editor), *The Critical Approach to Science and Philosophy* (Free Press, New York 1964).

14. BUNGE, M., 'The weight of simplicity in the construction and assaying of scientific theories', *Philosophy of Science*, 28 (1961), 120–149.

15. BURKS, A. W., 'The presupposition theory of induction', *Philosophy of Science*, 20 (1953), 177–197.

16. BURKS, A. W., 'On the presuppositions of induction', *Review of Metaphysics*, 8 (1955), 574–611.

17. CARNAP, R., *Logical Foundations of Probability**, 2nd. edition (University of Chicago Press, Chicago, and Routledge & Kegan Paul, London, 1962).

18. CARNAP, R., *Philosophical Foundations of Physics: An Introduction to the Philosophy of Science*, ed. Martin Gardiner (Basic Books, New York, 1966).

19. CHURCHMAN, C. West. (editor), *Measurement: Definition and Theories* (Wiley, New York, 1959).

20. COHEN, R. S. and WARTOFSKY, M. W. (editors) *Boston Studies in the Philosophy of Science*, 2 vols. (Humanities Press, New York, 1963).

21. COLODNY, R. G. (editor), *Frontiers of Science and Philosophy* (University of Pittsburgh Press, Pittsburgh, 1962, and Allen & Unwin, London, 1964).

22. COLODNY, R. G. (editor), *Beyond the Edge of Certainty: Essays in Contemporary Science and Philosophy* (Prentice-Hall, New York, 1965).

23. DANTO, A., *Analytical Philosophy of History* (Cambridge University Press, London, 1965).

24. DANTO, A. and MORGENBESSER, S. (editors), *Philosophy of Science** (Meridian Books, New York, 1960).

25. DAY, J. P., *Inductive Probability** (Routledge & Kegan Paul, London, 1961).

26. DRAY, W., *Laws and Explanation in History* (Clarendon Press, Oxford, 1957).

27. ELLIS, B., *Basic Concepts of Measurement** (Cambridge University Press, London, 1966).

28. FAIN, H., 'Some problems of causal explanation', *Mind*, 72 (1963), 519–532.

29. FEIGL, H. and BRODBECK, M. (editors), *Readings in the Philosophy of Science** (Appleton-Century-Crofts, New York, 1953).

30. FEIGL, H., SCRIVEN, M. and MAXWELL, G. (editors), *Minnesota Studies in the Philosophy of Science*, 3 volumes (University of Minnesota Press, Minneapolis, 1956–62).

31. FEIGL, H. and MAXWELL, G. (editors), *Current Issues in the Philosophy of Science* (Holt, Rinehart & Winston, New York, 1961).

32. FRANK, P. G. (editor), *The Validation of Scientific Theories* (Collier Books, New York, 1961).
33. GALLIE, W. B., *Philosophy and the Historical Understanding* (Chatto & Windus, London, 1964).
34. GIBSON, Q., *The Logic of Social Enquiry* (Routledge & Kegan Paul, London, 1960).
35. GOOD, I. J., 'The paradox of confirmation', *British Journal for the Philosophy of Science*, 11 (1960), 145–148; 12 (1961), 63–64; 17 (1967), 322.
36. GOODMAN, N., 'Recent developments in the theory of simplicity', *Philosophy and Phenomenological Research*, 19 (1959), 429–446.
37. GOODMAN, N., 'The test of simplicity', *Science*, 128 (1958), 1064–1069.
38. GOODMAN, N., *Fact, Fiction, and Forecast*, 2nd. edition (Bobbs-Merrill, New York, 1965).
39. GRENE, M., *The Knower and the Known* (Faber & Faber, London, 1966).
40. GROSS, L. (editor), *Symposium on Sociological Theory* (Harper & Row, Evanston, Illinois, 1959).
41. HACKING, I., *Logic of Statistical Inference* (Cambridge University Press, London, 1965).
42. HANSON, N. R., *Patterns of Discovery* (Cambridge University Press, London, 1958).
43. HANSON, N. R., 'On the symmetry between explanation and prediction', *Philosophical Review*, 68 (1959), 349–358.
44. HARRÉ, H. R., *Theories and Things* (Sheed & Ward, London, 1961).
45. HARSANYI, J. C., 'Popper's improbability criterion for the choice of scientific hypotheses', *Philosophy*, 35 (1960), 1–9.
46. HEMPEL, C. G., *Aspects of Scientific Explanation and Other Essays in the Philosophy of Science* (Free Press, New York, 1965).
47. HESSE, M. B., 'Theories, dictionaries, and observation', *British Journal for the Philosophy of Science*, 9 (1958), 12–28, 128–129.
48. HESSE, M. B., *Models and Analogies in Science** (Sheed and Ward, London, 1963).
49. KATZ, J. J., *The Problem of Induction and its Solution* (University of Chicago Press, Chicago, 1962).
50. KÖRNER, S. (editor), *Observation and Interpretation* (Constable, London, 1957).
51. KÖRNER, S., *Experience and Theory: An Essay in the Philosophy of Science* (Routledge & Kegan Paul, London, 1966).
52. KUHN, T. S., *The Structure of Scientific Revolutions* (University of Chicago Press, Chicago, 1962).

53. KYBURG, Jr., H. E., *Probability and the Logic of Rational Belief* (Wesleyan University Press, Middleton, Conn., 1961).

54. KYBURG, Jr., H. E., 'Recent work in inductive logic', *American Philosophical Quarterly*, 1 (1964), 249–287.

55. KYBURG, Jr., H. E., and NAGEL E. (editors), *Induction: Some Current Issues* (Wesleyan University Press, Middleton, Conn., 1963).

56. KYBURG, Jr., H. E., and SMOKLER, H. E. (editors), *Studies in Subjective Probability** (Wiley, New York, 1964).

57. LAUDAN, L., 'Grünbaum on "The Duhemian Argument"', *Philosophy of Science*, 32 (1965), 295–299.

58. MADDEN, E. H. (editor), *The Structure of Scientific Thought** (Houghton Mifflin, Boston, 1960).

59. NAGEL, E., *The Structure of Science* (Harcourt, Brace & World, New York, and Routledge & Kegan Paul, London, 1961).

60. NAGEL, E., SUPPES, P., and TARSKI, A. (editors), *Logic, Methodology, and Philosophy of Science* (North Holland, Amsterdam, 1962).

61. PALTER, R. M., *Whitehead's Philosophy of Science* (University of Chicago Press, Chicago, 1960).

62. PAP, A., *An Introduction to the Philosophy of Science** (Free Press, New York 1962).

63. POLANYI, M., *Personal Knowledge: Towards a Post-Critical Philosophy* (Routledge & Kegan Paul, London, 1958).

64. POPPER, K. R., 'Philosophy of science: a personal report', *British Philosophy in Mid-Century*, ed. C. A. Mace (Allen & Unwin, London, 1957).

65. POPPER, K. R., *The Logic of Scientific Discovery* (Hutchinson, London, 1959).

66. RESCHER, N., 'On prediction and explanation', *British Journal for the Philosophy of Science*, 8 (1958), 281–290.

67. RUDNER, R. S., 'Philosophy and social science', *Philosophy of Science*, 21 (1954), 164–168.

68. RUDNER, R. S., 'An introduction to simplicity', *Philosophy of Science*, 28 (1961), 109–115.

69. RUDNER, R. S., *Philosophy of Social Science* (Prentice-Hall, New York, 1966).

70. SALMON, W. C., 'Should we attempt to justify induction?' *Philosophical Studies*, 8 (1957), 33–48.

71. SCHEFFLER, I., 'Explanation, prediction and abstraction', *British Journal for the Philosophy of Science*, 7 (1957), 293–309.

72. SCHEFFLER, I., *The Anatomy of Inquiry: Philosophical Studies in the Theory of Science** (Knopf. New York, 1963 and Routledge & Kegan Paul, London, 1964).

73. SCHILPP, P. A., (editor), *The Philosophy of Rudolf Carnap* (Open Court, La Salle, Illinois, 1963). (Specially relevant are chapters by Hempel, Kemeny, Burks, Putnam, and Nagel, pp. 685–826, and Carnap's comments, pp. 71–81, pp. 944–998).
74. SCRIVEN, M., 'Explanation and prediction in evolutionary theory', *Science*, 129 (1959), 477–482.
75. SELLARS, W., *Science, Perception, and Reality* (Routledge & Kegan Paul, London, 1963).
76. SELLARS, W., 'Induction as vindication', *Philosophy of Science*, 31 (1964), 197–231.
77. TAYLOR, C., *The Explanation of Behaviour* (Routledge & Kegan Paul, London, 1964).
78. TOULMIN, S. E., *The Philosophy of Science* (Hutchinson, London, 1953).
79. TOULMIN, S. E., *Foresight and Understanding* (Hutchinson, London, 1961).
80. ULLIAN, J. S., 'More on "grue" and grue', *Philosophical Review*, 70 (1961), 386–389.
81. WATKINS, J. W. N., 'Between analytic and empirical', *Philosophy*, 32 (1957), 112–131.
82. WATKINS, J. W. N., 'A rejoinder to Professor Hempel's reply', *Philosophy*, 33 (1958), 349–355.
83. WIENER, P. P. (editor), *Readings in Philosophy of Science* (Scribners, New York, 1953).
84. WINCH, P., *The Idea of a Social Science* (Routledge & Kegan Paul, London, 1958).
85. WRIGHT, G. H. VON, *The Logical Problem of Induction**, 2nd. edition (Routledge & Kegan Paul, London, 1957).

INDEX OF NAMES

(*not including references in footnotes or the Bibliography*)